TOUCHING GREATNESS

MEMORABLE ENCOUNTERS WITH GOLFING LEGENDS

DERMOT GILLEECE

TRANSWORLD IRELAND

TRANSWORLD IRELAND
an imprint of The Random House Group Limited
20 Vauxhall Bridge Road, London SW1V 2SA
www.rbooks.co.uk

First published in 2008 by Transworld Ireland

A CIP catalogue record for this book
is available from the British Library.

ISBN 9781848270350

The author is grateful to *The Irish Times* for their co-operation in the
publication of this book, and to John Baker of Baker Sports Management.

Addresses for Random House Group Ltd companies outside the UK
can be found at: www.randomhouse.co.uk
The Random House Group Ltd Reg. No. 954009

The Random House Group Limited supports The Forest Stewardship
Council (FSC), the leading international forest-certification organization. All our
titles that are printed on Greenpeace-approved FSC-certified paper carry the FSC logo.
Our paper procurement policy can be found at www.rbooks.co.uk/environment

Typeset in 11/14pt Life by
Falcon Oast Graphic Art Ltd.

Printed and bound in Great Britain by
CPI Mackays, Chatham ME5 8TD

2 4 6 8 10 9 7 5 3 1

Mixed Sources
Product group from well-managed
forests and other controlled sources
www.fsc.org Cert no. TT-COC-2139
© 1996 Forest Stewardship Council
FSC

To Kathy, Tara and Mark

Contents

Foreword

I've been reading Dermot Gilleece since shortly after I picked up a golf club, about forty years ago, but it's only since I became a writer myself that I have been jealous of the rotten bastard. They say that the smaller the ball, the higher the quality of writing, and Dermot is living (I assume he's still living, although he won't return my emails) proof.

Like most of the great Irish prose writers, he has an oddly slanted view of events, which he translates into elegantly simple language, urging the eye to move on, sometimes too quickly, forcing the reader to go back to check if something could possibly have been described so beautifully. And it was. As I think I mentioned, I hate him. Of course . . . not really.

His series, 'The Making of the Game', was the first thing to which I would turn in the sports section of *The Irish Times*. To this day, I believe there is no finer writing on the game's colourful history, and all from this quietly spoken, almost invisible man, who, when I was playing for a living, was always around, even when it didn't seem to matter.

Unlike the vast majority of golf writers (in fact, make that sports writers), Dermot stayed out of the bar and actually walked the golf course, often with the parents or friends of those he was stalking. There was subterfuge in his behaviour, hidden intelligence disguised as innocent enquiry, and many were the times I read something about myself that even I didn't know! For instance, I learned that I got my imagination from my father, who apparently was making up stuff about me long before I did it myself. In fact, in a way, Dermot Gilleece is partly responsible for the success I had as a player, for I ended up believing a lot of my own press. Placebo effect my arse – if it works, it works!

As a child growing up in County Down, Dermot was the window through which I viewed my heroes, Irishmen like John O'Leary, David Jones, Eamonn Darcy, Des Smyth, Christy Junior, Hugh Boyle, Jimmy Kinsella, Eddie Polland, Fred Daly and, of course, the Lord God Almighty of Irish golf, Himself. There was Nicklaus and Palmer, and Trevino and Weiskopf, too, of course, but for me, they were the untouchables.

I would read of heroic Irish feats, disaster and idiocy, of John-O's win at the Irish Open at Portmarnock in 1982, and dream of playing there myself. The one thing that never entered my dreams was that one day Dermot might write about me. It never crossed my mind for, go on with you now, it was too good to be true!

David Feherty, broadcaster and hopelessly inferior journalist
Dallas, Texas 2008

Introduction

In the late fifties, when I was a trainee journalist in the now sadly defunct Irish Press Group, part of my job involved running messages for senior members of the staff. These included regular trips to the local bookmaker on Burgh Quay, placing bets for the group's main racing expert, Maurice Ring.

Though Ring enjoyed only moderate success, I was still fascinated by the notion of using one's expertise to make handy money. So I ventured to ask him why it was that he didn't quit working and take up punting full time. Peering up at me over a pair of horn-rimmed glasses, he paused for a moment before saying gravely, 'Young man, you must remember that horses are only human.' And I knew exactly what he meant.

Suddenly, horseracing lost much of its appeal as I contemplated my future as a sports reporter. In truth, though, there wouldn't be a sport of choice, not at that stage, anyway. About a year after the enlightenment from 'The Ringer', I was dispatched to cover my first golf tournament. In fact, it was the first game of golf I had ever seen, which approach was entirely in keeping with my employer's policy of firing youngsters in at the deep end. So it was that on a Monday morning in 1960, I covered the play-off for the Irish Hospitals Tournament at Woodbrook for the *Evening Press*. It involved Christy O'Connor Snr and Ken Bousfield, and O'Connor won with a course record 63 to the Englishman's 71.

As it happened, this was to be only a brief flirtation with the royal and ancient game. My main activity with the *Irish Press*, and from 1965 with the *Daily Mail*, centred on the reporting of soccer, rugby and GAA, as their Republic of Ireland representative. Still, leading amateur events, the Carrolls International and later the Irish Open offered the chance of a return to golf. As in June 1972, when I reported that British golfers Neil Coles, Brian Huggett, Bernard Hunt, Ronnie Shade and Peter Oosterhuis were opting out of the Woodbrook event because of an alleged IRA threat.

Then in 1974 there was the opportunity of reporting on the legendary Sam Snead in the Kerrygold Classic at Waterville and relaying the advice of Ryder Cup skipper Eric Brown to young hopefuls on tour. 'Stay at home for a few years and perfect your game before taking on the big boys,' he counselled at the Carrolls Celebration tournament in June of that year.

After leaving the *Daily Mail* in 1979, my involvement in golf blossomed once more when I joined Independent Newspapers for what proved to be only a sixteen-month spell. Though the term had yet to become ubiquitous, I was head-hunted by *The Irish Times* sports editor, Gerry Noone, and became the paper's golf correspondent in March 1981. Between then and 2001, when I took on the role of golf editor, I had the opportunity to meet all the game's leading players, while maintaining a close attachment to the amateur game, both men's and women's.

At *The Irish Times* I witnessed a dramatic change in the coverage of golf in these islands, from a time when the amateur was king, to the emergence of Tiger Woods as the most dominant figure in the history of the game. An illustration of this change was that in 1981, my first year in D'Olier Street, I was sent to Cypress Point in California to cover the Walker Cup, in which Irish teenagers Ronan Rafferty and Philip Walton were competing. Yet not a thought was given to the possibility of sending me to Walton Heath in London, where America fielded their greatest ever team in the Ryder Cup.

Even in 1985 I was sent to the Men's Amateur Home Internationals at Formby, Lancashire, rather than down the road to The Belfry in Birmingham, for what proved to be an historic European victory in the Ryder Cup. By the end of the decade, however, the growing popularity of tournament golf on television was being clearly reflected in our national newspapers. Meanwhile, I was having great fun putting together a weekly column called 'Golfing Log', which incorporated stories, short and not so short, which I had picked up on my golfing travels. A number of those stories have been worked into the various chapters of this book.

The dominant element of the ensuing chapters, however, centres on interviews with the great players whom I was fortunate to meet and on others who made a significant impact on me simply through the force of their personalities. In writing about Jack Nicklaus, for instance, I have concentrated on his career after 1986, when he captured the last of 18 major championships and was then faced with the crushing reality of declining skills. This process was even more painful for Seve Ballesteros, while other great players, such as Greg Norman and Tom Watson, seemed to be able to ease themselves more gently into their autumn years.

My love of golf history led me to explore Ireland's proud involvement in the Open Championship, from Michael Moran's breakthrough as third-placed finisher in 1913 to Padraig Harrington's glorious triumph at Carnoustie in July 2007 and at Royal Birkdale in 2008. The magnet of the past also drew me to a similar treatment of the Irish women's scene, in particular the glory days of May Hezlet and Rhona Adair, the so-called Golden Girls. Then there was the Irish golfing disapora, which enriched new frontiers of the game, especially in the US.

Through my good fortune in moving from *The Irish Times* to a golf correspondent's role with the *Sunday Independent* in 2002, my involvement with players at the highest level was maintained, almost seamlessly. So it was that more recent interview pieces were added to my files, some of them entirely new, while others lent embellishment to existing pieces. Then came the crowning glory of Harrington's victory in the PGA Championship at Oakland Hills, his third victory in six Majors. The process of putting it all together made me realize how truly blessed I have been in my access to so much golfing greatness.

The Irish Times have my gratitude for the opportunities given to me by Gerry Noone, initially, and then his successor as sports editor, Malachy Logan. I am also deeply indebted to Adhamhnan O'Sullivan for believing there was a role for me in the *Sunday Independent*, to his successor as sports editor, John Greene, and to Paul Kimmage, who was a true friend when I needed one. But a career in golf journalism wouldn't have been possible in the first place but for the wise and generous counselling of Terry K and Donal O'B, both of whom have gone from us to divot-free fairways in the great beyond.

CHAPTER 1

• • • • • • • • • •

A Different Celtic Tiger

'What golf needs is a black man with a great deal of personal magnetism and a whale of a game . . .'

CHARLIE SIFFORD, 1992

They had been promised an awe-inspiring spectacle, a place of breathtaking beauty, but on that memorable Friday in July 1999 all they could see from their helicopter was the ghostly outline of a promontory, shrouded in a stubborn mist that showed no signs of lifting.

Down below, the atmosphere around The clubhouse was alive with a mixture of expectation and concern. One of the young caddies fondled the familiar tiger head cover like it was a treasured toy from his not-too-distant childhood. The clubs had travelled by road and Cian Daly was told that their celebrated owner would be along in about an hour.

Inside, John O'Connor, president of The Old Head of Kinsale, darted from one room to another, the familiar look of serious contemplation a little more intense than usual. In sharp contrast, golf-course architect, Ron Kirby, sat quietly reading a newspaper, lifting his head on occasions to chat animatedly about the game that dominated his life.

The clubhouse clock was approaching noon when confirmation came that, in a manner of speaking, the tiger had landed. At a stroke, feelings of high anxiety were replaced by smiles of relief.

The elite six of Tiger Woods, David Duval, Mark O'Meara, Payne Stewart, Lee Janzen and Stuart Appleby had made the 30-minute chopper trip from Waterville, where they were based for much of their Irish stay, and were now negotiating the remaining few miles of the journey by road.

All involved at The Old Head were determined their visit would be suitably rewarding and sixteen-year-old Cian, described by caddie-master Noel Hurley as 'a gem of a kid', was certainly ready to play his part. Confused ambitions of becoming a concert violinist or joining the NASA space programme were temporarily forgotten while he dealt with the more immediate assignment of caddying for the world's leading player.

Then there was the relationship his fifteen-year-old colleague, Rory O'Brien, had established with another leading American sportsman. Clinging to O'Meara's bag as if fearing he would be set upon by thieves, Rory was wearing the rather special number 23 caddie bib. Why that particular number? 'Because that was Michael Jordan's number with the Chicago Bulls and I caddied for Michael when he came here on a recent visit,' Master O'Brien explained.

The Kinsale schoolboy had also worked that season with American businessman Rick Goings of the Orlando-based Tupperware company. And Goings happened to be a friend of O'Meara's, which explained how Rory got a gift by post the previous month of the eighteenth flag from Royal Birkdale, signed by the Open champion of 1998. And there was more. Much more. In fact, the teenager was overwhelmed to receive, by special delivery, a set of Cobra golf clubs, courtesy of Goings.

Opened officially on 1 June 1997, the course is situated on the stunning, 216-acre Co Cork promontory. It is where, on a May afternoon in 1915, in Atlantic waters 295 feet deep, the sleek liner *Lusitania* sank with the loss of 1,195 passengers and crew, victims of a German U-Boat attack off the south coast of Ireland. By a cruel irony, it occurred on a particularly pleasant spring day, warm enough to attract locals to the Old Head for a picnic.

Given its proximity to the disaster, it was almost inevitable that for years afterwards, mention of the Old Head would prompt thoughts of the tragic events of that fateful May afternoon. By the start of the nineties, however, the majestic promontory was in the process of adopting a far more desirable image. It was to be the location of a famously peaceful pursuit that could hardly contrast more sharply with the ravages of war.

Essentially, it is a headland course rather than a links, and it carries the marvellous bonus of offering what can be very welcome distractions from the more demanding aspects of the royal and ancient game, though not for players of the quality of its latest visitors. In the event, as lunchtime approached, the air was suddenly filled with the distinctly eerie combination of a lone piper playing the traditional Cork melody 'The Holy Ground' and the sonorous note of a fog-horn. The players and their Irish hosts, financiers Dermot Desmond and J. P. McManus, were at the club-house.

There was no sign of the fog lifting as they headed for the first tee in what the locals had hailed grandly as the 'Shamrock Shootout'. But the players didn't seem to mind and, with the caddies indicating the best lines to take, resident professional David Murray gave more specific guidance. One imagined the players revelling in the novelty of it all, like some sort of boyhood adventure.

Up the first fairway mist came sweeping in from the right, the eastern side of the Head. The green was visible, however, as the players hit their second shots and Tiger let out an excited 'whoop!' when his ball landed on the short grass. But there were challenges ahead for this child of the computer age, who would have to create mental pictures of where his ball might be landing, while also imagining what lay beyond.

As the sextet walked down the dramatic second fairway, the cliff-edge was just about visible. And still the mist came in, deepening Kirby's disappointment that these great players were being denied the spectacle and subtlety of a course he had helped create. Frustration became all the more acute when they played the 420-yard fourth, where the distant green was lost totally in the mist. Unwilling to make excessive demands of his imagination, Woods played a three-wood off the tee safely down the right half of the fairway, which left a second shot of only 123 yards.

While walking towards the green, he stopped momentarily and looked back. Too late he realized that, with a gentle breeze helping, he could have driven the green with the big stick. Reading his mind, Kirby smiled and called across to him, 'Maybe the next time.' They exchanged understanding nods. That damned fog!

Though the gallery increased with every hole, it remained probably no more than a hundred, making for crowd control of a decidedly gentle nature. For Stewart, who looked somewhat unfamiliar in regular slacks rather than the usual plus twos, it was quite a change from the heady excitement of his last tournament three weeks previously, at Pinehurst No. 2, where he embellished his position within the game's elite, through a second US Open triumph.

Now he was back in a land he had first visited in 1991, when he played in the Irish Open at Killarney a few days after capturing his first US Open at Hazeltine. And nobody could have imagined the tragedy which lay in wait for him three months hence, when he would be cruelly whipped from our midst by a freak air accident en route to Houston and the PGA Tour Championship.

In the event, there was no hint of quitting from the super-six as tee-shots were smashed down the long tenth, which Woods reduced, downwind, to a drive, nine iron and an eight-foot putt for the only eagle of the day. Soon they were back on the cliff-edge, only now they could actually see the 300-foot drop to churning Atlantic breakers below the tee at the spectacular, long twelfth, where drives were aimed over an elbow of the rock-face, towards a landing area way in the distance.

Oh blessed day! The fog was lifting and for the first time sound was accompanied by glorious vision. As if intent on outdoing each other in spectacular flight, cormorants, guillemots and peregrine falcons, varieties which would test even the most knowledgeable birdwatcher, swooped along the cliff-face before disappearing into one of the caves which traverse the Old Head at sea level. Appleby spoke into a camcorder as he filmed the scene. Then, laying the camera aside, he couldn't resist hitting three-iron shots down towards the rocks, sending golf balls on a route more likely to be travelled by the handicap player.

Kirby smiled quietly. 'He's doing what every golfer secretly wants to do: hit a ball into the ocean,' he mused. 'It's a special thrill to just aim it down there and let it rip.' As the Old Head was gradually revealed in all its magnificent splendour, the players could now appreciate what their trip was all about. And their patience found its reward in an afternoon that could hardly have been more beautiful. By the time they headed along the 459-yard fourteenth and back towards the ocean once more, the fog had disappeared completely. Now the drama of the finishing holes could be savoured to the full.

Only three of the players found the target at the treacherous, short sixteenth, where solid three-iron shots were needed to reach the green 199 yards away into a left-to-right crosswind that was pushing balls towards the cliff-edge. Then came the 626-yard seventeenth, where Woods hit a predictably long drive only to see it finish in the rough on the right. 'He's not up far enough to reach the green,'said Kirby. Whereupon Tiger let out a squeal of laughter after carving a driver second-shot high, wide and not-so-handsome, out towards the briny.

Kirby pointed out the line: the yellow, metal tower left of the lighthouse. Duval followed the instructions almost to the inch. Janzen also hit a good one. And there they were, preening themselves like spoiled children, when Stewart saw fit to demand their attention. 'Hang on!' he shouted. 'I'm the old guy who just won the US Open.'

After the seventeenth, which nobody reached in two, they proceeded to the extreme back tee at the eighteenth. Looking inland over the promontory, now clear of any hint of fog, the players' concern turned to Atlantic breakers crashing onto the rocks directly below them. Appleby joked, 'You wouldn't want to do a Gary Player off this tee,' in a reference to the technique the so-called Black Knight employed of walking into his shots. Meanwhile, Rory was recounting how Michael Jordan, on a visit earlier in the year, had reduced the 459-yard hole to a drive and nine iron, though the lad neglected to mention that it was with the assistance of a brisk, following wind. 'Not from this tee,' protested Stewart. Yes, from that tee, the US Open champion was told.

Tiger took a short line into rough up the left, from where he reached the green with an eight iron. Stewart, with that wonderfully seductive tempo, opted for a longer line down the right and didn't quite reach the fairway. Before settling over a second shot of 201 yards, uphill and into the wind, he agreed to be photographed with three delighted young local fans. Then, taking out a four wood, he feigned anger, while muttering, 'Michael Jordan hit nine iron my ass.' And as a beautifully struck shot sailed towards the elevated green, he gave a whoop of delight.

It was approaching six o'clock as they stood together on the final green, watched by a phalanx of spectators, strategically positioned along the terrace of the clubhouse. And as the audience applauded, one suspected it was as much for their patience with the weather as for their golfing skills. The relief from John O'Connor was almost palpable. 'Having these players here is something I always imagined would happen and the sun has never been more welcome,' he said.

After further picture-taking and autograph-signing, the players headed into the locker-room where the compliments started flowing. 'Those spectacular views towards the finish were worth the wait,' said Woods. Whereupon the friend he calls Marko added, 'With that breathtaking scenery, it's got to be one of the most dramatic locations for a golf course I've ever seen.'

Then Duval, in typically measured tones, remarked, 'I really love coming to your country. I've played Ballybunion, Lahinch and, of course, Portmarnock in the Walker Cup in 1991. I have always been made to feel so welcome.' He went on, 'Some of the holes we saw towards the end – their beauty would rival the best anywhere. I imagine it could be extremely difficult in high winds, especially some of those hills along the cliff, but the views are unbelievable. Standing on tees with a 300-foot drop is not something we do every day.'

Typically passionate, Stewart spoke about 'the beauty of this place', insisting that it would become 'a must of a golfing destination for tourists from my country'. He went on, 'For my own part as a professional, I feel really blessed to have had the opportunity of visiting this very special place.' Woods then interjected, 'Unfortunately we didn't see very much of the early holes but there were some spectacular views towards the finish. I think it's great that we've had this chance of such an amazing golfing experience.'

After changing their shoes, the players emerged to join club members and friends in a cup of tea and a sandwich, before their helicopter whisked them back to Waterville. It meant Cian Daly had to part company with a welcome burden, which had been close to his heart all afternoon. How well did he feel he had guided the world's number one through the fog? 'Tiger shot 71,' he said with a proud smile.

At the time of this greatest six-ball in the history of Irish golf, Woods and Duval were ranked first and second in the world. O'Meara was fifth, Stewart was tenth; Appleby was thirty-third and Janzen was thirty-fourth. Between them they had eight major professional titles: Stewart the 1989 USPGA Championship, 1991 US Open and 1999 US Open; O'Meara the 1998 US Masters and British Open; Janzen the 1993 US Open and 1998 US Open; and Woods the 1997 US Masters. Little more than a month later, Woods was to capture his second major when he beat off the challenge of Sergio Garcia in the USPGA Championship at Medinah. However, from a golfing standpoint, the autumn of 1999 was marked indelibly by the untimely passing of one of the game's favourite and most talented sons.

Stewart's tragic death was reminiscent of events thirty-three years previously, when another great American golfer was similarly cut off in his prime. Two years after capturing the Open Championship at St Andrews, Tony Lema and his wife were killed when their private aircraft crashed en route from the 1966 PGA Championship to a pro-am event elsewhere in the US.

On a visit to Ireland's south-west prior to the 1998 Open Championship, Stewart gained the distinction in the company of Woods and O'Meara of having a hole in one on the 217-yard, short third at Ballybunion. The club was a beautifully struck two iron into a stiff breeze and the outcome was doubly remarkable for the fact that Woods actually had a five at the hole. When has anyone been able to boast of outscoring the world's top player by four strokes on a par three? And during the 1999 visit, much of his time was spent in Waterville, where he entertained US Tour colleagues and delighted locals with rousing tunes on the harmonica. Small wonder the club decided to make him honorary captain for the year 2000, a distinction he was delighted to accept.

His last tournament appearance was in the National Car Rental Golf Classic at Lake Buena Vista, Florida, which started on 21 October. And during the second round, he was a little taken aback to be addressed by an Irish voice as he walked from the fifteenth green to the sixteenth tee on the Magnolia Course. Initially, he responded with suitable courtesy on being congratulated for his splendid victory at Pinehurst, but the player was clearly jolted when the spectator added, 'Congratulations on being next year's honorary captain of Waterville.' This time, Stewart asked, 'How did you know that? Are you a member of the club?'

At that stage, Dublin-based solicitor Tom Duffy, a native of Mullingar, explained that he was at Disneyworld on holiday with his wife and children, and had taken the day away from them to have a look at the tournament. Whereupon Stewart asked him if he had any advice to offer regarding Waterville. Duffy replied with a smile, 'Yes. Steer clear of committee meetings.'

This brought hearty laughter from the American, who was clearly aware of the ability of such bodies to make a camel out of a horse. With that, he hit off the sixteenth tee and was followed on the remaining holes of the round by his Irish fan. Their exchanges weren't finished. As Stewart walked up the eighteenth fairway, he spied his new-found friend once more, outside the fairway ropes. Coming over to Duffy, he enquired, 'Do you know J. P. McManus?' 'Not personally,' came the reply. 'I'm afraid I don't move in the same social circles.' 'Well, if you see him, give him my best regards.' And all of this while he was attempting to make the halfway cut, which, as it happened, he missed by a stroke after a second successive 71.

Neither man could have known this would be the last tournament hole Stewart would ever play. And by a remarkable coincidence, on that very day, he was among the leading names announced at a press conference in Limerick to compete in the

McManus Invitational 2000 Pro-Am at Limerick GC the following July. Duffy, whose brother Michael is a past captain of Mullingar GC, said, 'Though our exchange was helped by the fact that there weren't many people around the sixteenth tee, I was amazed by his friendliness and willingness to chat. And I was really stunned when he actually sought me out going down the eighteenth.' He concluded, 'Obviously it's dreadfully sad that he is now gone from us, but I will treasure these beautiful memories of a generous and charming gentleman.'

On the Monday after their meeting, a freak accident claimed the life of an open and generous man, who graced his craft with abundant skill, vitality and a marvellous sense of fun. There would be no more Irish visits and the sense of loss was especially acute at the McManus Pro-Am, after which a group of leading American players, including Woods, went to Waterville on a sad assignment. With Stewart's widow, Tracey, they honoured their fallen colleague at the unveiling of a larger-than-life bronze, erected in his memory.

It became a poignant postscript to a 1999 visit during which Irish people took him to their hearts. And those of us fortunate enough to have seen him and his five colleagues grace The Old Head can still picture his mock rebuke on the seventeenth fairway – 'I'm the old guy who just won the US Open.' And in the late afternoon, we laughed with him beneath a bright July sun on what had earlier been an extraordinary, foggy day.

Tiger, of course, won the millennium staging of the McManus Invitational, and I was in Heidelberg the following May when he swept to success in the Deutsche Bank TPC Open. His remarkable accessibility on Irish visits was brought sharply into focus by events on the Saturday evening after he had carded a sparkling third round of 63. A slim, dapper figure in sunshades gave brief and explicit instructions to the waiting television crews. 'Tiger will give three interviews,' said Mark Steinberg. 'You have two questions each. Nobody asks a third question or he walks.'

When the centre of attention descended the eight steps from the elevated score-recorder's area like a major showbusiness personality, there were further instructions from his manager.

'OK, this is the order: Sky, German, you [to Ken Brown, representing the US Golf Channel].' In such circumstances the interviewer knew he had to pick his questions carefully. Ask something like, 'Well, Tiger, you must be pleased with that round,' and question number one could deliver a brief 'Yes' in reply. These, however, were practised operators. The opening question was: 'Well, Tiger, tell us how the round developed for you.' No monosyllabic answer to that.

An exasperated TV cameraman exclaimed, 'What a circus!' Close by, a German worker was driving wooden stakes into the ground to accommodate additional security ropes. 'Crazy!' he remarked to nobody in particular. 'All zis for one person.' Brown, who was the last of the interviewers, shared his bemusement. 'It's an amazing situation,' said the former Ryder Cup player. 'As Tiger turned to be interviewed by me, he had this glazed look in his eyes, as if his mind was a million miles away. Once I started asking him questions, however, I had his complete attention. Then, when I finished, the glazed look came back and he turned automatically as if expecting another interview. Amazing.' Still, he conceded, 'Unfortunately, it has to be this way. The demands on Tiger are such that he would never get to the locker-room if all of our requirements were to be satisfied.'

Against this background it's not difficult to imagine my excitement at being told there was a good chance of a one-to-one with the great one, as part of the build-up to the 2005 staging of the McManus Invitational. When JP expressed the hope it would happen, I took it as a done deal. And so it proved, but not before I had received a sharp reprimand. I was driving towards a barbecue in a swish area of Augusta on the Monday of Masters week when my mobile phone rang. 'You're late,' said JP. 'He's been here since six.' How, I thought in self-mitigation, could I have known that Americans believed in arriving for an evening gathering in the late afternoon? Still, having made a decidedly inauspicious start to the evening, I wasn't about to dig a bigger hole for myself.

Suddenly, the situation received an unexpected lift in the delightful form of my quarry's Swedish wife. 'This is Elin,' (pronounced Eelin), I was informed of the stunning blonde who stood before me. Her warm smile and firm handshake were hugely encouraging. 'I am hoping to have a chat with your husband,' I ventured, quickly adding the reassurance, 'Don't worry, I won't give him grief.' Her smile never wavered.

Six days later, Woods would resume his pursuit of golfing immortality by capturing a fourth US Masters, to bring him level with Ben Hogan and Gary Player on a 'major' tally of nine. And he would reach double figures on a return to the Open at St Andrews, where, in millennium year, he had become the fifth player to complete a career grand slam.

Given the context of the interview, I had to accept that matters such as the various swing changes he had undergone during the last few years, the protracted drought of 'major' success which followed his US Open triumph of 2002 and his ill-fated Ryder Cup partnership with Phil Mickelson had already received a sufficient airing in the international media. So, as temperatures on a hitherto balmy, southern night dropped markedly, I focused instead on what had become his regular July visits to Ireland, prior to the Open Championship.

One of these visits had developed into something of a busman's holiday, when, five years previously, he spearheaded a highly successful McManus Invitational at Limerick GC, which culminated in donations of €20 million to local charities. He was now set to return to the latest staging at Adare GC on 4 and 5 July, directly after the Smurfit European Open. Also competing would be familiar faces from the Old Head in the form of O'Meara, Appleby and Janzen, along with Fred Couples and Robert Allenby, among others. Indeed, rival Ryder Cup captains, Ian Woosnam and Tom Lehman, were among the high-profile line-up.

The fourth staging of the richest event of its kind in Europe owed its existence to an apparent golfing itch, which has tended to afflict the eponymous organizer every five years since 1990. When asked to explain the five-year cycle, McManus replied, 'I couldn't afford to do it more often,' but before anyone could run away with the notion of the wealthy financier suddenly being strapped for cash, he added, 'It's very time-consuming.'

Anyway, back at the American barbecue, I was tucking into a particularly pleasant steak when a tap on my shoulder was followed by a whispered, 'You're on.' With that, I stood up to be introduced to the world's foremost golfer. Dressed casually in a red tee-shirt and black slacks, his bare head made him appear decidedly boyish. His grip was firm, his eyes were bright and his amazing smile was very different from the one I had become used to from countless press conferences. There was a warmth in his eye-to-eye contact which I hadn't detected in what could be described as 'work situations'. He seemed prepared to talk there and then in a busy hallway, where other guests were coming and going – which wasn't what I'd planned.

Putting an arm over his athletic shoulders, I gently eased him into an empty room which I had spied earlier. Just the two of us. There, standing casually with his back to a wall, his face lit up as we talked of Ireland. I reminded him that his first visit had been to Waterville in 1998, when he had gone on to be third behind O'Meara at Royal Birkdale, and of a more extensive visit the following year, when Stewart's presence would later give cause for so much sadness.

'That's right,' he said, beaming. 'That's exactly what happened. The first time I came over with Mark, we just hung out at Waterville. And it was just great fun. Playing golf and fishing, and being with one another. Just a nice, relaxing time, chilling out before a major championship. That's what you want to do. You don't want to burn yourself ragged going into a major.

'We had a great time with the people at Waterville and with the people at The K Club the following year. We went to the pubs with Payne, and he'd get up there and start singing.' Didn't this larking about seem rather strange to a middle-class native of Cypress, California? 'No, not at all,' he replied, 'because I had heard all the stories from Mark. He'd been there a few times and he told me how it was going to be. And we had just the greatest time. But in a special way, it's going to feel pretty weird, very poignant, going back again after the last time, when Tracey [Stewart's widow] was there. Payne, like the rest of us, loved everything about Ireland, especially the people, so nice and so friendly. And it became a wonderful way for me to prepare for St Andrews.'

Recalling the visit to the Old Head in 1999, he went on, 'We didn't see very much of the early holes, but those spectacular views towards the finish were worth the wait. Though the golf course was still very young at the time, it offered a fair test.' Interestingly, a recommendation he made that the left side of the eighteenth fairway be given greater definition was taken on board by Ron Kirby, who created extensive mounding on both sides of the buggy path, so separating it visually and physically from the seventeenth.

By this stage I felt bold enough to suggest that Woods had actually won the 2000 McManus event by default, no matter that he gave the winner's cheque of £33,330 to charity. He laughed heartily. 'I know, I know,' he acknowledged, laughing all the while. 'Stuart [Appleby] did win the tournament. There's no doubt about that.' 'So you're conceding it,' I said. 'Yes,' came the unequivocal reply. 'He won. Sure he was using a laser, but he still did the lowest score.' So he was now formally acknowledging being second best? 'Yes,' he said. 'We all do. Regardless of the DQ [disqualification]. That's the way it is.'

Perhaps I should explain. Though Woods carded rounds of 64, 68 for a 12-under-par 132 around Limerick GC, he was actually outscored by Appleby, who had the effrontery to produce 66, 63 for 129. But there was a problem. Unaware that normal tournament rules applied, the Australian used a laser measuring device on the opening day and was disqualified by Tony Gray, the PGA European Tour official in attendance, for a breach of Rule 14-3 covering artificial devices and unusual equipment. 'I honestly wasn't aware there was a professional competition,' said Appleby at the time. 'I thought I was playing only for my amateur partners, and I just wanted to entertain the public and keep my amateurs happy. But, naturally, I accept the decision.' Almost needlessly, he added, 'I didn't come here for the money.'

Given the number of tournaments Woods had played since then, it seemed remarkable that he could remember the 2000 event in such detail. As he pointed out, 'The whole idea was to help out JP and raise money for his charities, and the things he likes to do for the people of Ireland, especially the people of Limerick. And junior golf. It was pretty impressive. And it goes to show you the quality of the person JP is. We came together for him and for him only.' I suggested that McManus was very much a product of his home place. 'Correct,' agreed Woods. 'We all kinda are. We all love our home town. He supports his home town, which is very special.'

He went on to talk about the death of Stewart and the trip to Waterville in 2000. 'When Payne passed, it was very special for all of us to come together like that,' he said. He also noted how the Royal and Ancient seemed to be sharing a five-year cycle with the McManus International, where Open Championships at St Andrews were concerned. It brought to mind the lead into the 1999 Open at Carnoustie, when Stewart had told him, 'The British Open is the best. It's original golf. A lot of Americans speak out against it; say they don't enjoy it. I just tell them not to bother. To stay away.'

So it was that Tiger endured the frustration of a brutal course set-up for a share of seventh place at Carnoustie and returned with his enthusiasm undiminished in 2000. That was when a perform-ance of discipline, authority and staggering artistry delivered an eight-stroke victory without even a solitary visit to one of the 112 bunkers over the four days. A year later he was back at Limerick GC, this time for a private battle with McManus. 'That was fun,' he recalled. 'JP played a two-ball scramble and I played two-ball worse ball. The problem for me in having to use my worse ball was that the windy conditions made it harder to make birdies. So he just had to make [net] pars and wait for me to make mistakes. Eventually they caught up with me and he beat me fairly easily. In fact, as I remember it, I got smoked.' Conceding fourteen handi-cap strokes, he surely did – by a five and four margin.

On that occasion, he and O'Meara stayed at Adare Manor, though they didn't have the opportunity of playing the course. 'In fact, I didn't even get the chance of looking at it,' he said, 'though from hitting some balls on the range I could see it was in a really beautiful setting.' How did he feel about moving from Limerick's modest 6,562 yards to a strong, championship layout designed by the legendary Robert Trent Jones? 'Let's put it this way,' he said, 'I love the way it was run in Limerick. It was more of a local thing, family-oriented. It was pretty neat for me to see JP with the people he had grown up with. They told me stories about him when he was a kid and so on.

'That's what made that tournament so special. Moving to a bigger course at Adare, I don't think it's going to change the feel. The feel will still be the same. We'll all do anything we can to make sure that it's even bigger than it was in 2000.'

Finally, I wondered how the Irish connection, which had become so much a part of his life, actually came about. 'Well, basically, Mark introduced me to JP and Dermot [Desmond]. I don't quite remember where. We exchanged phone numbers and the times we'd come to Ireland, and the times they'd come to Florida, we just hung out. And a friendship grew from there.'

Of course Woods's Irish connection has extended beyond these annual, pre-Open visits. There were his Ryder Cup visits in the autumn of 2006 and two years before that he finished ninth behind Ernie Els in the American Express Championship at Mount Juliet, having captured the title at the same venue in 2002. In the week of the 2002 staging, the world's top golfer had dinner with the world's top hurler, when the pride of Kilkenny, DJ Carey, showed off the Liam McCarthy Cup to Tiger, and presented him with a hurley and sliotar. Something for his trophy case at Isleworth in Florida, observers mused.

When dinner was over, Tiger was seen in the car-park of the Hunter's Yard shortly after nine, knocking the sliotar around on the tarmac. 'Flip it up,' urged Mount Juliet PR consultant Padraig Slattery. As a Clareman who also happened to be the 2005 captain of Portmarnock GC, Slattery knew about such matters. 'Naw, I think I'll leave that,' was the prudent response from a sporting genius who demonstrated a remarkable solo effort of his own, flipping a golf ball in the air with a wedge, in the celebrated TV advert for Nike.

This was the fun-loving side of a player whom Mount Juliet owner Tim Mahony found to be a decidedly serious young man. 'I have been struck by his strong, silent personality,'he said. 'Within twenty minutes of meeting Jack Nicklaus, you hardly knew you were in the presence of the world's greatest golfer: he became a very ordinary guy. But Woods is different. There's a huge reserve there. He's not a talker and he doesn't feel any compulsion to talk.'

From my experience, I could readily understand that view. Our chat had been strictly about golf and there was no question of delving any deeper, but I was greatly impressed by his warmth and courtesy, away from the demands of the tournament scene. So it was that when we parted at that Augusta barbecue and he headed back to join his wife, I was left with the image of a different side to the greatest golfer of his generation, of a man who, for relaxation, likes nothing better than the company of friends, preferably in Ireland, if it happens to be early July.

Thoughts of Tennyson

In the wake of the 2005 McManus Invitational, I was commissioned to write a piece for a commemorative book on the event. Wondering how I might approach the assignment, I hit on the idea of doing it through the eyes of two teenage girls, the twin daughters of my brother Declan, who lives in Limerick. So, this is their story:

Standing beside the putting green in the sylvan splendour of Adare Manor, Jenny and Sarah decided to text their friends. 'Guess who we're looking at right now?' they teased. Then, unashamedly gloating, a follow-up message read: 'Tiger Woods and Keith Wood – that's who. What are you doing?'

The sixteen-year-old twins, who are junior members of Castletroy GC, were having a golfing experience to remember. When isolated, early cloudbursts gave way to glorious sunshine, their home place became a haven for major celebrities from either side of the Atlantic. And they glowed with the excitement of it all.

Especially neat from their perspective was how the spectacle catered for every age group, from toddlers to teenagers, like themselves, and then to the older folk with whom they would more readily have associated the tournament scene. And they marvelled at the accessibility of the players and how well organized everything seemed to be. And how it was all being done to help local charities.

How dare anybody put Limerick down, when it could play host to something as beautiful as this! And the girls would have found no argument among attendances which totalled almost 50,000 over the two days, creating an atmosphere more readily associated with the rare old times of the Irish Open. And they were treated to an appropriate climax when Padraig Harrington swept to a record second-round 63 for ultimate victory by a six-stroke margin.

As it happened, the Dubliner had set another record on the opening day – by using up a brand-new marker pen in only nine holes. 'I can't imagine how many signatures that would be, but it's just fantastic out there,' he enthused. 'A lot of people are involved behind the scenes in helping JP bring a great assembly of players together for worthy causes, in what must be one of the most lovely places in Ireland.'

Traversed by the charming River Maigue, the manor was indeed a delightful place to be on those memorable July days. And imagining how it might have looked in earlier times, one was reminded of the words of Tennyson – 'On either side the river lie/ long fields of barley and of rye/ that clothe the wold and meet the sky/ and thro' the field the road runs by . . .' Now, on the same land, the architectural skill of another old master, Robert Trent Jones, was presenting a golfing test for some of the world's leading practitioners.

Like the rest of us, Harrington recognized the event wasn't about birdies, bogeys or prize money: it was about making a real difference to the less fortunate in our midst. Yet he still found himself awestruck at the throngs of spectators flanking the fairway and green at the thirteenth, which was his finishing hole after a shotgun start.

Afterwards, he talked once more of the pleasure of plying his craft before wonderfully responsive galleries. Then, referring to his partners from Charleville Community Care, he captured the essence of the pro-am format by remarking, 'It's a great

distraction when you're trying to read your team's putts and generally supporting what they're doing.'

Trevor Immelman, a future US Masters champion, dominated play on the opening day with a sparkling, eight-under-par 64. But the gifted South African happily deferred to the drawing power of El Tigre, who had arrived with seven US Tour colleagues in appropriate style, having travelled by private jet from the Western Open at Cog Hill in Chicago. 'It's special for all of us to come to an event like this and support a good friend,' said the reigning US Masters champion. 'JP does amazing things and when he asks for your support, you can't wait to give it.'

And despite feeling feverish and sniffling uncomfortably, he proved his commitment to the cause by carding an admirable 67 which started with a birdie on the fifteenth – his opening hole. All the while, his warmth towards spectators prompted within us renewed respect for the older virtues of humility, dignity and style.

'This is a wonderful golf course,' Tiger declared. 'If they had the rough up, with a couple of tougher pins and faster greens, it would be a really great test.'

Later, before heading for a well-earned rest, he gently chided those who might have suspected his thoughts were miles away, on a celebrated location in the Region of Fife. 'This is not about preparing for the Open,' he said. 'This is about enjoying 36 holes of golf in good company.' Which, on the opening day, happened to include Martin McAleese, husband of Mary McAleese, President of Ireland.

Prior to departing the scene, however, there was candid talk of St Andrews. And priceless pointers for prospective punters about his prospects the following week, when he duly captured the Open for a second time.

Such matters were far from the thoughts of Jenny and Sarah. 'Seeing Tiger in the flesh was kinda weird,' they recalled. 'But the thing we remember best was how happy everybody seemed.' And for event organizers, tributes don't come better than that.

Entering the Tiger era

In his 1992 autobiography, Charlie Sifford wrote, 'What golf needs . . . is a black man with a great deal of personal magnetism and a whale of a game who can demonstrate that blacks can fit into the game.' Five years on, as if to order, Tiger Woods had launched the game into a new era with more talent than even Sifford could have imagined.

As the first black golfer to make an impact on the US tournament scene, Sifford was controversially overlooked for a Masters invitation. Now, in *The Augusta Chronicle* of the morning after the 1997 Masters, Earl Woods, the champion's father, was pictured being congratulated by Ron Townsend, the first black member of Augusta National. We were witnessing remarkable times.

South Africa's Gary Player, three times a Masters winner, saw an international dimension to the achievement. 'Tiger Woods has the opportunity to do something for the human race that no other golfer before him has,' he said. 'Imagine the black people of Africa – 400 million – watching Tiger win the Masters . . .' As *USA Today* put it in an editorial, 'The result is a moment of enchanting transition, when a new generation arrives with new ideas and standards. Such moments may be traumatic, of course. But in golf as in all sport – as in all of life – the changeover is thrilling to witness. After all, when you make history, you make the future, too.'

Meanwhile, the hero of the hour was gracious enough to suggest that he never imagined winning by the unprecedented margin of twelve strokes. 'It's not what I envisioned,' he said. 'You envision duelling it out with say Faldo or Nicklaus or Watson – someone who's awfully tough to beat down the stretch. You dream of doing that or getting into a play-off. But never in the fashion that I did it.'

We had entered the Tiger era.

Heroic deeds at Torrey Pines

Consider these words: 'It's when I get the unbelievable shooting pain, and that's usually right at impact and just beyond it.' And these: 'I've got a few painkillers on board right now, definitely some anti-inflammatories going . . .' Yes, they come from Tiger Woods, but the interesting bit is that they're not from Torrey Pines in June 2008, but from his appearance in the American Express Championship at Mount Juliet four years previously.

This was when he talked of how proud he was to have confronted, a day at a time, the problem of extreme back spasms of the intercostals while getting through four rounds against the odds. And he played well enough for a ninth-place finish behind the winner, Ernie Els. But why did he do it? 'What keeps me going, I guess, is that I'm very stubborn,' he replied.

It was this stubbornness which carried him through an incredible 91 holes of the US Open for the reward of a fourteenth major title, bringing him within four of the record target of Jack Nicklaus, his *raison d'être* as a tournament golfer. And the gambling nature of the man was also revealed by Woods's coach, Hank Haney, who said of the injured knee, 'By last week there wasn't much left to damage, frankly.'

Now, the newly crowned champion had to face a fourth operation on the left knee, this time involving reconstructive anterior cruciate ligament (ACL) surgery. Though it would keep him out of action for the remainder of the year, he was assured by his medical people that the long-term prognosis was 'very good'.

'I think he's making the right choice in getting it done,' said his long-time friend Mark O'Meara. 'I know his doctors, and they're the best in the world. In six months he'll be better than new. It's time to realize the game is the thing that will benefit.' Though O'Meara would be returning to the scene of his 1998 triumph, Woods faced a very different July. Apart from the ligament damage, he had to recover from a double stress-fracture of the left tibia which has been attributed to the intense rehabilitation he subjected himself to in the build-up to the US Open.

All of which made his Torrey Pines performance nothing short of astonishing. Looking back on his limping, stifled shouts of pain and general discomfort almost from the outset, it seemed inconceivable that he could have lasted 91 holes. And the fact that he did, victoriously, made one wonder whether he was exaggerating the damage. This is not uncommon among elite sportspeople, if only to protect themselves mentally against the possibility of failure.

So, in my view, the comment attributed to Retief Goosen, whereby the South African suggested a certain degree of play-acting by Woods, wasn't as insensitive as it may have appeared. It was based on the assumption that no mere mortal could have endured such apparent agony over five days of physical exertion on the longest course in US Open history.

Once again, Woods had left us flabbergasted, this time by his powers of endurance. 'I know much was made of my knee throughout the last week, and it was important to me that I disclosed my condition publicly at an appropriate time,' he said. 'I wanted to be very respectful of the USGA and their incredibly hard work, and make sure the focus was on the US Open. Now, it is clear that the right thing to do is to listen to my doctors, follow through with this surgery, and focus my attention on rehabilitating my knee. I have to do the right thing for my long-term health and I look forward to returning to competitive golf when my doctors agree that my knee is sufficiently healthy. My doctors assure me with the proper rehabilitation and training, the knee will be strong and there will be no long-term effects.'

Where most observers thought he was recovering from key-hole surgery to remove fragments of cartilage from the knee two days after this year's US Masters, it transpired that the underlying problem was damage to the ACL sustained while running at his home in Orlando after returning from Carnoustie last July. And it wasn't a sudden breakdown insofar as he had been warned of a 'deficient ACL' as far back as ten years ago.

With his self-confessed stubbornness kicking in, he decided to play through the pain. Then, moving into Superman mode, he proceeded to win five of the next six events, including the WGC-Bridgestone Invitational, the PGA Championship, the BMW

Championship, the US Tour Championship and the Target World Challenge, while also finishing second at the Deutsche Bank Championship. And the streak was carried over into 2008, with victories in his first four events of the season.

But he was still experiencing pain and it was with a view to playing for the remainder of the season that he opted for surgery in April, a procedure which had been planned well in advance. The necessary ACL surgery could be postponed until the end of the year. In the meantime, the plan was to make a comeback in the Memorial Tournament on 26 May.

According to his manager, Mark Steinberg, in the *Washington Post*, the player felt a sharp and different pain prior to the Memorial, to the point where it became excruciating. An MRI scan showed a double stress-fracture of the left tibia for which the suggested treatment was three weeks on crutches, then three weeks of inactivity followed by rehabilitation.

This would mean missing the US Open and possibly Birkdale as well. His best hope would be a return to action in early August at Oakland Hills, where he would attempt to defend the PGA title after almost four months' inactivity. And if he played in the Ryder Cup at the end of September before eventually undergoing the ACL surgery, he could place the 2009 Masters in jeopardy.

All the while, Woods had his heart set on Torrey Pines. 'I was determined to do everything and anything in my power to play in the US Open on a course that is close to where I grew up and holds many special memories for me,' he said. Notwithstanding that it was contrary to medical advice. As Steinberg admitted, 'The doctor wasn't too encouraged about him playing in the Open. It wasn't that he could do extensive new damage to the knee. The doctor just doubted anybody could stand the pain.'

For Woods, the prospect of a US Open triumph on a course where he had no fewer than six Buick triumphs to his credit was irresistible. And he has no regrets. 'I'm not really good at listening to doctors' orders too well,' he admitted. 'Although I will miss the rest of this season, I'm thrilled with the fact that last week was such a special tournament.'

His absence from the Ryder Cup could be viewed as not quite

the blow some people may have imagined. However remarkable his talents, Woods is simply not a team man and without him the American players would probably mould together as a more effective unit. And, of course, there was the added impetus of winning back the cup 'for Tiger'.

In the meantime, he left us with the memory of quite extraordinary events last weekend. Curiously, the play-off victory on the Monday became something of a postscript to the real meat of the 108th US Open. If there was to be a lasting image of Torrey Pines, it would surely be the 12-foot putt on the 72nd green last Sunday, which Woods studied for 40 seconds from one perspective and then 30 seconds from another, before holing it to tie with Rocco Mediate.

Here was a stroke which separated golf from all other sports at the highest level. There could be no realistic hope of producing one of Woods's 320-yard drives, nor the spinning precision of his short irons. But even the humblest of practitioners has known the feeling of holing a 12-foot putt under pressure, even if it was for the Mid-Weekers singles. In the immediate aftermath, Woods described it as 'two and a half balls outside the right lip' and over a surface that was 'a bit wobbly'. Just like your average club green, you might say. The huge difference on this occasion, however, was the near-certainty of the outcome. You just sensed he wasn't going to miss. And that borders on the miraculous in such variable conditions.

Then there was the player's reaction. The electricity, the nerve-tingling excitement infused by Woods into such situations, makes for the sort of compelling viewing that brought record television audiences in the US that weekend. Indeed CNBC reported, one suspected only partly in jest, that while Woods and Mediate were battling in the play-off last Monday afternoon, eastern time, trading on the New York Stock Exchange slipped by 9.2 per cent.

Small wonder that the money-men from golf's commercial side were looking anxiously at the immediate future.

It also explained why Woods had been the top-earning American athlete on *Sports Illustrated*'s 'Fortunate 40' list for the last five years, with earnings of $128 million this past year alone, from prize money, endorsements and appearance fees.

Meanwhile, the NBC Network had their best Monday rating for golf in thirty years, while the play-off gave ESPN the most-viewed telecast in the history of cable television. Indeed, as a general view, NBC acknowledge that their ratings rise by more than 50 per cent every time Woods plays and the increase becomes even more pronounced when he's in contention.

And the attendance of 24,000 was double that which watched Goosen beat Mark Brooks in the last play-off for the title at Southern Hills seven years ago. Which, among other things, meant that the much-criticized intransigence of the USGA in sticking by its eighteen-hole play-off format, rather than the four-hole procedure introduced for the British Open in 1989, was certain to survive in the immediate future.

Former CBS sports executive Neal Pilson was quoted in the *Los Angeles Times* as saying, 'As hard as it is for some of us to remember, Tiger Woods hasn't been playing golf for ever. It was true for Michael Jordan and the NBA, and Muhammad Ali in boxing. Golf will survive and do very well without Tiger Woods. But at some point people have to understand that Tiger isn't going to play for ever. It's a natural phenomenon and we're all aware of it – advertisers, sponsors, golf tournament directors and other golfers.'

Finally, Torrey Pines 2008, with Woods, Mediate and England's Lee Westwood as the three leading challengers for the title, had me thinking of history repeating itself in remarkable detail. Back in 1990 at Medinah, Nick Faldo missed a putt on the 72nd hole to get into a play-off, just as Westwood did. And Hale Irwin and Mike Donald proceeded to battle out a play-off over nineteen holes, just as Woods and Mediate did.

One crucial difference, however, was that Irwin, at forty-five, captured the title: Mediate, at forty-five, didn't. A seriously injured Tiger simply wouldn't succumb.

Nine days later, on 25 June 2008, IMG issued a statement regarding the wellbeing of their most valuable client. It read: 'Tiger Woods underwent successful reconstructive surgery on the Anterior Cruciate Ligament (ACL) in his left knee on Tuesday in Park City, Utah. The surgery was performed by Dr Thomas D. Rosenberg and Dr Vernon J. Cooley, who did arthroscopic surgery on Woods' same knee in April 2008. "We were confident going into this surgery and I am pleased with the results," said Dr. Rosenberg. "There were no surprises during the procedure, and as we have said, with the proper rehabilitation and training, it is highly unlikely that Mr. Woods will have any long-term effects as it relates to his career."

'A rehabilitation schedule and projected timetable for Woods' return to competitive golf has yet to be determined, but will be announced at the appropriate time. "It was important to me to have the surgery as soon as possible so that I could begin the rehabilitation process," said Woods. "I am very appreciative of Dr Rosenberg and Dr Cooley and his staff's guidance and look forward to working with them through the necessary rehabilitation and training. I also want to thank everyone for their well wishes over the past week. I look forward to working hard at my rehabilitation over the coming months and returning to the PGA tour healthy next year." '

● ● ● ● ● ● ● ● ● ●

CHAPTER 2

Great Courses and their Makers

'The great pity of it is that we don't play enough strategically demanding courses like Augusta National.'

PAUL McGINLEY

'Aim a foot right of the pin and it's quick, sir.' This was the opening instruction from a gentle black man named Douglas who, for a fee of $35 'plus my tip', was to be my caddie for the golfing adventure of a lifetime. The putt was struck solidly with an assured touch, which had been fine-tuned on winter parkland greens back home at Clontarf Golf Club. Douglas let out a gasp and in the same instant began to pull out a wedge for the pitch shot he was convinced I would have from off the far side of the green.

Clearly a man of little faith, I thought, as the ball gathered break-neck speed with every turn, before crashing against the back of the hole and then popping miraculously down into the cup. 'Great read, sir!' beamed Douglas. And notwithstanding my excitement at the outcome, I still spied him surreptitiously slipping the wedge back into the bag. In that instant, a potentially great partnership, possibly the rival of Musgrove and Lyle, Langer and Coleman, Fanny and Faldo or Woods and Williams, had been sundered.

Meanwhile, I found myself reflecting smugly on Nick Faldo's play of that same opening hole in 1989, when he set off on the final round of the US Masters. Given my start, rather than the double-bogey with which he had begun a magnificent round of 65, he would have saved himself the agony of a play-off for the title with Scott Hoch. But what could he have expected, without my price-less experience of Irish winter greens!

Anyway, this was Monday, 11 April 1994 and I was savouring my reward as a winner of the golf writer's equivalent of the Lotto. At the time, from an entry of about four hundred scribes and photographers covering the first major of the season, a draw was made from which a fortunate forty were given the chance to play Augusta National on the morning after the tournament ended. After five failed attempts, oh joy of joys, my name had come out of the hat.

Very few of the world's golf courses will set pulses racing among jaded scribes. I can remember the buzz when it became known that the visiting media could play Cypress Point on the eve of the Walker Cup in 1981. And there was the crushing disappointment of losing out to a British colleague in a chance to play the Old Course at St Andrews during the Dunhill Cup, while playing Valderrama has always been a special treat. But Augusta National is different. And the point was illustrated perfectly by Paul McGinley during Masters week 2001, when he confessed that he had turned down several opportunities to play there as a member's guest. 'Though I'm absolutely fascinated by what I've seen on television, I have declined all invitations,' he said, on a visit to Dublin that week. Why so? 'Because I want to earn the right to be there,' he replied.

As one of Ireland's top three tournament professionals, McGinley went on to acknowledge it as a particularly difficult week for him. Darren Clarke had played the Masters every year since 1998, while Padraig Harrington, who made the break-through in 2000, was back there again. And it was no consolation knowing that the only other Irishmen to have competed there by that stage were Joe Carr, Christy O'Connor Jnr, Garth McGimpsey, Ronan Rafferty and David Feherty.

'The great pity of it is that we don't play enough strategically demanding courses like Augusta,' added McGinley. 'And I would be lying if I said it doesn't bother me not being there. But the solution is in my own hands. I know what I have to do.' In simple terms, he had to lift himself into the top fifty of the world rankings, which he did by the end of that year. So it was that the Dubliner eventually made his Masters debut the following April, when he had the distinction of carding rounds of 72,74,71,71 for a share of eighteenth place behind Tiger Woods. The only downside was that he missed gaining an exemption for the following year's event by the slender margin of a stroke.

How much easier it was for me! My instruction was to arrive at the club at seven a.m. and it was still dark when I got there at six thirty. I would play in a fourball with three British colleagues and . . . our tee-time would be nine. The long wait afforded ample time for observation. Like eyeing the fetching derriere of Jan Stephenson poured into leopardskin slacks, while I wondered if Augusta's members realized what they were missing by excluding women from their number. Another LPGA favourite, Patty Sheehan, also arrived for an early start, as did members of the CBS television crew. Then, who should we see outside the professionals' shop, where he had returned to be expertly fitted for his green jacket, but the newly crowned champion, Jose-Maria Olazabal. 'We're playing the course,' we chorused happily. 'Piece of cake,' he replied, with an even bigger smile.

Some time later we were waiting behind the first tee when Royal and Ancient secretary Michael Bonallack (he didn't have a knighthood back then) arrived in a buggy, having completed the back nine. How had it gone? I enquired, desperately seeking a crumb of comfort. 'I was in the water at the twelfth, thirteenth and fifteenth,' he replied with admirable candour. Which had the effect of gently massaging my tingling nerves until the implications of what I had just learned suddenly dawned on me. Serious grief had been inflicted on a five-time winner of the British Amateur Championship and three times a competitor in the Masters, albeit without making the cut. What pleasures did it have in store for me? Had I sufficient ammunition? I checked my bag for the umpteenth time. Eleven balls. Should more be acquired from the pro shop? If so, how many? If only I had remembered to pack the ball retriever which had saved me countless pesetas on golfing trips to the Costa del Sol, yet it seemed unthinkable to go fishing for balls in the sacred waters of Augusta National. Not a moment too soon, the starter's voice rang out. 'You're next on the tee, sir,' he said, and so we set off where Olazabal had gone the day before.

Local experts estimate that in normal Georgia weather the grass grows 1.5 millimetres per day during the month of April. So, when myself and my fellow Monday marauders were let loose on the hallowed sward, the bent grass on the uncut greens was 50 per cent longer than the Spaniard had encountered in a splendid closing round of 69. Which was scant consolation insofar as they remained wickedly quick. And we were facing the same pin placements.

Anyway, by a rather interesting route – my drive was marginally longer than 92-year-old Gene Sarazen had struck as one of the ceremonial starters four days previously – I came to face that opening putt – a 20-footer, right to left across the slope of the green for a bogey. My strategy down the long second was particularly interesting. In a manner of speaking it involved hitting two drivers, one was of the persimmon variety, while the other happened to choose a most ill-conceived spot on the service road to stop his drinks truck. Though he had the good fortune to be saved by the high bonnet, the wretch still left me with a dreadful lie.

But enough of these trifling asides. A key element of my overall strategy was a decidedly casual approach to the short fourth and sixth holes. After all, where would be the excitement in having a hole in one on an outward journey, which wasn't seen on television at that time? Who would care? If I was to have an ace, it had to be on the twelfth, the scene of so much torment for Masters aspirants. With this in mind, I bunkered my tee-shot at the short fourth. And at the treacherous sixth, the ball was hit deliberately into the MacKenzie ridge, which traverses the green, with the result that my birdie putt was from 25 feet, up the steep slope to the pin on the upper tier. My par putt was from 35 feet, up the steep slope to the pin which was still on the upper tier. Miraculously, I got it to 4 feet and sank the putt for a bogey that felt like an unqualified triumph.

At this point cheering could be heard from the direction of the fifteenth green. Not quite a Masters Sunday cheer, but a fairly enthusiastic effort nonetheless. It later transpired that the excitement concerned the exploits of a particularly gifted fourball, one of whom had emulated Sarazen by recording an albatross two, while a colleague had an eagle three. These were undoubtedly splendid efforts, even if they lacked the sort of painstaking study of putting surfaces to which I had applied myself.

So we progressed to the seventh, where my deft execution of an eight iron from beneath overhanging branches on the left had sent the ball 5 feet from the pin, directly above the hole. 'Straight in, sir,' Douglas commanded, almost dismissively, as I contemplated the cavernous bunker directly down my line, off the front of the green. For a split-second I was tempted to see if my caddie were reaching for a sandwedge. Then came the ludicrous thought that he might have some moderately powerful tranquillizers secreted in those generous white overalls, for situations like this. Somehow the putt held its line and trickled into the cup off the left lip: a birdie. 'The grain sure done tried to take that one outa tha hole,' said the caddie. He was right. It was the first time I had become aware of nap on the Augusta greens.

Buoyed by this success, I determined to make the most of a birdie opportunity on the fiendishly difficult ninth, where my approach came to rest in the left-front fringe, about 15 feet below the hole. A simple task: stroke the ball nicely but firmly up the 90-degree slope to the flat area where the pin was located. Ah the boundless optimism of the handicap golfer! What extraordinary naivety! The reality was that I sank a very tricky 8-footer for a seven.

Intervening shots comprised a series of chips which defiantly refused to clear the slope. My British colleagues, meanwhile, had collapsed in a paroxysm of laughter, assuring me, between their breathless gasps, that I had outdone Tommy Cooper at his incomparable best. For my own part, I had discovered the true difficulty of Augusta's greens. Downhill putts were so intimidating that one developed a mortal dread of hitting the ball firmly. As a consequence, getting the ball up a steep slope became an almost insurmountable mental challenge.

After extremely slow progress, we eventually got to fabled Amen Corner. The front nine had taken us two and three-quarter hours, but this snail's pace seemed eminently worthwhile when Rae's Creek came into view. The eleventh had been negotiated in a straightforward par (how could Raymond Floyd have dumped a seven iron into the water there in his play-off with Faldo in 1990?). Now pulses were seriously racing as we walked towards the twelfth tee.

Japanese seemed to be everywhere. Hitting shots into the water, hitting shots over the water and shooting pictures all the while with a vast array of photographic equipment. After quite a wait, it was our turn. Sadly, only one of our fourball hit the green and as my five iron shot found the creek, I reasoned, without any conviction, that I might well have had my hole in one had the organizers taken the advice of Tom Kite, who had suggested with heavy irony that the pins be placed in the water to make the course even more difficult. However, after re-loading, I did manage two putts from 30 feet for a five.

I remember deciding there and then that it was unquestionably the most intimidating par three I had ever faced. Its difficulty lay not so much in being fronted by water with a gaping bunker and trees at the back. The real problem was presented by the shallowness of the green, which appeared like no more than a sliver from the tee. Then there was the way it angled away towards the right, increasing the span of water all the while. Scores seemed unimportant, however, as we walked over the Hogan Bridge, which, it should be noted, is limited to the players and their caddies during the Masters. This entire area of Amen Corner is roped off. The same applies to the Byron Nelson Bridge on the thirteenth and the Sarazen Bridge at the fifteenth.

One of our group, a four-handicapper, got a birdie at the fifteenth but generally our play of these holes was poor, largely because we felt obliged to go for the green from extremely difficult positions, including sidehill lies at the thirteenth and downhill lies at the fifteenth. So, a generous contribution of balls was consigned to the deep. In between was the fourteenth, with what I found to be the trickiest green on the course. When I came up short in two,

Douglas suggested I should aim my chip about 20 yards left of the pin, in its Sunday position on the right. Having done as instructed, I stood mesmerized as the ball took a 90-degree turn before finishing about 15 feet behind the hole.

The sixteenth was relatively easy by comparison. Then, in my anxiety to avoid the notorious Eisenhower tree at the seventeenth – so called because of the torment it inflicted on the late President of the US – I headed up the fifteenth fairway on my caddie's advice and found I had a clear pitch for my third shot to the green. By the time we got to the eighteenth tee, we had been almost five and a half hours on the course, in sweltering heat. The claustrophobic effect of the lines of trees flanking the entrance to the fairway, where gaping bunkers dominated the player's vision up the left, was a revelation, too. Though I had taken in that view several times during previous visits to Augusta, it now looked entirely different; unbelievably threatening, with a driver in one's hand.

Finally, as we progressed up the steep slope (as high as a seven-storey building) to the green, there was a deep sense of history, of all the great players who had trod this celebrated turf, from Jones and Sarazen to Hogan and Snead, to Palmer, Player and Nicklaus. And to the wonderful Europeans, Seve Ballesteros, Bernhard Langer, Sandy Lyle, Faldo, Ian Woosnam and, most recently, Olazabal, who had given us such a sense of pride in our continent.

Our scores for the round? Not a word was mentioned. It was as if there were an unplanned pact of silence akin to the rugby practice of what-happens-on-tour-stays-on-tour. The only notes we compared were about putting and I was moderately pleased with my total of thirty-six putts, including three singles and three three-putts. In a general assessment, I rated the course about ten strokes more difficult than an average club layout here at home, largely because of the fear factor. But it was a wonderful experience. One imagined that, at the outset, Douglas must have feared the embarrassment of having to replenish his master's supply, but, miraculously, I had nine balls left in the bag. Now he was beside himself with pride at the splendid job he had done.

So to the matter of his tip. I had learned that such details are treated seriously in America and especially so at Augusta National, where longtime locker-room attendants Richard Germany and Roland Gray could give a serious run-down on the generosity – or parsimony – of Masters champions through the years. They were clearly delighted in 2000, when Vijay Singh peeled off several $50 bills by way of a parting gesture, and a positive bonanza was in store four years later, when Phil Mickelson, a locker-room legend, donned the green jacket in his first major triumph.

Mickelson has been known to tip $50 for an on-course drink and in the locker-room he gives a standard tip of $500 if he misses the cut; $1,000 for a top-ten finish; and $2,000 to $3,000 for a win. He has also been known to tip a further $500 to security guards, so we can imagine the extent of his largesse after achieving a long-awaited breakthrough.

So what has all this to do with your impoverished scribe and the dutiful Douglas back in 1994? Suffice it to say that he was left with a good impression of this fair land. 'Look forward to seeing you the next time, sir,' were his parting words. But there hasn't been a next time. In fact, I have not entered the ballot since then, for the simple reason that nothing could ever compare with my baptism in the cathedral of the pines.

Finding Bobby Jones in Dolphin's Barn

Back in 1967 at his shop in Dolphin's Barn, Dublin, Cecil Whelan took a trade-in of five interesting-looking golf clubs against a new set. By his own admission, the allowance was decidedly modest, given that it would have been possible to buy a very fine set of irons at the time for less than £100.

At The K Club thirty years later, in an auction in aid of the Hospice Foundation, those modest discards were beautifully displayed in a specially designed glass case, following the Smurfit Christy O'Connor Pro-Am. And they were knocked down to an

American buyer for €12,700 after the under-bidder, who happened to be Ian Woosnam, stopped at €12,065.

I should mention at this stage that the irons, two to six, were from a matching set carrying the stamp 'Robt T Jones Jr − Spalding'. They were, in fact, from the first ever matching set of irons, manufactured by Spalding in 1933, in co-operation with the Grand Slam winner of three years previously.

When I contacted Kathy Robbins at the company's headquarters in Massachusetts, she very kindly filled me in with details from their catalogue of the time. Whelan's clubs had steel shafts to which a so-called bamboo lacquer was applied, giving them the look of hickory. The catalogue carried the information that a Bobby Jones signature set − one to nine − of 'Spalding Registered Cushion Shaft Irons Steel Shaft' for men and women could be bought for US $60. It was also possible to buy a set of six women's irons for $40.

Individual irons were also available at $5 each and they carried the promise: 'With your eyes closed, you cannot tell which of these clubs you are swinging. From driving iron to mashie niblic [sic], they all feel exactly alike when swung through the arc of a stroke. So, instead of trying to master six or nine different swings, you perfect one.'

When capturing the so-called 'impregnable quadrilateral' in 1930, Jones had sixteen clubs in his bag, all of them selected by feel from a variety of club makers. So, when Spalding tested them while in the process of launching matched sets for the first time, they were amazed to discover that they all matched perfectly, with the exception of the mashie-niblick or seven iron. On being told this, Jones made the intriguing disclosure that 'I've always had trouble with that particular club.' He and Spalding then entered into an agreement whereby the company continued to produce his signature irons until 1973, two years after his death.

'I didn't see them having any commercial value at the time, but in the back of my mind I thought I might one day use them to raise money for charity,' said Whelan, the indefatigable secretary of the Links Golfing Society. 'They lay in a corner of the shop for years, until I eventually brought them home.'

Meanwhile, their delighted new owner, Irish-American Michael O'Halloran, expected them to fetch as much as $75,000 when he auctioned them for charity in the US. All of which proves that it sometimes pays to keep up with the Joneses.

Footnote: At the same auction, memories were revived of the only occasion that Ben Hogan, Byron Nelson, Arnold Palmer and Sam Snead played together. It happened in the 1965 First Invitational Exhibition at the Preston Trails club in Dallas, Texas. On a visit to the US, the remarkable Cecil managed to get not only a photograph of the illustrious quartet, but the balls they used – which were autographed, naturally. Beautifully presented, the display, including balls, was bought for € 7,620 by Dr Michael Smurfit for display in the Arnold Palmer Room at The K Club.

Pete Dye and the Man Upstairs

Given that most of us tend to mellow with age, it's unusual to find a seventy-nine-year-old radical, but Pete Dye is such a man. Among his pet dislikes are the notion of golf as an elitist game and the soaring costs of green fees on both sides of the Atlantic.

When we met during the 2004 USPGA Championship at Whistling Straits, Wisconsin, the man who has been given millions to design some of the game's most dramatic courses spoke of how his favourite layout has generated millions for its local community. 'It's the one I did in the Dominican Republic,' he said.

In the Casa de Campo golf complex, Dye has designed, in fact, three courses – Dye Fore, The Links and the world-renowned Teeth of the Dog. 'The Man Upstairs built ten holes, which meant I had only to build the other eight,' he said of his favourite. 'But what really warms me is that there wasn't even a paved road when I went down there; now 50,000 people have jobs as a result of golf.'

Environmentalists, who can be a lot more extreme than Dye

when promoting their particular viewpoint, might do well to consider such factors before condemning golf course developments in this country. Indeed, as the designer proved when transforming a Florida swamp into the Stadium Course at Sawgrass, and featureless land on the shores of Lake Michigan into the amazing Whistling Straits, golf and nature can be made to work extremely well together.

However, Dye claims the game is becoming too costly, largely because of an unrealistic emphasis on the condition of courses. 'While the spread of golf in Ireland has been unbelievable, it is also true that where you were once paying $2 in green fees, the cost is now closer to $200,' he said.

'I hate to see this happen, not only in Ireland, but in the United States as well. Average green fees should be from $35 to $50 at the most. But here's the problem: rising costs have to do with the way we're maintaining courses nowadays. I've been screaming about this, but nobody appears to be listening.' He explained, 'It seems like everybody these days is talking about green speeds. I heard talk of a green speed of twelve during the PGA at Whistling Straits. Ben Hogan won the US Open at Oakmont in 1953 on the fastest greens in the history of the United States and if they had a Stimpmeter at the time those greens would probably have measured about five or six.

'Augusta National has a lot to answer for. With a budget that would choke a mule, they present their course in superb condition for the Masters each year. And every greens chairman from Milwaukee to New Orleans is looking at it on TV and wants to know why his own greenkeeper can't do the same. So the greenkeeper does it to keep his job and maintenance costs go sky-high. When you cut greens low, you eliminate grain, which should be part of the game of golf. The eighteenth green here [Whistling Straits] is about 18,000 square feet and not a blemish on it. No heel marks, no brown spots, no poa annua [meadow grass]. It's so doggone true that if the ball is set on the correct line, it's going to go in. In those conditions, I'd expect players to shoot the lights out.

'Professionals have a harder time putting on greens of seven or eight than they do on the really fast ones. On slow greens, you could have three different speeds, downgrain, up-grain and cross-grain, to contend with. With mowers now costing $20,000, there's no question but that you could slash maintenance costs if you reduced the speed of greens. It's like everything else in golf. The demand comes from club members and their officers looking at the big events on television.'

Aidan O'Hara chuckled knowingly. 'I agree with Pete Dye,' said the greens superintendent at Mount Juliet, where, incidentally, an instruction came from the PGA European Tour that green speeds for the 2004 American Express Championship be increased to 12.0 on the Stimpmeter, from 11.5 in 2002. To borrow Dye's words, that was when Tiger Woods putted the lights out, with a 25-under-par winning aggregate of 263.

'Our fairways are now being treated the same as greens were on an average course fifteen years ago,' O'Hara went on. 'I remember when Mount Juliet became the first Irish course to top-dress fairways in 1993, visitors were demanding that greenkeepers at their home clubs should do the same. And when we successfully drained Fota Island, other clubs in the area wanted to copy us.

'When I first came into golf, the norm was to mow greens on Mondays, Wednesdays and Fridays, and the fairways once a week. Now, greens are mown every day and fairways three times a week. And it all costs money. Only recently, my directors asked me why it was that maintenance costs had soared over the last three years. And my explanation was that the cost of equipment, pesticides, sand and fertilizers had gone through the roof. And wages have risen, too. In Ireland, payroll represents about 60 per cent of maintenance costs as opposed to 55 per cent in the US.'

While accepting that leading tournament venues such as Mount Juliet, The K Club, The Heritage, Adare Manor and Druids Glen are exceptional, with annual maintenance costs as high as €1.5 million, O'Hara said, 'I would consider it desirable but not practical for ordinary courses to be aping Augusta National. Otherwise, golfers must accept that such standards are bound to lead to higher green fees.'

As for Dye, he concluded, 'If speeds of eight or nine were

accepted as the tournament norm, a lot of grain will come into the greens, which would be a gift to the good players. But the real bonus would be that the cost of maintaining those greens would nose-dive.'

Ireland's golfing saint

In July 1991, a frail old man who had become a veritable institution in Irish golf visited the Old Head of Kinsale to examine the feasibility of building a course there. It would be a high-profile development involving an outlay of several million pounds, yet Eddie Hackett's expenses included the item: two nights' accommodation in Kathleen Humberstone's B and B – £34.00.

This was the sort of thoughtfulness for his clients' resources which made Hackett a unique figure in Irish golf-course development over a period of close on thirty years. Money was always a secondary consideration. His prime concern was to do justice to a site at an outlay which would fit his client's pocket. Regarding a commission to build the splendid Connemara links at Ballyconneely, he said, 'They had no money, you know. I told them if you're that keen on golf, I'll go down, and I'll put a stone in for a tee and a pin in for a green, and you can pay me when you can.'

That was in 1970. Thirty years later I made a return visit to Connemara to look over the spectacular new nine holes which Hackett designed along the coast. Sadly, he died before the project was finished and, on his recommendation, the work was completed by Walker Cup player-turned-architect Tom Craddock, who has also departed to divot-free fairways in the great beyond.

'Oh, Eddie Hackett was a saint, you know,' said Fr Peter Waldron, secretary of the Connemara GC Ltd. 'He was totally self-effacing and had more integrity than almost anybody I ever came across. And he worked for pennies.' Hackett's response to this was, 'I know I've charged too little all my life, but starting out I didn't have the confidence in my abilities.'

His early involvement at the Old Head stemmed from a friendship between the new owner, John O'Connor, and Paul Mulcahy, nephew of Jack Mulcahy, the former owner of Waterville who died in September 1994. Hackett was justifiably proud of the majestic links in south Kerry, where his prospective employer had given him the blunt instruction: 'I want you to design for me the best golf course in the world.'

Like all things golfing, the merit of Waterville is very much a subjective matter. But there is no doubting its status as one of the world's great links courses and it remains as a towering monument to Hackett's marvellous design skills. Typical of a meticulous attention to detail was the manner in which he protected the bunkers. Aware that the course could be windswept, especially during winter months, he made the unorthodox decision of containing the sand through the use of peat dust from the local bogs instead of soil.

Hackett described Waterville as 'a beautiful monster'. But so respectful was he of all his clients that he wouldn't dare express a preference for one of his courses over another. It was clear, however, that the Kerry links remained very dear to his heart until his death in December 1996. And, appropriately, it is still his most famous work, though his overall contribution to Irish golf as a whole has been incalculable.

Born in Dublin in 1910, the son of a publican, he got his break into golf as a clubmaker with Fred Smyth at Royal Dublin. From there, he went to Belgium as assistant to the great Henry Cotton at Royal Waterloo. Later, he became secretary of the Irish Professional Golfers' Association and the resident professional at Portmarnock until 1950. But it was only in the 1960s that he discovered his true golfing vocation. Bill Menton, the then general secretary of the Golfing Union of Ireland, was flooded with phone calls from clubs throughout the country, enquiring about coaching and architectural work. Essentially, this was the result of a tremendous upsurge in interest in the game in the wake of the Canada Cup at Portmarnock in 1960, allied to the *Shell Wonderful World of Golf* series on television.

Hackett, whose health had always been fragile and whose activities at the time were limited to some coaching, was seen by Menton as an ideal candidate. So it was that a career which would have a profound influence on the development of golf in this country over the last three decades was launched. As it happened, his first project was at Letterkenny GC where the Donegal Irish Women's Open was staged in 1999.

From on-the-job experience, his design skills were developed to the extent that he became widely acknowledged as Ireland's only golf course architect, being responsible for such seaside gems as Murvagh (at Donegal), Connemara and Carne. 'In the early days, there was no one else to go to in this country, and it was very expensive to employ an English architect,' he would remark simply. He would also insist that 'nature is the best architect' and by way of proving the point, would follow the lie of the land, siting holes wherever 'the Good Lord provided'. It has to be acknow-ledged that lack of finance would have fostered this philosophy. Either way, earthmoving was generally kept to a minimum on a Hackett course.

When asked if a certain hole might be a little unfair, he would look somewhat perplexed while answering, 'It is what was there, you see.' Indeed, I remember him recounting complaints he had about the tee on the sixteenth at Waterville, from golfers who claimed they couldn't feel comfortable on it. Eddie's reply was, 'You're not meant to feel comfortable there.'

A soft-spoken, extremely gentle man with a deep spirituality, he possessed an extraordinary resilience, despite having been the victim of TB early in his life and meningitis at a later stage. And as I have indicated, his design fees would now be considered no more than loose change to his successors in the craft.

His involvement in more than a hundred design projects in this country ranged from a totally new creation to the revising and upgrading of existing work. Or it might have been the expanding of a nine-hole course to eighteen holes. Some of these projects were undertaken with the minimum of publicity and extremely modest payment. For instance, at the 'old' Adare Manor club, he helped in laying out a testing eighteen-hole stretch in a decidedly limited area. And, as usual, new friends were made in the process.

The hundredth course he designed was at West Waterford GC in Dungarvan, where the Spratt family commissioned him to create a championship-standard layout on 150 acres of delightfully rolling terrain. When it was officially opened in 1993, the extent to which he succeeded could be gauged from a searching challenge which almost invariably surprises the unwary visitor. And I can recall visiting his wonderful creation at Carne, Belmullet, shortly after it was completed and being staggered by his skill in finding a routing through towering dunes. Afterwards, in the charming clubhouse, one of the staff pointed to a chair and table strategically positioned for a perfect view of the links. 'That's where Mr Hackett would sit on his visits here,' she said with a quiet reverence.

He once remarked, 'I could never break up the earth the way they tell me Jack Nicklaus and Arnold Palmer do. You disrupt the soil profile and, anyway, it's unnatural. Within reason, I try to use what's there, and you can never do with trees what you can do with sand dunes.' From Waterville to Connemara, Carne, Rosapenna and Murvagh, Hackett has some wonderful links courses to his credit. And his admirable versatility is also evident in such fine parkland stretches at Malahide, Beaverstown, Old Conna, Charlesland, Djouce Mountain, Athenry and Ballinrobe.

There are no gimmicks with a Hackett layout, no attempt at creating a so-called signature hole. Rather they are characterized generally by elevated tees, clear, visible landing areas, large greens, and the absence of blind drives and hidden hazards. Perhaps typical of his thinking was the short twelfth at Waterville. 'When I was making that hole, local contractors told me they weren't going to touch the ground because Mass was once celebrated in the hollow,' he recalled. 'And we never touched it. Its plateau green is natural and there are no bunkers. It doesn't need one and that's the best tribute you can pay a hole.'

Given his remarkable enthusiasm and application, however modest the project, it's not surprising that Hackett should be revered by his many clients. But a true measure of his place in Irish golf is to be found in the respect and admiration of his peers.

'Whatever our involvement in the game, we owe Eddie Hackett an enormous debt of gratitude,' said club professional and golf-course architect Bobby Browne. 'He was one of a kind.' Indeed he was. And at this remove, we can fully appreciate the stroke of inspiration which guided Jack Mulcahy towards the gentle Dubliner, when he set about turning his wild dreams about Waterville into glorious reality.

CHAPTER 3

● ● ● ● ● ● ● ● ● ●

When Winning Becomes a Cherished Memory

'Victory is everything. You can spend the money but you can never spend the memories.'

KEN VENTURI

Skies over Augusta National darkened ominously as the leaders played the opening nine. It was Saturday, 13 April 1996 and while threatened thunderstorms never materialized, winds gusting to more than 25mph heightened the challenge of notoriously difficult greens, especially for the leading contenders in the sixtieth US Masters.

Greg Norman, whose rounds of 63 and 69 had given him a four-stroke lead over Nick Faldo at the halfway stage, was paired with the Englishman in the third round. It was the first time they had come together in a major championship since the third round of the Open at St Andrews six years previously, when Faldo outscored his rival with a sparkling 67 to Norman's 76. On this occasion, however, 'the Shark' was very much in command.

Though Faldo had birdied the seventeenth, the fact that he faced a 10-footer for par on the eighteenth made it likely that Norman's fourth-round partner would be Phil Mickelson, who was the leader in the clubhouse on 210 after a third-round 72. But, typically, the Englishman holed the putt for a 73 to Norman's 71: the final pairing would be unchanged for Sunday, even if the gap had now been extended to six strokes. 'I think if you're right there, you can keep a close eye on things,' said Faldo afterwards. 'And by playing with Greg I could gauge things so much better, especially when I happened to get a couple of shots closer. It was unquestionably crucial for me to play with him on Sunday.'

At that time, it was the custom of Augusta National to play host to the so-called international media at a clubhouse reception on the Saturday evening of the Masters. And to ensure that we would be suitably spruced up for the occasion after a working day, we scribes generally availed ourselves of the locker-room facilities. So it was that as the runaway leader of the tournament emerged from the changing area, he was met by Peter Dobereiner, the doyen of British golf writers. And perceiving a rather anxious look, brought on perhaps by events on the eighteenth, 'Dobers' threw an affectionate arm around the Shark's shoulders before uttering the immortal words: 'Don't worry, Greg, old son. Not even you can fuck this one up.'

Covering American golf tournaments for a newspaper on this side of the pond can be a very trying exercise, given the time difference, so I was among those who greatly welcomed Norman's commanding position. We could give this overdue Augusta breakthrough by the Shark appropriate treatment in Monday's *Irish Times* and I remember feeling decidedly smug as I headed towards the first tee at around three in the afternoon to see the leaders drive off, having written four background pieces on Norman to fill a broadsheet page by way of a special tribute. As Dobereiner had decided, this was one he simply couldn't lose.

With the lead cut to two strokes halfway through the final round, however, the sports editor had become decidedly anxious. 'Is this guy going to blow it?' he asked down the phone. 'No, no,' I tried to reassure him without any great conviction. 'He's just had a few stumbles.' But, of course, those stumbles were to become a total collapse, which defied normal, competitive logic. Not only did Norman lose; incredibly, he crashed to a closing 78 against a 67 from Faldo to finish a full five strokes adrift.

Augusta had never witnessed anything quite like it. For sharply contrasting reasons, Faldo and Norman were both in tears, standing on the eighteenth green. 'I just said I don't know what to say

— I want to give you a hug,' Faldo explained afterwards. He then added, 'There were other little things, but I'm storing them away.' The gesture did much to cushion what was clearly a devastating blow for Norman. 'I was extremely impressed,' he said afterwards. 'It brought tears to Nick's eyes and to mine. He's gone way up in my estimation after that.'

In cold, clinical terms, Norman crashed to the worst collapse in the sixty-year history of the event, worse even than the failure of Ed Sneed, who let a five-stroke advantage slip away in 1979 before losing a play-off to Fuzzy Zoeller. Yet in a positive sense, the Shark left me with indelible memories of a post-round reaction that was only slightly less remarkable than what had happened on the course during a pulsating afternoon. Though his eyes had a glazed look and there was a pale hue to the normally tanned face, he took his disaster with enormous grace and dignity. 'I screwed up; it was my own fault; I screwed up; this was one that I let slip away,' he said.

But almost immediately, there came the insistence that we shouldn't feel sorry for him. 'I wouldn't like to see a player do what I did,' he went on. 'Sure, I would like to be putting on a green jacket, but it's not the end of the world. I have a good life. Honestly, I'll be OK. It was the most disappointing round of my career, but I'm not going to fall off the face of the earth because of what happened here.' I was among those moved close to tears by his gracious acceptance of what must have been a heartbreaking reversal for such a proud man.

The headlines in the local papers the following morning were fairly predictable. 'Not again, Greg!' declared the *Atlanta Constitution*, over a picture of Norman collapsing on his back after an attempted eagle chip had grazed the hole at the long fifteenth. 'Shark skinned!' ran the banner headline in the *Augusta Chronicle*. And Faldo was proved right in his Sunday assessment that while he hoped the event would be remembered for his best-of-the-day 67, the more likely reaction would have to do with the manner of Norman's squandering a seemingly unassailable lead.

Ken Venturi, the former US Open champion turned CBS commentator, who lost a four-stroke lead in the final round of the

1957 Masters, said, 'I thought no matter how badly he [Norman] played today, he couldn't lose the tournament.' NBC rival, Johnny Miller, had a different slant, saying, 'Greg is a very interesting guy to watch. It's like a car race. You want to see the best drivers win, but a lot of people in the stands want to see a car wreck. They don't want to see anybody die or hurt, but they love to see wrecks. And Norman gives us lots of wrecks.' Significantly, the only lead-- ing player who remained unconvinced through the weekend was Jack Nicklaus, Norman's one-time confidant. When asked midway through the final round what it would mean to the Shark to win the elusive green jacket, Nicklaus replied, 'He hasn't won it yet. The challenge of this course is 100 per cent mental.'

Then there was the Faldo factor. I felt certain we would have witnessed an entirely different Norman had he been paired with any other player on the final day. But Faldo clearly bothered him, perhaps because they are direct opposites in so many respects. Norman would have felt capable of overwhelming most opponents through his skill and aggression. Against Faldo, however, he knew that no matter how well he played, however big his lead, the Englishman would still be there, grafting away relentlessly, even in a seemingly hopeless situation. Mind you, it was also very reveal- ing that Faldo three-putted only once over the four days.

Either way, after an extraordinary weekend we were left to ponder the unpredictability of sport. And the fact that Norman succumbed to the ice-cool skills of Faldo, 84 years to the day since an unsinkable ship, the *Titanic*, lost its battle with a different sort of icy obstruction on 14 April 1912.

Sensing the groundswell of sympathy in the media centre on that fateful evening in Augusta, Norman had assured us, 'It's not the end of the world for me. My life is going to continue.' And sure enough, two tournament victories, including the Andersen Consulting World Championship, had been added to his formid- able haul by the time I interviewed him in late February 1997 in Dubai, in the build-up to the Desert Classic. I remember thinking, 'The man's truly a marvel' and whatever one's suspicions about his competitive qualities, there could be no doubting his innate courtesy and extraordinary resilience. Both qualities were evident when he agreed not simply to grant me an interview, but to talk frankly about the painful events of the previous April. It was a time when his marriage seemed solid as a rock, some years before he took up with Chris Evert, and his wife Laura stood beside him throughout our conversation.

It fascinated me that one of his first reflections on the sixtieth Masters involved a total rejection of the Faldo factor. He claimed the identity of his final-round playing partner was of no consequence, despite some bitter experiences, notably in the 1990 Open and the 1992 Johnnie Walker World Championship. Having turned for reassurance to Laura, he fixed me with his penetrating, pale-blue eyes. 'When I awoke that Sunday morning – and Laura will testify to this – I was calm, I was cool and I was relaxed,' he said. 'We did all the normal things. There wasn't one thing in my head that was likely to throw me.'

Now that the ice was broken, it quickly became clear he had no problem in discussing what he had acknowledged as the most disappointing single round of his career. 'People think that after a set-back it takes you a while to get your game into shape,' he said, 'but my philosophy is: once a competitor always a competitor. It's like riding a bike. So, I meant it when I said last year that it wasn't the end of the world for me. I had a strong belief at the time that something good was going to come out of it and I still believe that. I saw it simply as a test. I've had a lot of reporters write to me saying how impressed they were with my interview afterwards. Which is nice. And sure, it's going to be interesting when I go back there. In fact it's already started, with the fan mail coming in.'

He went on to talk of the enormous fund of goodwill he experienced from the general public, golfing and otherwise. 'Before leaving home recently, I had ten boxes of mail to answer,' he explained. 'Mail from people wishing me well and telling me "Do it this time." Stuff pretty much like that.'

So, was he already mentally heading down Magnolia Lane for a seventeenth successive Masters challenge since 1981, when he finished fourth behind Tom Watson on his Augusta debut? 'Oh sure,' he agreed. 'I have no ghosts in the closet and no fears of going back there. I'm not lying about that. I'm building towards

Augusta. I want to win the Masters. Indeed, I'd also like to win the British Open every year and the US Open as well.'

As part of his preparation, however, he planned to protect himself by avoiding any newspaper or magazine articles about the game. He had also instructed that no golf magazines be delivered to his home at Hobe Sound, Florida, and should one slip through the net, Laura would hide it. 'A lot of the stuff written about me is totally untrue,' he said. 'And it has the effect of hurting me and hurting my family. But I'm not going to walk away from playing in the Masters. I was prepared to face the music after what happened a year ago and I've no intention of hiding now, though that's probably the only way I could avoid everything that goes with it. Imagine what people would write if I were to do that. So I take things on the chin. I accept the responsibility for screwing up, not only on the golf course, but off the golf course. I believe it helps make me a better person.'

Then, by way of stressing the unfairness of taking his Masters collapse out of context, Norman went on, 'People like to put you under a microscope as if to say, "Okay, let's see what he's like right here, over these eighteen holes." And if you don't prove what you're supposed to prove in that test, then you're not a good person. The fact is that there's more to life than just playing golf and winning. Maybe I'm my own worst enemy, but it's my nature to lay things out this way. I say what I believe. Sometimes that's not the right thing to do, but you've got to have the courage and the confidence to do so. And it would be nice, once in a while, if people were to talk about the good that you've done, which hasn't all been necessarily on the golf course.'

While talking in this typically dynamic manner, he always maintained eye contact. 'You see, what happened at Augusta last year was physical – it wasn't mental,' he went on. 'I can honestly tell you that. It became mental on about the ninth hole when I missed that second shot by 18 inches. I thought a lot about it afterwards. When that happened on the ninth [where his approach shot spun back and off the front of the green for a bogey], I knew my swing wasn't doing what my mind wanted it to do. And I knew every shot was just a little bit off. So then it became a mind thing for me.

I started pushing. As I see things now, the problem was more physical for the first eight and a half holes. And it became mental from then on, because I kept pushing myself. Pushing myself. And you can't do that in this game, especially around Augusta National. The combination of both those things brought the worst possible outcome. I'm not a negative person, but as each hole went by, it became harder and harder not to let that negative feeling take hold. I've thought long and hard about it, and that's the way I have figured things out. Basically, there's nothing more to say.'

But there was, though not specifically about the 1996 Masters. I suggested the experience might have given him a greater sensitivity with regard to the pain of others. This certainly appeared to be the case during that week in Dubai where he was especially caring in his comments about the troubled Spaniards, Jose-Maria Olazabal and Seve Ballesteros. He then admitted that he had written letters to Olazabal and phoned him a few times in the course of his illness and consequent absence from the game. 'When somebody's down and out, I'm the first to try to get them back up again,' he said. 'I see myself more as a giver than a taker.' Olazabal later confirmed this by saying, 'Greg was always in touch. He also wrote a note and was obviously anxious to know what my position was.'

At one stage during the summer of 1996, when the events of Augusta National were still very fresh in the memory, the pain in Olazabal's feet became so severe that he was reduced to crawling on his hands and knees just to go to the bathroom. That was before Dr Hans-Wilhelm Muller-Wohlfahrt, a Munich-based specialist in locomotion, discovered that the problem had to do with several misplaced vertebrae pinching the nerves of his lower back, rather than with the earlier diagnosis of rheumatoid arthritis.

In April 1999, we had another Sunday at Augusta and another hug between the leading combatants on the seventy-second green. This time the principals were Olazabal and Norman. And once again, the Shark was vanquished. After a solid drive up the middle of the final fairway and an eight iron to the front fringe, the Spaniard stood, fighting back tears. Then, as he and Norman walked side-by-side up the 70-foot climb towards the green, the

Shark could hardly credit how natural the whole thing seemed. And he found himself thinking, 'It's as easy as that; he's won the tournament.' Given his own horrendous disappointments in pursuit of a coveted crown, one could readily understand his bemusement. While expecting something extraordinary, he had failed to recognize that the mark of greatness is to make things look easy. By his own admission, all he could think of was 'what I would have to do to beat him'.

When he left the course on that Sunday evening, Norman headed for the local airport, where his private plane was waiting to fly him back to Hobe Sound. 'There was no replaying of the last round,' he said. 'There was no reason to.' And by way of emphasizing his astonishing resilience, he kept an appointment at eight thirty the following morning to give a clinic at the Medalist course which he designed near his home. 'When I contacted my office they told me they had received hundreds of faxes from people wishing me well for the future,' he said. 'That's the thing about the Masters; it seems to generate so much emotion.'

Meanwhile, runaway winner of the most inane question posed after the final round on what was yet another memorable Sunday at Augusta had to be the one by an American scribe, who asked, 'Greg, can you describe the difference between the one [hug] today and the one you got in 1996 [from Nick Faldo]?' A bemused Shark eventually answered, 'Well, Jose's a lot thinner.' What he didn't say was that when he and Olazabal embraced each other, the Spaniard whispered to him, 'Keep hanging in there. You'll get it.' But it hasn't happened. Indeed, indications are that his appearance in 2002, when he was tied thirty-sixth behind Tiger Woods, will prove to be his last. If so, he bade farewell to Augusta National with an appropriate flourish, claiming two crystal goblets for an eagle three on the long fifteenth in a final round of 75.

There was no crystal for his great rival on that occasion, but Faldo was still in a familiar position, ahead of him on the leaderboard in a tie for fourteenth, and 1996 seemed a distant memory.

Nicklaus: the autumn years

Little more than three months after a landmark sixth Masters triumph, the mind still marvelled at the breathtaking scenes from Augusta National. For most enthusiasts on this side of the Atlantic, those memorable images were on television, but this was real life, which probably explained the sense of unreality at Royal Dublin on Monday, 21 July 1986 when the voice of Niall Toibin, in the role of MC, articulated the most famous name in golf over the public address system. Imagine it. Jack Nicklaus was about to hit his first golf shots on Irish soil.

This was the so-called Toyota Challenge of Champions, an exhibition match which brought the great man into opposition with Seve Ballesteros, holder of the Irish Open title. With an attendance considerably larger than the planned limit of 5,000, Nicklaus displayed a keen sense of occasion by dressing in a white shirt, yellow sweater and green slacks, the Irish national colours. And familiar though the blond head, solid frame and warm smile may have been, I can still sense the tingling excitement I felt at what was about to unfold.

Though it had been a long time in the making, especially in the context of earlier Irish visits by illustrious contemporaries such as Arnold Palmer, Gary Player, Tom Watson and Lee Trevino, the occasion permitted Nicklaus to make the unique comment: 'I never imagined having lunch in Dublin, Ireland, and dinner in Dublin, Ohio, on the same day.' Which he did, on leaving our shores for Muirfield Village. Meanwhile, it mattered not a whit that Ballesteros won the match by sinking a typically outrageous 45-foot birdie putt on the eighteenth for a 2-under-par 70 to a 71 from 'the Bear'. Entering into the spirit of things with obvious enthusiasm, both players made it a marvellous occasion.

In the context of some stunning achievements by Tiger Woods over the last ten years, it is interesting to recall Nicklaus being asked later in the afternoon, at Royal Dublin, if it were possible for a player to equal his record of eighteen major championship triumphs. 'When I was Seve's age [Ballesteros was twenty-nine at the time], I had seven major professional titles. Seve has four. That's not such a big difference. If any player is to do it, I think Seve is the one.' We would later discover that the Dollymount experience planted the seed of Nicklaus handiwork of a different kind. 'The design deal was actually done in the car-park at Portmarnock,' Tim Mahony, head of Toyota Ireland, later recalled. 'I was speaking on my car phone to Jack in Helsinki when we tied everything up.'

So it was that having carded a final round of 68 in the Open Championship at Royal Lytham on Monday, 18 July 1988 (bad weather had caused a day's delay), Nicklaus joined the ABC commentary team for the remainder of the afternoon and then flew in his private jet to Waterford, with his wife, Barbara. Two years after he had first set foot on Irish soil, he was about to embark on what would become a lasting relationship with this fair land. 'I am not at liberty to disclose details of my Irish trip,' he said guardedly at Lytham, before taking to the skies. 'That would be a matter for my client. All I can say at this stage is that I am flying into Waterford Airport.'

Had my golf-writing colleagues and I been newshounds worthy of the name, we would have made a link with the events of Royal Dublin in 1986 and Mahony's acquisition a year later of a breathtaking estate at Thomastown, Co Kilkenny. Instead, it was a further twenty-four hours before news emerged that the Bear was heading for Mount Juliet where, in fact, he and Barbara were guests of Mahony and his wife, Maeve. And on seeing the property, he duly signed a design contract for $1.25 million.

From then onwards, Mahony had regular meetings with his new-found golf partner, notably on the Bear's thirteen visits to Mount Juliet. 'I would like to think that we have become friends, but you never really know with Jack,' the businessman admitted later. 'I found him to be an unusually intelligent man, absolutely straight in all our dealings. He is essentially a very serious person, thoroughly dedicated and with marvellous powers of concentration.' Mahony went on, 'In his presence, you're never conscious of being with a major sporting celebrity, but there is an innate strength about him. He is not a man I would wish to cross.'

Meanwhile, Nicklaus was always open and courteous when we scribes kept tabs on his progress during those visits, even when questions concerned some decidedly caustic comments about his design work elsewhere in Europe, notably at St Mellion in Cornwall, where the Benson and Hedges International Open was played from 1990 to 1995. David Feherty famously exclaimed, 'We've been diddled. This one was designed by Barbara [the great man's wife].' And Bernhard Langer observed that while the left-to-right nature of the layout was fine for Nicklaus and his natural fade, it was very different for a player who drew the ball. In response, Nicklaus permitted himself the acid remark, 'I would assume that Langer would have to learn how to fade the ball or change his schedule.' He added, 'An accomplished professional should be able to move the ball any way he wishes – right to left, left to right, high or low.

'My view of the St Mellion criticism is that there are always ten guys who will bellyache. We have them in the States, though, in fairness, I would not have considered Bernhard to be among that group. I designed it [St Mellion] mainly for a fade shot, because I considered that draw shots would be too difficult to control on such a hilly site.' Then, by way of a general response to his critics, Nicklaus said, 'There has been a lot of jealousy and it drives me crazy. People haven't been able to criticize my golf too much over the years, so they've chosen to pick at my courses. I don't like to say it, but I'm afraid it's true. If you don't want to be criticized, you should say nothing, do nothing and be nothing.'

It represented a rather unhappy commentary on life in the lime-light. Yet he didn't dwell on such matters and we were given the wonderful admission, 'Golf is still what I dream about at night. Playing golf, that is. It is good after all these years not to feel the game grinding you down mentally. Because it can do that. I don't feel a strain when I play, but, in between times, the level of per-formance and attainment is always a worry.' Then there was the assertion: 'I haven't abused myself. I've lived good and clean, and kept my discipline. I love the outdoors and I love golf best of the things I do outdoors. The way I live and the way I keep my mind strong are the key things in keeping competitive in golf. Yeah, I'm a very competitive person. People haven't always liked it and haven't always liked me, but the character you have is what makes you the golf player you are. You can't separate one from the other. I can go away and work on courses, but if my mind is strong, I can pick up my golf to a satisfying level when I come back to it.'

The official opening of Mount Juliet on Sunday, 14 July 1991, was captured beautifully by a Kilkennyman with a perception worthy of the county's great hurling tradition. On hearing that there was to be an exhibition match between Nicklaus and Christy O'Connor Snr, which would be refereed by Joe Carr, the local remarked, 'Be God! That's like having Christy Ring, Mick Mackey and Jimmy Langton [all-time hurling greats] in the same half-forward line.'

There were other charming elements to a hugely enjoyable occasion. Like the concern expressed by Nicklaus at the idea of O'Connor, then sixty-six, playing off the back tees against a player fifteen years his junior. 'I wouldn't worry about Christy,' said Carr. 'He's still well capable of taking care of himself.' The accuracy of Carr's assessment gained rich emphasis later in the day when, in the official score for the match, O'Connor won by 72 to 74. In fairness to Nicklaus, however, it was noted that 'Himself' was permitted a Mulligan at the first hole where the ball from his opening drive was blocked right, never to be seen again. (The word locally was that it was picked up by an unscrupulous spectator who kept it as a souvenir.)

During that period, I found myself considering the notion that, unlike the rest of us, every leading sportsperson faces two deaths, one competitive, one natural. But even as his supreme skills began to desert him, Nicklaus continued to give wonderful interviews. I have a special memory of the US Masters in 1995, before Tiger Woods burst onto the professional scene. After Nicklaus had given a lengthy, official press conference, I happened to be in a small group of golfwriters who had an informal chat with him in the interview area. Among the questions we asked him was who was the best golfer of all time? His reply was typically direct. 'Hogan was the best I ever saw,' replied the Bear. 'I never saw Jones, so I can't comment on him. As for myself, that's for others to judge.'

It seemed that the time had come to make these sort of judgements when I had my next extended chat with him at Chateau Elan, Georgia. At the scene of the 1996 Sarazen World Open, Nicklaus's public appeal was shown to be undiminished, as he stood for an hour and twenty minutes outside the score-recorder's tent in a chilly November wind, autographing caps, photographs and scraps of paper for an adoring audience, lined six-deep. They didn't seem to care that he had just shot a miserable third round of 79, which placed him last in the tournament, but he certainly cared, very deeply indeed.

At fifty-six, the notion of being treated as a ceremonial golfer was abhorrent to him. So he felt obliged to point out, 'I just don't play well in cold, windy weather anymore. And it doesn't help when you lose your ball off your drive at the first hole.' Still, there was a generous smile and a typically warm handshake. We talked of Tim Mahony and his hopes of staging the Ryder Cup at Mount Juliet, which brought the enthusiastic response, 'I think Mount Juliet would be a very fine venue for the Ryder Cup. There is plenty of space in the old estate and the accommodation is there to house the players. It would be a strong venue. Absolutely.' Warming to the notion, he then enquired, 'When was the last time you had the Ryder Cup in Ireland?' He could hardly credit that it had never been here. 'You mean you haven't had one! Then I feel you should push real hard for it.'

Staying with the Ryder Cup, I wondered what sort of a captain he believed Seve Ballesteros would make at Valderrama the following year. This time his response came with a somewhat accusatory look. 'You guys put a lot into the business of being a captain and I don't happen to agree with that,' he said.

And further evidence of the huge gulf which exists for Nicklaus between the competitive and administrative sides of the game came in the words, 'I was captain twice [1983 and 1987] and from what I remember my main concern was that I had a lot of tees, ball markers, towels, gloves and spikes for the shoes and things like that. That's the sort of thing you do. Then you put the pairings together and you go watch them play.

'It's a great honour, but you don't actually do a lot. Obviously it's fun being part of it, but I honestly don't think it matters all that much who happens to be captain of either side. Everybody tries to do a good job.' Still, he was prepared to concede that 1987 was something of a watershed in the history of the event insofar as it marked the first European victory on American soil. 'Unfortunately I happened to be the captain that year,' he grinned, 'but if you accept that it was bound to happen somewhere, I suppose I'm glad it happened at my course, Muirfield Village. We had a good team, but my recollection of the match was that the Europeans showed themselves to be tougher coming down the stretch. It certainly gave them a great boost, which I suppose carried through to Oak Hill [1995]. And for the future of the event, I happened to think that that result was fine.'

He then talked of Tiger Woods, whom he had famously predicted would win more US Masters tournaments than himself and Arnold Palmer combined (ten). Interestingly, he sympathized with Woods over the flak the player received for failing to accept an invitation to play in the Buick Challenge. 'I remember the first time I did something like that I was nineteen,' he said. 'I was playing the US Masters and I wanted to play in the Azalea Open at Cape Fear the previous week. So I called up and said I was Jack Nicklaus, a Walker Cup player, and was there any way I could get into the tournament. And the guy said, "Yes, we will give you an exemption," and I was to come over and play.

'But when I got there, they didn't give me the exemption and I was ticked off a little bit to discover I had to qualify. Anyway I got through and shot 147 to be fourteenth after the first two rounds. It was real windy and if I shot 70,70 for the last two rounds I would have won the tournament. But I said I had to prepare for the Masters. See you later. And I'm off, thank you very much. I was a kid, not much younger than Tiger. Anyway, when I got to the Masters, I was told by my elders: "Jack, you can't do that." "Do what?" I asked. "You can't do that on tour." So you learn. I haven't done it since. And I don't think you will see Tiger do it again. We all go through things we wish we hadn't done.'

By the time Nicklaus made his only competitive appearance on this island in the British Senior Open at Royal Co Down, a further five years had elapsed. And the end of his playing career seemed all the more imminent, when he suddenly winced in pain from a seized right leg as he rose to leave the media centre on the Sunday. It was a moment which offered all the explanations one could reasonably have required regarding his reluctance to commit himself to any future appearance here.

The important thing was that the legendary name was there in the results, tied third behind the Australian Ian Stanley. His countless admirers would have preferred he was there as the winner, but the Bear still left a lasting imprint. 'I don't know how much golf I will play in the future,' he said. 'I have no tournaments on my schedule for the rest of this year. I want to get a couple of these physical problems fixed. I will play if I can play, but not if I am continuously hurting.' In this context, the partially torn right hamstring, which caused him to withdraw after a first round 77 in the Ford Senior Players Championship in Dearborn, was no more than an irritation. A far more serious concern was a herniated disk, which had been causing shooting pains and general weakness in his right leg.

As for Royal Co Down, he said, 'Everybody has been fantastic; the people couldn't have been nicer. My wife and I have enjoyed it greatly, but I would like to have won, too. I wanted to be greedy.' He clearly enjoyed elements of an extremely challenging links, which he described as 'pretty skittish'. But he went on, 'Is it the best course I have played in the British Isles? Probably not, because there are too many blind shots. But throw that aside and it is an enjoyable course, a great strategic test where you really have to play golf. I thoroughly enjoyed it.' Would he like to see changes? 'You don't change a course like this,' he replied. 'You wouldn't want to change St Andrews, which was built a long time ago and still stands the test of time. This is the way they built courses 100 years ago and you accept them as they are.'

Meanwhile, the struggle between natural competitiveness and anno domini continued. And Des Smyth, himself a highly competitive person, got a rare insight into the Nicklaus psyche after carding a sparkling third-round 66 in the Senior British Open in July 2003 at Turnberry. While winding down from the excitement of the round, the Drogheda man found his attention drawn to the television screen and the sight of Nicklaus standing over a 12-foot putt for a birdie at the fourteenth. The game's greatest competitor was on a roll at six under, with the prospect of shooting his age, a magical 63. But the putt slipped tantalizingly past the target. And when Smyth then observed an apparently good tee-shot break right of the green for a bogey at the short fifteenth, he knew the chance had gone. So, off he went to meet his wife, Vicki, and son, Gregory, who were with him at the event.

'About an hour and a quarter later, we were driving out of the car park when I saw Nicklaus walking towards us,' he recalled. 'And when I lowered the car window to ask how he had finished, he leaned in, said hello to Vicki and then started to talk. For the next twenty minutes, arms resting against the car, he passionately told me every shot he had hit from the fourteenth, leading eventually to a disappointing 67.

'He was absolutely gutted, because he knew he had had the makings of a terrific round, with the chance of shooting his age. And as he talked, I couldn't help thinking that here was the greatest golfer the game has ever seen – unless Tiger outstrips him – baring his soul to a fellow pro; devastated that he didn't shoot the number he wanted. Finally he said, "It would have meant so much to me." Then, before leaving us, he added, "Maybe tomorrow. Though the worry is that those chances don't come around too often these days."''

On returning to the Champions Tour in the US that autumn, Smyth recounted this story to new-found American colleagues. 'Their reaction was that people tend to forget how much the game has meant to Jack, especially when he's playing well and the competitive juices start flowing,' he said. In the process, Smyth realized, not for the first time, that the same could be said of himself and the vast majority of golf's so-called pensioners.

There were to be regular Irish visits by the Bear in the wake of Royal Co Down, but not as a player. Notable among these was a visit he made five months after that Turnberry meeting with Smyth. It came in December 2003 when a blinding, watery sun forced its way through heavy cloud-cover on what had been a damp, depressing morning. Quite properly, nature had made a special effort to welcome an illustrious visitor to Killeen Castle at Dunshaughlin, Co Meath.

Nicklaus had just flown in from Florida for what was going to be a long day. And as his activities neared an end, I observed an unprecedented sight: the indefatigable Golden Bear actually yawning. The daylight hours were spent going through the early design stage of a new, high-profile golf development for the Dublin company of Castlethorn Construction. And given the site and the budget, it wasn't difficult to imagine it as a glittering addition to the portfolio of one of the most imaginative and demanding exponents of his craft. Later, during an evening which became considerably darker than planned, Nicklaus was made an honorary life member of Sutton GC, where longtime friend Joe Carr held a dinner in his honour.

'There are similarities yet marked differences between here and Mount Juliet,' he said of his second Irish design project. 'I would describe Mount Juliet as a crested property, meaning that it had a high point from which we worked down. Here, on the other hand, the changes in elevation are not so marked, yet wonderfully attractive in their own way. With the castle as a unique feature, this is certainly a very nice piece of property where space is not an issue, though you would still be careful not to waste the owners' land.'

The ancestral castle, home of St Oliver Plunkett, which dates back more than eight hundred years, would be transformed and enlarged into a luxurious five-star hotel of 202 bedrooms, along with a leisure centre including a 20-metre swimming pool, tennis courts, a 3,025 square-metre conference centre, golf clubhouse and club lounge. The castle, together with 460 acres of surrounding lands, was bought by Castlethorn in 1995 and it later acquired the adjoining Loughmore Stud, giving a total area of 562 acres. Interestingly, the golf course design was originally offered to Seve Ballesteros, when Roddy Carr was his manager, and though the proposal was later abandoned, Carr returned from the US in 2007 to become a key member of the Killeen staff.

During a break for lunch on that December visit, we adjourned to a charming house close by the castle. There, having discarded his jacket, the Bear looked admirably trim in a navy sweater, though at sixty-three he was clearly finding it a challenge to remain that way. The chicken casserole was very much to his liking, but he took only small, sample portions of the desserts on offer. And when photographer David Conachy playfully attempted to snap him in the act, he shied away, hiding the dish like a guilty child while protesting, 'I don't want this getting back to a certain person named Barbara. She might not be amused.'

Before he headed back out in the Range Rover for further inspection of the site, I wondered about the need for another high-profile parkland course in this country, however admirable the design specifications. 'What you're achieving in Ireland now is a mixture of different courses which offer a wide appeal to the travelling golfer,' said Nicklaus. 'And the great advantage you have here is that they're all accessible. We have some new seaside courses in the States, but they're out in places like Oregon. How the hell do you get there? You can't even find them on the map.

'On the other hand, my sons Steve and Jack came here to Ireland in September and they played Portmarnock, Co Down, Mount Juliet, Ballybunion, Waterville, the Old Head and Lahinch. Now there's a great mixture. Jackie really likes Lahinch. Last year they went to Scotland and played Loch Lomond, St Andrews, Carnoustie and Turnberry. That's the sort of selection the discerning golfer wants.' Another son, Gary, was on this latest trip, but headed on to London on business, before returning to Dublin that evening. Gary had failed to regain his US Tour card at the recent qualifying school and to indicate how narrow the gap is between success and failure in tournament golf, it was only three years since he lost to Phil Mickelson in a play-off for the BellSouth Classic. Now he had no playing rights.

Meanwhile, stage two of the Bear's Irish visit was an intimate gathering at Sutton GC at the invitation of the great J. B. Carr. Picking my way gingerly down the steps from the car park at about six thirty, I wondered about the absence of light. That was when the club captain, Colm Moriarty, explained with an outstretched hand that there was an electrical blackout of the entire area. Now there are unavoidable glitches which can be imagined when welcoming a famous guest such as Nicklaus, but the absence of electricity is not something to be bargained for, especially with a hot meal on the menu.

Still, people understood, especially the guest of honour. Typically thoughtful, he said without amplification, 'I'm sorry you had this problem here tonight. But who really cares? Sometimes it's the problems that make an evening more interesting.' A charming sense of fun was also evident in his gentle teasing of Carr, who had earlier talked of the regular contributions he once made to Barbara Nicklaus's cashmere-sweater fund, when losing bets to the Bear during practice rounds for the Open Championship. In fact, the Bear recalled how an exasperated Carr had finally pleaded, 'Jack, don't you think Barbara could afford to buy her own cashmeres?'

Nicklaus went on, 'I remember coming here in 1990 for the club's centenary celebrations. I hadn't seen Joe for some time and it was a delight to see him again.' Then, with a wicked chuckle, he added of his 81-year-old host: 'Can you believe his sense of humour, his mind, has not changed a bit over the years? I just hope that when I'm ninety-four I'll be just as sharp as you are, Joe.' (Sadly, Joe would be dead within six months of that visit, but not before receiving a phone call from Nicklaus to his hospital bed and there was a wreath sent to his funeral.)

As things transpired, the first course of an unplanned candlelit dinner was barely completed when the lights came on. And Nicklaus was correct: everybody coped wonderfully well, especially the kitchen staff. Soon it was time for the visitors to get some well-earned rest. They included Dirk Bouts, a design associate, who explained that the Bear's Gulfstream would be flying the following morning to the south-east of Spain, to survey one of the six courses they were designing in the region of Murcia. Finally, there was Ron Kirby, familiar in this country for his work at Mount Juliet, the Old Head of Kinsale, Skellig Bay, Dromoland Castle and most recently at Castlemartyr. He had made his own way here from Florida and planned to return home on a scheduled flight. 'But things have changed,' Ron informed me. 'Jack asked me if I'd like a ride and I said, "Sure." ' Just like you might offer someone a lift down the road in your car. In the international world of golf-course development, the Atlantic was but a trifling hurdle.

By that stage we had become familiar with the Bear's repeated concerns about the dramatic improvement in the golf ball. 'We've got to stop it, period,' he said during a recent Masters. 'Some day, somebody's going to do something about it, because we're just running out of land. Wouldn't you love to see Tiger Woods play the same golf course that Lloyd Mangrum played? About the only course in the world you can do that on is St Andrews. And about the only way St Andrews holds up is because of the weather and getting the greens cut fast enough to where they're hard as a rock and you can't do anything.'

After my wife, Kathy, and I had spent three weeks in Hawaii in January 2006, we returned home via West Palm Beach where we had been invited to stay at the Bear's Club. The sixty-sixth birthday of the great man on the previous Saturday was followed twenty-four hours later by a family celebration at the Club, before he joined Tony Jacklin for the official opening of 'The Concession' on the Monday. All three events had passed by the time we arrived on Monday afternoon, but there would be compensations. Meanwhile, concerns about the golf ball had gained a disturbing new dimension.

Among memorable aspects of Hawaii was the sight of a group of elderly, oriental enthusiasts playing so-called ground golf in a public park near Waikiki Beach. I was to discover that this Japanese-invented pursuit is highly organized in the Honolulu area. The equipment is a wooden club in the shape of a putter, but with a considerably larger head, which strikes an object about the size of a tennis ball. Unlike croquet, the stroke is made in the conventional golfing way and balls can be teed up and hit in the air. Holes range from fifty to more than a hundred yards and the target is a wire contraption, not unlike a bird cage sitting on the grass, with openings through which the ball is slotted and where the sound of chimes signals success.

Some way down the road in the Sony Open at Waialae Country

Club, the remarkable exploits of Bubba Watson could not have offered a more dramatic contrast. The latest sensation to hit the PGA Tour was smashing the ball incredible distances on his way to fourth place in the tournament. At twenty-seven, the 6ft 3in left-hander, weighing 14st, was a graduate of the 2005 Nationwide Tour where, hitting a power-fade, he averaged 367.3 yards in one particular tournament – as he did on occasions in the Sony – and 334 yards for the year. John Daly plays pat-a-cake golf by comparison with the so-called 'White Orangutan'.

Using a Ping driver with a 44-inch shaft and a 460cc head off the tee, his second shots to the 561-yard eighteenth at Waialae were with clubs ranging from lob-wedge to pitching wedge, over the four days. Indeed his closing eagle on the Sunday was the product of a drive, wedge and five-foot putt. Elsewhere, the 466-yard fifth was reduced to a two iron and nine iron, and at the 353-yard tenth his drive landed 15 yards from the green and Watson's playing partner, Fred Funk, claimed to have been out-driven by 140 yards. Ian Baker-Finch, the 1991 Open champion who now commentates for CBS, happened to be in the Nicklaus headquarters when I arrived there and he viewed Watson's power-hitting with deep concern. 'In ten years, there will be guys of 6ft 3ins and 220lbs who will totally finish the game of golf as we know it,' he said. 'By hitting the ball 360 yards in the air, the Bubba Watsons are going to destroy golf courses and shotmaking.'

When Nicklaus joined us, the Australian pointed out that the Bear had been warning of this for years. 'There will be no more Corey Pavins,' Baker-Finch remarked. Nicklaus then showed obvious concern, adding, 'And there will be no place in the game for a man with the skill and commitment of Gary Player. Imagine not being able to accommodate the winner of nine major championships! You could also rule out Hogan. All that skill being destroyed by power!' He went on, 'I played quite a few times with Hogan, including the last round of the 1960 US Open when Arnold [Palmer] won, and in the 1966 Masters when I won. Sure, I out-drove him, but in those days length was only a part of the game. Now, it *is* the game.'

Nicklaus pointed out that in his pomp he was using a driver

weighing 13½ ounces, compared with 12 ounces nowadays, and with a 41-inch shaft, compared with 44 or 45 inches. 'Guys nowadays can hit it miles, but they've got no game,' he said. In fairness, this wasn't directed towards Watson, with whom he was not familiar. The Floridian is known among his contemporaries as a player of considerable skill, who can shape shots at will. Indeed, a childhood friend remarked, 'Bubba's liable to hit a 10- or 15-yard hook with his lob wedge or a 30-yard cut with his driver.'

Predictably, both Nicklaus and Baker-Finch emphasized as a matter of urgency the need to limit the modern golf ball and the Australian also advocated reducing the current 'ridiculous' size of driver heads to a maximum of about 270cc. It was the sort of enlightened golfing talk which seemed to fit beautifully with a stay at the Bear's Club, where I rested my head in the St Andrews suite. Conceived by Jack and his wife Barbara, it was officially opened at the end of the millennium on 31 December 1999 as a joint venture with thirty-four other wealthy shareholders and is essentially a golf course and clubhouse with lavish, limited accommodation.

The entrance to the locker-room left one in no doubt that it was unashamedly a shrine to the most dominant player in the history of the game. There on the right was a stuffed polar bear in a suitably dominant pose, standing on a base of glistening, mock ice and with a clear, golden hue to its white coat. This is how Nicklaus explained its significance: 'In 1966 I was playing in the PGA Grand Slam of Golf event at Kemper Lakes GC near Chicago. Our foursome consisted of the four major championship winners of that year. As I was walking down the fifteenth fairway, a young lady ran under the ropes toward me, threw her arms around me and began to cry. "Jack, my father is dying of cancer. He is such a fan of yours. Would you do me a big favour and call him?" My answer was, "I can't stop right now, but I would be happy to talk with him after the round is completed." She met me after the second round and we called her father. When we spoke, her father said, "Jack, I know I sound fine but I only have a few months to live."

'He went on to tell me that he had taken a polar bear in Alaska and, at the time, it was said to have been the fourth largest ever taken. He added, "The bear has a golden hue and it has always reminded me of you. I have been a great fan of yours and when I pass away I would like for you to have the bear as a gift from me." I told him how much I appreciated his kind gesture and assured him I would find a good home for the "golden" polar bear. When my dream of the Bear's Club became a reality, it seemed appropriate to me that the bear's home should be here, in memory of a special fan – Dr Walter J. Murawski.'

Over at the Concession, Jacklin expressed the hope it would play host to the Ryder Cup in far-off 2020. Either way, he had realized the ambition of creating, with his once great rival, a memorial to the climax of the 1969 matches at Royal Birkdale. That was where Nicklaus famously conceded him a two-foot putt on the last, thereby ensuring that the overall match was tied. This time, when the pair played a gentle exhibition, thirty-six years on, there were tears of gradidute from Jacklin at the involvement of the great man, but then Nicklaus has always known instinctively how to do the right thing.

When I next met the Bear in December 2006, the contrast in surroundings could hardly have been more stark. During a bright, sunny lull before the onset of a fierce storm, he was in Donegal, relishing the prospect of a treasured ambition actually becoming a reality. It was a sight to revive memories of great links battles in the Open Championship, as the Bear set about crafting thirty-six holes from 350 acres of spectacular duneland known as St Patrick's, near Carrigart. Against the backdrop of Sheephaven Bay, the commanding figure also conjured up images of how the poet Keats pictured stout Cortez, as Nicklaus stared with his eagle eyes at 'the opportunity of a lifetime for any golf course architect'. Then he mused, 'I've always considered these islands to be the home of golf and for years I've wanted to do a seaside course. This is it.'

It was a Wednesday and he was making his third visit to the property. After staying overnight in Downings in the company of members of his design staff, he headed south to Waterford. There he looked over two other projects, one near Tramore involving the developer Gerry Conlon before his Gulfstream took off for Croatia and then on to Greece. With a total of sixty projects in hand, he showed no signs of slowing down, though he was only a month short of his sixty-seventh birthday. 'Because of the special nature of the site, I would have to say that this is one of the most exciting projects I've been involved in,' said Nicklaus of St Patrick's. In a way, it had its beginnings for him in May 1959, when he first experienced links terrain in the Walker Cup at Muirfield, before playing in the British Amateur at Royal St George's a week later.

'On seeing Muirfield I had no idea what I was looking at, but I enjoyed it,' he recalled. Then, capturing the essence of the links challenge, he went on, 'We had an east wind all the time we were there, but when I returned to Muirfield for the British Open in 1966, the wind was from the west – until the last day, when it switched to the east.' That was when he had the first of three Open triumphs and I marvelled at his memory for such detail. 'Oh sure,' he said by way of response. 'Wind is a very significant part of links golf, which is why we will have generous fairways here. Usually, you find that links golf has two wind conditions, either a shore breeze from the ocean or an off-shore breeze. Weather patterns are very different inland, where the wind just goes around the clock.'

While acknowledging that the British and Irish concept of this sort of terrain related specifically to the linkland between arable land and the seashore, he expressed certain reservations. 'I liked Co Down a lot, except that you had more than twenty-five full shots which were blind,' he said (although that is hotly disputed by the club). 'You couldn't tell where anybody was on the course. Hit it over the top of a hill and you might kill somebody. You can't have that in this day and age. Not that I have any objection to blindness as such. It is part of links golf, but it must have definition, not this business of hitting over a white stone.'

With working titles of the Ocean and Inland courses, what then was his plan for St Patrick's, which has a dramatic spine of towering duneland and where Eddie Hackett designed one of the layouts back in 1982? Nicklaus, who expressed a particular liking for Kingsbarns as 'a modern links', replied, 'Each course here will measure between 7,200 and 7,500 yards and will be a little different from the old links courses that I've played in the British Open. There won't be the same bunkering. And definitely no revetting. What I like about this piece of property is all the blow-outs, where the sand has piled up through the years and the wind has stripped away the grass, creating what is essentially an open fracture in the ground. You will see some examples at Sandwich. It is an ever-changing feature, which this golf course has in abundance.'

On his first visit earlier that year, he spent six hours on the site. The second visit lasted twelve hours and this time it would be eight. 'Normally, I would have made only one visit by this stage,' he said, by way of emphasizing the appeal of the project. 'We are attempting to complement a great links tradition and to have thirty-six holes, unencumbered by real estate, on the water, in Ireland, which makes this a very special and interesting project.'

Within months of this visit, the word on the golfing grapevine was that the project would have to be shelved because of lack of finance. Construction work had stopped early in 2007 and the chances of continued involvement by Nicklaus appeared decidedly bleak. So it was with a certain apprehension that I broached the subject while at the World Golf Village for the induction of Joe Carr into the Hall of Fame in November 2007. To my surprise, Nicklaus was remarkably forthcoming. 'It's too good a piece of property to leave lying there,' he told me. 'We're working with three or four groups right now that are all interested in buying a piece of it. I see a bright future for the project. Absolutely.' He went on, 'I'm not prepared to put a timetable on it. It could be a month from now; it might take longer. Either way, I'm convinced it will happen in one form or another, possibly as a founder's club.' This would be with wealthy investors, like his exclusive Bear's Club in West Palm Beach. Could we take it, then, that the Nicklaus organization wouldn't be letting it go? 'We're not letting it go,' was the Bear's emphatic reply.

It has been more than twenty-two years since Royal Dublin and Nicklaus had gone through the painful transition from being a champion, nearing the end of his competitive career, to a highly respected golf course architect seeking new challenges. In the process, a lasting bond had been established with this country.

Watson and Newt

Tom Watson had no ghosts to exorcize when he travelled to Carnoustie for the 1975 Open Championship. Like Ben Hogan at the same venue twenty-two years previously, he was making his debut in an event which would ultimately capture his soul, while establishing him as one of the toughest competitors in the history of the game.

In what was his fourth full season on the US Tour, he would have seen himself as a promising twenty-five-year-old, attempting to learn his craft. But American observers were less kind. His seeming inability to get the job done, as they like to phrase it, had been highlighted at the 1973 Hawaiian Open, where he squandered a three-stroke lead. Then there was the ten-round World Open for a then staggering first prize of $100,000 at Pinehurst No. 2, where he led by six strokes after a stunning 62 in the fifth round, only to eventually finish fourth.

A similar story emerged from the major championships. After three rounds of the 1974 US Open, Watson led by a stroke from Hale Irwin, with Arnold Palmer a further stroke back in third place. This was the championship where the severity of the course prompted Dick Schapp to write the book *The Massacre of Winged Foot*, about a brutal test which Irwin won with a seven-over-par aggregate of 287. For his part, Watson made a wobbly start to the final round, with bogeys at the fourth, fifth and eighth, and by his own admission 'blew it' in a closing 79 to be five strokes behind the winner in a share of fifth place.

But there would be better times ahead, as he gradually acquired the elusive quality of competing. Later in June 1974 he had his debut victory in the Western Open, coming from six strokes behind with a final round of 69. Still, comparable form continued to elude him at 'major' level. A final round of 73 knocked him back to a share of eighth place in the 1975 US Masters. Worse was to come in the US Open at Medinah, where he had rounds of 67 and 68 to lead Ben Crenshaw by three strokes at the halfway stage, only to collapse to 78 and 77 for an eventual share of ninth behind Lou Graham.

These could hardly have been considered encouraging credentials for a young man attempting to emulate the great Hogan. Even with a win in the Byron Nelson Classic earlier in the 1975 season, Watson didn't need reminding that the demands imposed by major championships were rather different to those of a regular tour event. Incidentally, it was around this time that Pat Heneghan, the dynamic press officer for what would be the inaugural Carrolls Irish Open at Woodbrook in August of that year, signed up Watson on an appearance fee, little imagining what lay in store.

Though Watson could boast no better than a moderate amateur golf career in his native Missouri, Jack Newton was an extravagantly gifted sportsman who represented Australia in rugby and cricket as a schoolboy, before a rugby injury prompted him to concentrate on golf. Born in Sydney on 30 January 1950, he was almost five months younger than Watson, but very much more successful as a tournament golfer when he headed for Carnoustie.

I remember him from the Kerrygold Classic at Waterville in September 1975, when we happened to be staying in the same hotel. He finished down the field after a closing 82 and while giving him a lift to the golf course during the tournament, I discovered he wasn't one of the world's great communicators. Indeed, the number of words he proffered on the twenty-minute journey could have been counted on the fingers of one hand. Taciturn he most certainly was, but a sportsman's build, shaggy, blond hair, a warm smile and an ability to enjoy himself made him extremely popular with both sexes. And he had a golf game to match that appeal.

As is the way with Australians, he found himself obliged to become an international player and, between his professional debut in 1971 and the middle of 1975, he had six tournament victories – the Dutch Open, Benson and Hedges Festival and City of Auckland Open in 1972, the Nigerian Open and Benson and Hedges Matchplay in 1974 and the Sumrie Better-Ball with Ireland's John O'Leary in May 1975. He was newly married to his English wife, Jackie, by then.

Going into the Open Championship that year he possessed an

irresistible putting stroke, courtesy of the game's greatest player. 'I picked up something watching Nicklaus in a practice round,' he recalled. Meanwhile, having lost money to Newton in an exhibition match in Australia some time earlier, Tom Weiskopf threw down a challenge of a re-match during the build-up at Carnoustie. 'Bring a good partner,' Newton teased. It could be said that Weiskopf took the advice very much to heart in that he brought Nicklaus along. Newton chose O'Leary, his successful Sumrie partner at Queen's Park GC, Bournemouth two months previously.

After two early birdies, Newton made a grave error by turning to the so-called 'Towering Inferno' and teasing, 'We're going to kick your butt, Tom. Better go back to the clubhouse and get a new partner.' Newton claimed that the ill-judged taunt was overheard by Nicklaus, who turned to Weiskopf and remarked, 'Let's teach this young bastard a thing or two.' With that, Weiskopf proceeded to turn on the heat with a 64 while the Bear had a 65. And though Newton far from disgraced himself with a 67, he lost £300. Later, however, Nicklaus decided that, having been taught a lesson, the young Australian could ill-afford to lose that sort of cash. So, typically sporting, the Bear settled for a sandwich and a drink, and turned his attention to the more serious challenge ahead.

During a conversation I had with Watson prior to the Open Championship of 1999, he produced one of his famous Huckleberry Finn grins and declared proudly, 'Carnoustie? Yes, I'm the defending champion. Have been for twenty-four years. Back in 1975 I remember the weather was good for the first three rounds, but for the final round on Saturday the wind blew down the eighteenth.'

It should be noted that this treacherous hole, dominated by the serpentine Barry Burn and the source of so much grief for Padraig Harrington on his way to victory in 2007, was a 525-yard par five after James Braid had remodelled the course in preparation for the 1931 Open, won by Tommy Armour. For the 1975 Open, however, it was shortened and played for the first time as a par four, which was later stretched to a formidable 499 yards for the 2007 Open.

As Watson recalled the play-off against Newton, the fearsome eighteenth was directly into the wind. 'And it blew hard,' he said. 'The golf course certainly showed its teeth. That's why it was so important for me to have scrambled as well as I did. On the seventy-second hole, I remember looking up at the scoreboard and seeing Newton was three ahead, but he still had the sixteenth to play. And seventeen was right into the wind. And I remember thinking to myself, if I make this [birdie] putt, Newton still has a lot of work to do. As things turned out, he had bogeyed the sixteenth before I putted, so the gap was now two. And then I made the putt to go one behind. Meanwhile, Bobby Cole [overnight leader] had made double-bogey at fifteen. So, given the conditions, I knew I could be in a play-off.

'There was no need to psych myself up for the [eighteen-hole] play-off the following day in that I had a lot of confidence in the way I was striking the ball. Still, I hit a terrible drive on the first hole before knocking it on the green and two-putting for par. At number two I knocked it stiff, about three feet, while he hit his approach almost into the ocean – 80 yards off line. Then he hit a wedge to four feet and made that putt for par. And that's the way it developed. It was nip and tuck. He was ahead of me by a stroke and I remember chipping in for an eagle at the fourteenth to draw back to even.

'Then we both bogeyed sixteen and eventually came to the eighteenth hole tied once again. I hit my approach first and got it on the green, and he hit his shot into the bunker and I thought, "Well, let's see what happens from here." He played a good bunker shot out to about 12 feet from the hole. I knocked my approach putt about three feet by and, to put the pressure on him, I decided to finish, knocking it right into the hole. And he slides his by. And I've won.'

In the context of the money match prior to the championship, it was interesting that Newton and Nicklaus happened to play together in the third round, where Australian Jack shot a course record 65, to the Bear's 68. As can happen so often on links terrain, however, competitors were rocked onto their heels by the ferocity of the weather for the final round, in which none of the leaders broke 70. Playing with Cole – 'Bobby was probably as nervous as I was' – Newton found himself with the championship lead, as the South African slumped towards a 76.

The Australian recalled, 'I came to the sixteenth tee [235-yard par three] and there were three groups waiting. It was like a *Who's Who* of golf: Jack Nicklaus, Ray Floyd, Tom Watson, Johnny Miller. I don't think the long wait did me any good.' Finally, he needed a par four on the eighteenth for a play-off, and got it. Then, referring to the play-off, Newton went on, 'Two things that day turned out to be the opposite of what the US press had been writing. They'd been saying that Watson was a choker and that he was a suspect putter. But he never looked like missing a putt the whole damn day.'

Within a few minutes of sinking the winning putt, Watson was pleasantly surprised that his name was already on the Open Trophy, the famous claret jug. This could be attributed to the canniness of the Royal and Ancient's official engraver, Alexander Harvey from Perth. As he explained later, 'I was able to engrave the last two letters beforehand as both names finished with "on".' So he got the name of the new champion right, which, incidentally, was more than the R and A captain managed to achieve when he publicly congratulated 'Tom Kite'.

Watson's proud claim in 1999 of having been the Carnoustie champion for twenty-four years stemmed from the fact that the famous links went off the Open rota after 1975, largely because of insufficient accommodation in the area and inadequate infrastructure for the increasing demands of an Open Championship. However, its rehabilitation as a major venue began with the staging of the Scottish Open in 1995 and when the tournament returned there the following year, those of us present would not easily forget the horrific conditions of high winds and squally showers sweeping in off the North Sea.

Nor would we easily forget the sight of Colin Montgomerie as he trooped into the media centre after carding a wretched 81 on the final day. His matted hair, bedraggled appearance and the sound of his golf shoes tramping over the wooden floor conveyed an image far removed from that of a jolly big giant. In fact, he looked as if he had just emerged from a car wash on full cycle, without a car.

As he sat down to face us, the first question was put to Monty by a notoriously eager scribe who asked him innocently, 'Tell me, Colin, was the wind a factor?' Hardly believing his ears, the Scot mumbled to himself, 'Was the wind a factor?' Then, realizing the inanity of the question, he repeated, 'Was the wind a factor?', before thundering 'WAS THE WIND A FACTOR?' This has since become a celebrated story among golf scribes and Montgomerie has come to appreciate the humour in it. Indeed, sometimes, when he happens to be in a good mood, scribes have been known to ask him, 'Was the wind a factor?' and then share in a quiet chuckle.

For Watson, winning the 1975 Open represented a very significant step in his development as a top-rank player. However, he claimed, 'It didn't bring about any miraculous transformation in my competitive strength. That hadn't really changed. I left Carnoustie still learning how to win. It was only when I won [his second Open] at Turnberry in 1977 that I felt I belonged. At that moment [after eventually beating Nicklaus in a titanic struggle] I felt I was ready to play with the big boys. That was when I gained the confidence in myself that I could win at the highest level.'

With rounds of 68, 70, 65, 65, Watson won by a stroke. And he had to birdie the seventy-second hole to do it, after hitting a glorious seven-iron second shot of 162 yards to within three feet of the pin. The memory still stirred him, twenty-two years later. 'For me, that was the ultimate, because I was playing against the best golfer in the world,' he said. 'That was where I wanted to be. Going behind was not that big a deal, because I was supposed to be behind. But being able to come back, and then back again and win, made me believe I could play with the best in the world from then on.'

All of which was essentially down to Nicklaus. 'I've seen some great swingers; far better swingers than I could ever have hoped to be,' said Watson. 'But they didn't seem to have the talent to negotiate their way around a golf course. Nicklaus was the best at it that I've ever seen. By far the best. Trevino was pretty good, too. He knew how to play a golf course. They would go out on a golf course with a target score in mind. I think that's awfully important towards being successful at the highest level.

'Nowadays they call it focus. They talk about [President] Clinton's focus groups as one of the reasons for his successful presidency in that he has the insight to be able to tell people what they want to hear. On the golf course, great players have good focus. It means that on every shot you know where to hit it and where not to hit it; you can picture the shot you want to play. That's essentially what you have to do to win major championships.

'That's one of the reasons Payne Stewart won [the US Open at Pinehurst a month previously]. His rhythm is the best thing about his golf swing. And when the heat came on, his wonderful rhythm was awfully important. That's Payne's strength. And you can see it in an NBA basketball final. You see people get out of rhythm when they're shooting. You can see it happen. It has to do with all sorts of things, but mainly pressure.'

For Newton, the crushing disappointment of Carnoustie was reflected in only one further top-ten finish during the second half of the 1975 season and that was eighth place behind Christy O'Connor Jnr in the Irish Open. Incidentally, his only other Irish Open appearance was a year later, when he was twenty-third behind Ben Crenshaw at Portmarnock. A cherished ambition was fulfilled, however, when he became a member of the USPGA Tour, where he captured the 1978 Buick Open. And although he went on to win the 1979 Australian Open, his best subsequent performances in the US would be as runner-up to Craig Stadler in the 1980 Greater Greensboro Open, and to Seve Ballesteros – 'He's a great bloke' – in the US Masters, a week later.

But now that Watson had learned to compete, he seemed to win almost at will. Indeed, by his own admission, he 'backed into' a fourth Open triumph at Royal Troon in 1982, when Nick Price famously squandered the chance of victory. In attempting to explain the precise nature of competing at the highest level, Watson claimed afterwards that it was essentially about decision-making. Observers had the notion of pressure manifesting itself in trembling hands or a tortured stomach, but to Watson it was about recognizing the wrong messages which came from an addled brain, and that could be acquired only by experience.

In the event, he hit a glorious two iron to the seventy-second green at Royal Birkdale on Sunday, 17 July 1983 to retain the Open crown and record his fifth victory in all, one short of the milestone set by Harry Vardon. It was to be his last major triumph and he was still two months short of his thirty-fourth birthday. But Birkdale 1983 was memorable for a more amusing reason, as Sir Michael Bonallack later recalled. Bonallack took over as secretary of the Royal and Ancient from Keith Mackenzie in September of that year and, in the context of the Open, he had something of a dry run at Watson's triumph.

'On joining the R and A, I went straight to Birkdale at the end of June, when the final preparations for the Open were in full swing,' he said. 'Having stayed until the championship was over, I then went back to St Andrews. That was when I was understudy to Keith, who had devised a new plan for the prize presentation. It involved a mobile stage which could be dismantled in sections. Rising to about two or three feet off the ground, there were steps onto it.'

Bonallack went on, 'It was an enormous thing, very heavy, and the idea was that it would be erected quickly on the fairway, 50 yards short of the eighteenth green after the last putt had dropped. Given its prime position out there on the course, everybody in the stand would be able to see the presentation. So, four little dots were placed on the fairway to mark exactly where it would go. And they had a rehearsal with people rushing out from the side of the stage and putting it up there, which, of course, was fine when there was nobody else around.'

When the big moment arrived and Watson came up the eighteenth fairway with playing partner Craig Stadler, Mackenzie took Bonallack to the back of the green to watch the grand plan go smoothly into action. 'Unfortunately, he hadn't bargained for one of the most traditional happenings on the final day of the Open,' the understudy went on. 'Horrified, he saw the crowd do their usual breakthrough before coming straight down the middle of the fairway, where the stage was meant to be. He then grabbed me by the shoulder and said, "They can't do that. Go and stop them." With that, he turned round and went straight back into his office.

'Well, there was clearly nothing that I or any of the marshals could do in the face of a determined charge by 3,000 spectators down the middle of the fairway. And the people who were waiting by the sides of the eighteenth, ready with the sections of Keith's stage, were fully aware of this. Still, out of a sense of duty I suppose, they eventually struggled out there and assembled it as best they could, where it was originally planned to go. With that, a section of the crowd climbed up on it to get a better view. While all this was going on, the presentation was actually set up at the back of the green, in front of the clubhouse window.'

On the following day, at the wind-down press conference to the Open, Mackenzie was asked what the odd-looking platform erected on the eighteenth fairway was for. This is how Bonallack remembered the moment: 'Without batting an eyelid, Keith said he was concerned that the spectators coming down the final hole didn't really get a proper view of the presentation ceremony. So, the idea was that with this easily assembled platform, the problem would be overcome. I remember thinking that he got out of it very well.' Two months later, Mackenzie had retired, Bonallack had taken over and nobody was any the wiser about the special plans for the Royal Birkdale victory ceremony.

In far-off Australia, on 24 July, the Sunday after Watson's last Open triumph, a tragedy occurred which would have a profound impact on the world of golf. It involved Newton, who was about to board a chartered light Cessna aircraft at Sydney Airport, for the short flight back to his hometown of Newcastle, having attended an Australian Rules match with three friends. It was raining as the engines idled and the propellor blades whirred, preparatory to take-off.

In a catastrophic instant, Newton was caught by a propellor. Though the pilot instantly slammed the engines into reverse, it was too late. The golfer lost his right eye, right arm, half his liver and serious quantities of blood. Indeed, but for the skill of a medical team from the Prince of Wales Hospital in Sydney, he might have died. 'The injuries to his arm and eye were minor compared to his stomach,' his wife, Jackie, later recalled. 'He got septicemia and had to have a temporary colostomy while his bowel healed. Then there were the various grieving stages he had to go through for his lost limb. But Jack's attitude was extremely good. In fact he was quite an easy patient under the circumstances.'

Newton's astonishing acceptance of his fate remains one of the most noble and heroic of sporting stories. As he reflected philosophically, 'I had two young kids and a great wife and a great family. And the golfing world really got behind me. So I don't believe I had any choice. I mean I had two choices: I could go and sit in a corner for the rest of my life or I could get on with it. To get to the top in golf you've got to be pretty tough and a lot of the experiences I went through in the game really helped me. Then I was lucky, because I started doing some TV commentary and I enjoyed that, because it kept me in contact with the guys I used to play against, and that's probably the single biggest thing that I miss.'

He went on, 'Some people might accuse me of having a warped sense of humour, but there was one thing I noticed above all else while I was in rehabilitation – and I was there for nearly a year because I was in and out of hospital for various operations. It was that among people in there with brain damage, and arms and legs off, and all kinds of problems there was a common thread in that they all maintained a great sense of humour.

'That's a pretty good lesson for everyone. We all seem to take ourselves a bit too seriously, whereas if you can have a laugh and a joke, the world becomes a better place. I actually think it wouldn't be a bad experience for eighteen-year-olds to spend a day in a rehabilitation place and just see another side of life.' Yet there was almost a palpable sadness as he admitted, 'I'd be a liar if I said I wouldn't mind sticking my arm back on and getting out there amongst it, because I'm a competitive bloke. But I had fourteen great years on the tour and some terrific experiences doing things in golf that not too many other people have done.'

Newton went on to play one-handed golf off 15-handicap and was capable of beating most 12-handicappers. He also pursued a career in golf course architecture, quite apart from his broadcasting activities. Then there was his writing – 'bloody difficult, too, with a cigarette and a glass in your only hand'.

During Open week in 1999, Watson and Newton met again outside the new hotel at Carnoustie, close by the eighteenth green where fate had dealt them sharply contrasting hands twenty-four years previously. Private moments were shared about 1975 and the different roads their lives had taken, and one could imagine Watson's deep concern for his old rival and Newton bravely dismissing any sympathy, possibly with the words, 'No worries, mate.'

On 11 June 2007, Newton was awarded the Medal of the Order of Australia for services to golf, particularly through a range of executive youth development and fundraising activities. He and Jackie have two children. Clint Newton plays rugby league for Hull Kingston Rovers, while their daughter, Kristie, is now a golf professional, having had an impressive amateur career.

Millennium Captain!

The decision to honour Tom Watson as the millennium captain of Ballybunion was formalized at the club's AGM on 26 February 1999 on the nomination of incoming captain Fintan Scannel. 'When Fintan and myself contacted Tom to tell him the news, he had no hesitation in accepting,' said the club secretary/manager, Jim McKenna. 'He is familiar with the structure of club golf in this part of the world, so he knows what the role of captain involves. We're currently working out a schedule for him of the club's main functions during the millennium year and the feeling is that he will make at least four or five trips over here.'

McKenna went on, 'Apart from the fact that Tom is a member of the club, there is a precedent for the bestowing of this type of honour. Sean Walsh was nominated as the centenary captain in

1993 in acknowledgement of his immense contribution as the club's long-time secretary/manager.' Ballybunion were keenly aware that Watson had contributed enormously to a dramatic growth in Ballybunion's green-fee revenue, especially from golfers in the US where the gospel was spread at every opportunity. And, as McKenna put it, the millennium captaincy is the club's way of saying 'thank you'.

Watson shared the distinction of being an honorary life member of Ballybunion with his good friend Sandy Tatum, a former president of the USGA, and with US President, Bill Clinton, among others. In his capacity as a tournament professional, it was also a charming coincidence that he would be the club's captain during a year when Wentworth bestowed the same honour on Bernard Gallacher. He and Gallacher will be recalled as rival Ryder Cup captains at The Belfry in 1993, when the Americans gained what would become a rare victory in the biennial event.

Word was that it took Watson 'no more than a minute' to accept and he got a clearer picture of what might be described as the job specification during his customary July visit in 1999. 'Captain of Ballybunion! How about that!' he enthused. 'I got the call just before Christmas [1998] and I was only too delighted to accept. It's quite an honour.' His first visit to the club as part of his preparation for the 1981 Open at Royal St George's sparked a love affair which led to Watson declaring that Ballybunion was no less than the best course in the world. As he later put it, 'I have come to love the golf course, the golf club and the people. Everything about the place.'

The inspired deal by Pat Heneghan duly culminated in Watson's appearance at Woodbrook as the reigning Open champion of 1975 and he shared thirteenth place behind the winner, Christy O'Connor Jnr, and was three strokes behind Newton. Later, on being asked how much Irish he had in him, he avoided the usual grandmother stuff so much favoured by his countrymen. Instead, he replied with typical candour, 'I haven't found that out yet, but you could say that I'm Irish by injection.'

He and his son, Michael, played Ballybunion by way of links preparation for the 1998 Open at Royal Birkdale. But, sadly, it failed to inspire the required magic and a second-round 76 pushed him three strokes outside the half way cut. Later, when I told him of the possibility of Ballybunion staging the Murphy's Irish Open during his year of captaincy, he commented, 'That would be wonderful. What a place for the Irish Open! And there's always the possibility I could play in it. We'll see what happens.'

When the 2002 Open Championship came to Muirfield, the familiar, jaunty walk had lost some of its spring as he trod fairways which had been so productive for him back in 1980. But the smile remained as warm and welcoming as ever. Looking out over the scene of his 1980 triumph, he said, 'You know an interesting thing about links turf? Wherever you go, they all have the same smells. I wish I could have played Ballybunion under championship conditions, when the Irish Open went there in 2000. Unfortunately, there was a conflict with senior commitments I had in the States.' But he was there for his captain's prize on the Saturday after the Open, 29 July, when, because of the huge response from members, there were three shotgun starts – a unique format for a unique occasion.

Now, with boyish looks finally giving way to middle age and with his fifty-third birthday less than two months off, there were still fresh fields to be conquered, such as a debut appearance in the Senior British Open at Royal Co Down the following week. He considered himself extremely fit for a man of his years, a fact he attributed to 'a strict workout regimen and good genes'. And though links terrain exacted a punishing toll on mind and body in his thirtieth appearance in the Open, there was little indication that his affection for the championship might be waning.

In fact, his enthusiasm reminded me of an incident at St Andrews in 1984, when his ball was found by a grizzled local after he had mis-hit his drive at the twelfth. 'Was he a Royal and Ancient type?' Watson was asked afterwards. 'More ancient than royal,' came the reply. Then there was his acceptance of an alleged participation in an incident at Muirfield, which would not have reflected credit on those involved. Twenty-two years on, he finally came clean on what actually happened on the evening of his Open win in 1980. 'I wasn't kicked out of here,' he acknowledged with a smile. 'That was [Ben] Crenshaw. It's always repeated that I was part of the story, but I wasn't. I was already eating.'

It will be recalled that Watson was reputed to have received his marching orders by the then redoubtable secretary, Paddy Hanmer, a retired Royal Navy captain. The story went that with Crenshaw, Tom Weiskopf and their respective wives, the newly crowned champion returned to the course where the men played the seventeenth and eighteenth with old hickory clubs. 'The problem was that Penny Crenshaw was aerating the eighteenth green with stiletto heels,' Watson added. 'My understanding is that Captain Hanmer emerged from the clubhouse and said to Ben, "Mr Crenshaw, this is not allowed. I want you in my office at six forty-five tomorrow morning." I don't know what transpired after that, except that it made for a wonderful, wonderful story.'

More solidly based in fact was how Watson and his mentor, Byron Nelson, made a special visit to this country in the early summer of 1989 when, using a helicopter, they played Ballybunion, Co Sligo and Royal Co Down on what was intended as a farewell visit for one of the game's legendary figures. A photograph on the clubhouse staircase at Newcastle commemorates the visit. On a trip to the west of Ireland five years earlier, Watson had hoped to play Connemara, but was unable to do so because of time constraints. So, on meeting club officials at the PGA Golf Show in Orlando in February 2000, he listened carefully when they invited him for an overdue look at Eddie Hackett's handiwork.

Later that year, Watson finally arrived at Connemara and played the course along with his wife and American friends, and with Connemara's European Youth silver-medallist, Derek McNamara, as his caddie. Watson's verdict? 'It's a true championship course where the elevated greens, particularly on the back nine, are spectacular.' Regarding his trip with Nelson, he said, 'There was no particular reason why we did it then; I just wanted to be sure we did it some time, because Byron loved coming over here. He loved the atmosphere. And when he was a commentator with ABC television, he thoroughly enjoyed the way the game was played on links courses. Running the ball along the ground and playing quickly, that was his way. He was a marvellous player.

Unfortunately his hips were bothering him on our visit, but he still played, though he wasn't very happy with his golf game. And when a great golfer plays poorly, it hurts the soul.'

He then explained his latest visit: 'I'm going to the British Seniors essentially because it's being played at Royal Co Down. On my visit, I had the feeling that I wanted to experience tournament conditions there and see how I could handle what I saw as a very, very difficult links challenge. As for its blindness, most links courses have their blind shots. There are a few at Muirfield, which means you must have some local knowledge. Unless you're a great chess player, which sadly I'm not, you've got to learn very quickly where to hit it. The winds, the firmness of the turf and the bounces make it almost impossible to establish a strategy until you have played the course two or three times.

'So, at this distance, I can't do justice to Royal Co Down, because I've played it only the once. But I remember the short seventh with the shoulder off the left of the green. I played a wonderful short-iron shot in there and I remember thinking, "My Lord! What a difficult hole this is with this type of wind." And I imagined how much tougher it would be to get on the green if the wind were blowing stronger. Of course, I also remember the famous view down the ninth, looking towards Slieve Donard and the Mournes. But to be honest, I remember the seventh more. In fact, it's usually the short holes I remember the most on a course I've visited for the first time.'

Royal Co Down wasn't especially kind to Watson in 2002. Having been in a challenging position for fifty-four holes, he slumped to a closing 79 which left him tied for fourteenth place behind wire-to-wire winner Noboru Sugai. Twelve months later, however, a cherished title came his way. And it seemed richly appropriate that his first Senior British Open triumph should have come at Turnberry, a course which bestowed such rich favours on him as to rival Ballybunion for his affection.

Seve and the pain of departed skills

Seve Ballesteros was only nine months away from his fortieth birthday when he came to Druids Glen in July 1996 to fulfil what had become an admirable commitment to the Irish Open. He couldn't have known that his winning days on the European Tour were behind him; that he had crossed a golfing rubicon when relinquishing his Spanish Open title to a rookie Irishman by the name of Padraig Harrington at Club de Campo in May of that year.

The proud Spaniard was unquestionably aware, however, of a serious decline in his game. Indeed, the danger signs had been in evidence all of three years previously on his native terrain in the Majorca Open. That was where a clearly distressed Ballesteros repeatedly bit his lower lip while attempting to cope with a cruelly destructive game. All the while, his caddie, Billy Foster, was becoming increasingly upset by his master's torment at figures soaring towards 20-over-par. Finally, he could take no more.

In a voice trembling with emotion, the young Yorkshireman turned to him on the tenth tee. 'Let's go in,' he urged. 'There's no point in torturing yourself any more.' Whereupon Ballesteros replied, 'No, Billy, we are professionals. We must battle, regardless. We will carry on and finish the job.'

On being asked the secret of golf on that fateful visit to Druids Glen, he replied pensively: 'To forget.' Yet the regal air and extraordinary charisma remained, as he and his family relaxed in a suite in a County Wicklow hotel. 'There will be no more coaching,' declared the player who had captured a third Irish Open at Portmarnock ten years previously. 'I've had enough coaches over the last few years. There will be no more.'

This was the one-time conquistador who, in another significant happening in 1996, had made peace with owner Jaime Patino over Valderrama's selection as the venue for the 1997 Ryder Cup. It happened during the week of the Volvo PGA Championship at Wentworth and had to do with what was, in my view, the Spaniard's illogical campaign against Patino, while championing the claims of Novo Sancti Petri as a rival venue. Arguably the most remarkable press conference I have ever attended started with him in the media centre at Wentworth, pulling a small, crumpled piece of paper from his pocket as an improbable 'prepared' statement.

Ballesteros then proceeded to address the assembled media with the unforgettable words, 'There will be no questions, only answers.' This was followed by the most fulsome apology imaginable. All of which prompted me to suggest in print that he had 'poured so much oil on troubled waters, as to be in danger of creating an ecological disaster to rival the Exxon Valdez'. Most players would have been heavily criticized for what he did to Patino, but, being Seve, his apology was readily accepted and we forgave him.

We knew he was suffering grievously on another level. 'My game cannot get any worse,' he had said dejectedly, after shooting rounds of 78 and 79 in the Moroccan Open at the start of the 1996 season. 'I used to overpower the golf course and now the golf course overpowers me. It's very painful when you have to talk all the time about these things. It's not easy – why this, why that, and what are you going to do and why don't you do this. It drives you crazy. It's not good, when everything is negative, negative, negative, because the mind is very powerful.'

It was hardly surprising that he had spent the four months since Morocco trying to forget. 'I want to look to good things, to happy memories,' he said. Yet expert observers took the view that Ballesteros couldn't regain his former competitiveness without undergoing a major swing change. 'Even at his best, I always thought Seve was living right on the edge,' said Lanny Wadkins who, as US skipper, watched him struggle desperately in the 1995 Ryder Cup at Oak Hill. 'He erased a lot of mistakes with his short game.'

Bernhard Langer was more blunt. 'Seve's problem is his swing,' said the German, with typical directness. 'He must change it.' Those who knew about such matters believed that while the Spaniard's swing may have been aesthetically pleasing, it was not grounded in sound mechanics, and that for years he played on talent and heart, until a shaky foundation eventually betrayed him. Essentially, his swing path into the ball was too steep. From the top, he failed to flatten his plane into the sort of rounder, sweeping motion which is to be found in the majority of consistent hitters.

It was a world away from the 1979 Ryder Cup at the Greenbrier in West Virginia, which was notable for two key reasons: Lee Elder had become the first black player to represent the US, while the newly formed European team contained two Spaniards. This latter development led to the legendary Sam Snead, one-time professional at the host venue, sneaking back purely to see a remarkable twenty-two-year-old whom he had come to admire only from a distance. As it happened, the feeling was mutual. Then the reigning Open champion, Ballesteros couldn't wait to see the famous leg kick. And the old 'Slammer', an incredibly fit sixty-seven-year-old at the time, duly obliged, raising his right leg level with the Spaniard's upstretched hand. When he demanded that Ballesteros do likewise, however, the reply was a firm 'no'.

On the afternoon of the first day, the young conquistador and compatriot Antonio Garrido played against Fuzzy Zoeller and Hubert Green in the second foursomes. As a foretaste of many a Ryder Cup battle to come, there was an incident on the sixteenth green where the Spaniards wrapped up the match by 3 and 2. After conceding a putt to Green, Garrido scooped the ball back to him with his putter. The two of them then began arguing and getting progressively agitated. Ballesteros later recalled, 'I remember I had to stand in between them. At that moment I could see that the Ryder Cup was important. Even though we didn't play for money, we played for pride.'

Americans never fully comprehended the deep-seated antipathy they instilled in the young Spaniard by choosing to give him a difficult time during his early years on tour there. From that first meeting at the Greenbrier, he decided they should be beaten at all costs. And he enjoyed a number of glory days against them, specifically in his two US Masters triumphs, three Open victories and, most of all, in the Ryder Cup.

Against this background, it is hardly surprising that despite being the world's most dominant player during the 1980s, when he was widely regarded as a genius with a short iron in his hand,

Ballesteros often captured the public imagination more for his exploits as Europe's talisman in the biennial showpiece than for other tournament performances. Except in this country. It is doubtful if even his native Spain owed as great a debt of gratitude to Ballesteros as Ireland did. As three-times winner of the Irish Open, he made it, almost single-handedly, second only to the Open Championship in European appeal. And the irrepressible, swashbuckling nature of his play seemed to find a special place in Irish hearts.

The feeling was mutual, though sometimes expressed in mischief. Like during the presentation ceremony for the Dubai Desert Classic in 1990 when Des Smyth observed that Ireland would have had a clean sweep of the leading positions but for the interference of 'some bloody Spaniard'. Whereupon Ballesteros piped up, 'It was me, it was me.' This was the occasion when Eamonn Darcy won the tournament, David Feherty was runner-up, and Smyth was forced to share third place with the 'bloody' Spaniard.

However, these are but glimpses of a truly great player, who dominated much of my golf-writing career and whose decision to retire from tournament play during the week of the 2007 Open Championship at Carnoustie provoked mixed feelings from all who know him. Some would have hoped that he could finally find peace after more than a decade of torment, while others knew they would seriously miss his charismatic presence in the game.

Speaking of the profound influence Ballesteros had on the 1991 Ryder Cup team at Kiawah Island as its most charismatic senior member, David Feherty said, 'No player but Seve had the ability to make my hair stand on end simply by watching him play. By that time, I had idolized him for the best part of fifteen years, since he first hit the headlines at Birkdale in 1976. I found his presence to be quite extraordinary and I can still picture him prowling around, prodding players, grabbing them by the back of the neck, hugging them.

'He's a very physical person; personal contact is very important to him as a means of communication. At Kiawah, he made a particular point of coming to the newcomers in the side, players like myself and David Gilford, Paul Broadhurst and Steven

Richardson. He deliberately made himself feel small in our company so as to strengthen the bond between us. He bared his soul to us, telling of his own vulnerability, so that we might think of him as an equal, as just another member of the team. His motivational powers were phenomenal and as far as he was concerned, we were all in this thing together, all pulling together.' Tony Jacklin, the Spaniard's captain in four previous Ryder Cup stagings, said, 'Seve's passion and conviction have been so fantastic that he has made things happen which couldn't otherwise have happened. It is something only a really great player could do and it's been wonderful to see.'

As a Ryder Cup captain in his own right, Ballesteros was seen at his mischievous, manipulative best at Valderrama in 1997. Looking towards that memorable staging, he remarked of his appointment, 'I said yes, because so many people wanted me to take the job. And I gained so much from golf in Europe that, really, I had no choice.' When the time came, he threw himself into the whole endeavour with typical passion. Among other things, he claimed to have been responsible for the fact that golf's biggest event would be coming to Ireland, telling me, 'I was the first one to recommend that the Ryder Cup should go to your country. It was a great decision by the Ryder Cup committee.'

And there was humour. Like in his account of the lengthy trip he had on the Sunday of Ryder Cup week from Santander to the Costa del Sol, including an unscheduled two-hour delay in Madrid. By way of reaction, a prominent British scribe enquired, 'Did you happen to see my luggage?' 'Ah, you travel BA again?' suggested the Spaniard, with a sly grin. 'No, I travelled Iberia,' the scribe replied acidly, naming the official carriers to the Ryder Cup. Eyeing the man's well-rounded physique, Ballesteros responded, 'Too bad my clothes won't fit you, otherwise I would lend you some.'

The captain's mood had been buoyed up, one suspected, by having received the agreement of US skipper Tom Kite for a change of format in the week's matches, whereby play on Friday and Saturday would start with fourballs rather than the traditional foursomes. Why the change? 'It was just an idea,' he said innocently. Just an idea! Only those with equally devious minds saw a connection with Europe's struggle to produce only two halves from the opening four foursomes matches in defence of the title in 1989, and the fact that Ballesteros and Jose-Maria Olazabal, the illustrious Spanish Armada, were the only winners in the same series in 1991, when the trophy was relinquished.

I always thought of Ballesteros as being one of the brightest sportsmen I had ever met, but Peter Dobereiner, the celebrated English scribe, attributed this sharpness to native cunning. Either way, he never failed to impress his then business manager Roddy Carr. Like when he arranged special treatment for his players' spanking-new dress shoes prior to the gala dinner, the biggest social function of Ryder Cup week – an attendant at the European Team's headquarters was instructed to systematically roughen the soles and heels with sandpaper.

'That was Seve's way of guarding against any player slipping and injuring himself,' said Carr, who saw it as a particularly thoughtful touch. 'It's common sense, of course,' he added, 'but that's typical of the way Seve thinks. He also decided to hand out earplugs to each of the players, so they could use them to block out all noise on the first tee when the tournament started. In this way, the players remained *tranquillo* in what could be the most pressurized situation of their career.'

Was he a difficult task master? 'Not particularly,' Carr replied. 'But he likes things to be done a certain way and, with so many demands on his time during Ryder Cup week, the last thing he needed was for some important detail to be overlooked.' His dealings with the European players that week could best be described as interesting. For instance, there was the occasion during practice when Darren Clarke found himself on the downslope of a greenside bunker at the ninth. Complaining that there wasn't much sand in the trap, Clarke thinned two recovery attempts, but his captain decided that a lack of sand wasn't the problem.

Ballesteros, who was known to be a moderately useful exponent of the wedge, noticed that instead of following the line of the sand on the follow-through, the player was raising the club at impact. 'I told Darren to keep the clubface lower than the ball and straightaway it was a perfect shot,' said the Spaniard. Clarke's reaction? 'Sure, Seve's a genius at those shots and I was only too happy to take his advice. We sorted it out in a matter of seconds.' Ballesteros then insisted that if he saw problems when battle commenced, he would not wait for a player to seek his advice. 'Even if it is Nick Faldo, I will take action immediately,' he said.

For another rookie, Thomas Bjorn, a lasting memory of Valderrama came from his singles with Justin Leonard. Four down after four to the reigning Open champion and trying desperately to get back into the match, the Dane didn't quite welcome the interjection from Ballesteros, reminding him of Europe's agreed strategy to play the course rather than the opponent. Bjorn recalled, 'He was sitting on a buggy and I said to him, "Hang on a second, Seve. I'm one over par and four down. I don't need to know if I'm playing strokeplay or matchplay. I just want to get around here as good as I can." Then I added that I didn't need to see him for the remainder of the match.' As a parting shot, Ballesteros told the Dane to relax. 'I AM RELAXED,' the player shouted in reply, much to the amusement of onlookers. And to his great credit, he managed to gain a halved match.

By that stage, one of the most feared competitors in the major championships could now play in only two of them, as a former champion, and the Spaniard's last cut in the Masters was when he finished forty-third in 1996, though he managed a highly creditable share of twenty-first place in the Open at Royal Birkdale two years later. If a ray of sunshine were to return to his competitive life, it was much more likely to come in matchplay, at which he had few peers. And it happened in the inaugural Seve Trophy at Sunningdale in April 2000 when, in a clash of the respective captains, he beat Colin Montgomerie by 2 and 1. Afterwards, he made the profound observation: 'A good match-player is sensitive to the exact emotional state of his opponent. By doing that, he can gain the advantage.'

Curiously, there was a time when he almost despaired of being able to handle the special challenge of man-to-man combat. Indeed, he had the 1979 Open Championship and 1980 Masters title to his credit before enlightenment came. This could be attributed partially to his never having had a competitive amateur career. Either way, the secret eluded him until the semi-finals of the 1981 World Matchplay Championship at Wentworth. This was when he met Bernhard Langer in what was clearly a needle match between Europe's top players. Recalling how he took the lead by holing a long birdie putt at the short tenth, the Spaniard said, 'When that happened, Langer looked tense. He looked like he did not expect to win.' Ballesteros won the match by 5 and 4, and went on to beat Ben Crenshaw in the final.

On being given a wild card only a few days earlier, he had freely acknowledged his failure in five previous matchplay tournaments – and it infuriated him. 'I should be a good man-against-man player, because I like to beat people,' he said, 'but I'm not. Maybe in matchplay I give the other man confidence. He knows I will always make a big mistake.' Then, after studying the techniques of Hale Irwin and Gary Player, whom he considered to be outstanding match-players, he concluded that while making the odd mistake, they hardly ever made big ones. 'Irwin goes par-par and sometimes birdie,' he said. 'This creates much pressure. I know, I felt it.'

As luck would have it, he was drawn against Irwin in the first round and beat him by curbing his own natural aggression. So came the breakthrough for a player who went on to equal Player's record haul of five World Matchplay titles. And it was fascinating to note, on that Sunday in millennium year, even with a game in serious decline, well-formed competitive instincts allowed him to produce the shots for a similarly controlled performance. All the while, his spirits were lifted by an ongoing study of Montgomerie's discomfort, just as had happened with Langer, twenty-nine years previously.

Meanwhile, there is a special reason for recalling another Druids Glen appearance in 2001 to promote the staging of the Seve Trophy there a year later. It was, in fact, the silver jubilee of his first-ever visit to this country, in the Irish Open at Portmarnock in 1976, when he finished fifth behind the winner, Ben Crenshaw. As part of the Druids Glen promotion, we had the sight of a Seve special, when he went down on his knees and whacked a three-wood onto the island green at the 190-yard seventeenth hole. And it won him a bottle of Rioja, his favourite tipple, on the foot of a bet made over dinnner the previous night with John Dully, chief executive of what was then Bord Failte.

'It wasn't as good as the shot at Royal Dublin,' he conceded, in a reference to the clinic he gave, free of charge, on the Tuesday evening of Irish Open week in August 1983. 'That was a really good one,' he added with a broad grin, about a driver hit off his knees onto the green at the 255-yard sixteenth. Another memory of that evening was watching him play miraculous recoveries from a greenside bunker on the eighteenth, with an open-faced two iron.

From my perspective, it was also a time when I was decidedly fortunate in avoiding the opportunity of exchanging words with him. It should be noted that the Royal Dublin staging marked an eagerly awaited return to the tournament for Ballesteros, who had missed the 1981 and 1982 events because of a row with the European Tour over appearance fees. So, when he offered to mark his comeback with the clinic for youngsters, I noted in *The Irish Times* that it was no more than he was entitled to do, given his two-year absence.

Having played in the US the previous week, Ballesteros came to Dublin via London and, as my luck would have it, the only newspaper he could lay his hands on during the flight here was the one I wrote for at that time and he became extremely angry after reading what he viewed as a very unfair piece by your humble scribe. Indeed, he was still seething when he was met at Dublin Airport by Paddy Rossi of the sponsoring company, Carrolls. 'Who this man Gilleechay?' he stormed, brandishing a copy of the offending paper. 'Why he do this thing to me?' Then, with Rossi attempting to calm him down, he demanded there should be a printed retraction.

Given that the Carrolls man apprised me of this little contretemps, you will understand why I made no special effort to meet one-to-one with the the bold Seve that week. And as the tournament progressed and he achieved a dominant position en route to ultimate victory, his memory of my criticism began to fade. Indeed, he has never ever mentioned it to me, despite our countless meetings since then, including an invitation to join him for lunch in Dubai fifteen years later, when Harrington joined us.

He was the first real star of European golf, with looks and demeanour to match. I always thought of him as having remarkable, manipulative skills in his dealings with the media and, from our perspective, we were extremely fortunate in having such an accessible and fascinating player dominating golf, certainly on this side of the pond. He once remarked with typical passion, 'If you ever feel sorry for somebody on a golf course, you better go home. If you don't kill them, they'll kill you.' So, in choosing the likely winner of a tournament, his name was generally the first to spring to mind. Which once led a colleague of mine to chide, 'I suppose you'll tip Seve to win the Grand National.'

As Feherty and Jacklin indicated, he had no peer as a motivator. I remember Muirfield Village in 1987 when he and Olazabal came together for the first time as the embryonic Spanish Armada. Fearing he would be only a burden because of his poor form in practice, Olazabal asked Jacklin to stand him down. Whereupon Ballesteros assured his young compatriot, 'Don't worry, Jose. I play good enough for both of us.'

Augusta, where he triumphed in 1980 and 1983, claimed a very special place in the Spaniard's heart. It would have a similar impact on Olazabal, though, by his own admission, he was a mature eighteen-year-old before he saw images of Ballesteros achieving his 1980 Augusta breakthrough. 'After I played an exhibition with Seve at Pedrena in 1984 he gave me a video of that win,' recalled Olazabal. 'I took it home and spent a couple of hours watching it. They were the first pictures I ever saw of him winning. His first British Open win of 1979 was never shown on Spanish TV, which meant that Spain wasted the influence of a great player.'

Though considerably grander, Augusta reminded Ballesteros of the rolling, tree-lined fairways of Real Club de Golf de Pedrena, where he had learned the game as a youngster, first as a caddie and then as an aspiring professional. He seemed destined to prosper among the Georgia pines, given that the tournament generally coincided with his birthday on 9 April. And through his successes, the famous green jacket became familiar attire among his European colleagues. Over a twenty-year period, starting with his ground-breaking win of 1980, six Europeans won the Masters on eleven occasions.

When Olazabal was preparing for his final round in 1994, he read a note in Spanish which was pinned to the door of his locker. Written on Augusta National notepaper, it assured him, in so many words, that he would win the title because he was the best player in the world. And it was signed 'Seve'.

In a way, it was a predictable gesture from one Spaniard to another. It might also be seen, however, as having its roots in a note left by Gary Player on the locker door of a young Masters aspirant before the final round fourteen years previously. That particular note from the South African to Ballesteros had read, 'Buena suerte, compadre' – good luck, colleague.

Despite those wonderful performances at Augusta, it is generally agreed that Seve's finest triumph was the 1984 Open at St Andrews. 'This game is great and very strange,' was his bemused comment after finishing with a birdie which was witnessed by his mother, Carmen, among delighted thousands. Two strokes back, second place was shared by his great rival, Langer, and Tom Watson. It was Michael Bonallack's first Open as secretary of the R and A and he recalled it with particular affection. 'Everything seemed to go like clockwork and a heatwave added to the appeal,' he said. 'We had that wonderful finish with Seve holing the putt on the eighteenth green and punching the air like a matador. And afterwards there was the party that went on in the whole of St Andrews that evening, making it probably a bit like Paris must have been like after the World Cup, except on a smaller scale.'

Ballesteros will have a treasured place in Irish golfing hearts for the great memories he created on countless visits to this country. So, on his retirement, we take a lead from Player and wish him, 'Buena suerte, viego amigo' – good luck, old friend.

El Gato, buíochas le Dia

It's four o'clock on a Wednesday morning in May 2005 and, with a pro-am assignment, Eduardo Romero is due on the practice ground at Carton House in another three hours. However, instead of being asleep in his hotel in Maynooth, he is on the phone to Buenos Aires, dealing with a matter far more important than golf – a matter of life and death.

Earlier on he had learned through a phone call from his wife, Adriana, that one of their 'children', a six-year-old with Downs Syndrome, had had a heart attack. Now he was on to a doctor friend of his back home, who was offering to have the child flown by private aircraft from Corboda to the Argentine capital city for immediate surgery. The first round of the Nissan Irish Open would be dominated by thoughts of the boy and the latest news from the hospital, which wouldn't surprise anyone familiar with this delightfully caring man.

Meeting him, one is struck by the warmth of a smile which, at full wattage, could light up a large room. Then there is the charm of his broken English, which would be ideal as the voice-over for a Speedy Gonzales cartoon. That, I hasten to add, is from a male perspective; women are absolutely bowled over by what they would view as an irresistibly romantic treatment of words, especially first names.

That Monday he played with three women in the Des Smyth Classic, organized by the Links Society at The K Club. And they positively delighted in his pronunciation of their names – Terree, Patreecia and Ruthay – while remarking afterwards on his caring, helpful attitude as their professional. So, there was general approval from competitors and guests when, at a function that evening, he was pronounced an 'International Ambassador for Golf' and presented with a stunning piece of Waterford Crystal by Cecil Whelan.

Romero feels at home in Ireland, even to the extent of speaking our language; the self-same tongue which a curious number of Irish parents cause their children to believe is a waste of time. 'Conas a tá tu,' he beamed. Then, before I had a chance to answer, he continued, 'Tá mé go maith.' He paused before adding with boyish glee, 'Buíochas le Dia.' Indeed.

'Des Smyth, Padraig Harrington and Paul McGinley tell me those words,' he said proudly. 'And I teach them Spanish – you know, buenos dias, things like that.' Clearly he had forgiven Harrington for beating him in a play-off for the 2002 Dunhill links championship at St Andrews. 'It was not a big disappointment,' he said. 'I play very good, but Harrington play better.'

Romero was born in July 1954 in Villa Allende, which, despite its population of 45,000, he describes as a village, five miles from Cordoba in northern Argentina. His father, who died in 2002, was a golf professional and so is Eduardo's brother, while he has a married sister who plays off six handicap. 'I first play golf when I'm five,' he said. 'And that is when I get my name "Gato", the cat. Go to Cordoba and ask for Eduardo Romero and people look at you funny like and scratch their head. Everybody call me Gato because when I am young I like to climb trees all the time. I live in trees. And my grandmother say, "That kid, he is like a cat." So I become Gato Romero.'

Which explains why the Gato Romero Fundacion is so called. It is a hospice which he runs for homeless children in Cordoba, a city of 2.5 million inhabitants. There is accommodation for a hundred orphans while 150 others, poor children from the streets, will go there for breakfast, lunch and tea, and for shoes and clothes if needed. 'My wife and my daughter help me,' he said. 'They are our children – and one of them is very sick right now. You touch the door at my foundation and maybe a kid only two years old come to the door. So many poor kids. I pay. I've been doing it for three years now. It's a lot of money, but I love it.'

He also helped a local hospital in Cordoba, which he hoped to provide with a mammogram before the end of 2005. It cost US $50,000 and when we spoke there was only about US $10,000 in the kitty. But the money would be found, partially from a local charity pro-am to which he lends his name every November.

A caring nature runs in the family. His daughter, Dolly, who studied law, finds it impossible to pass a stray dog in the street, which means that at the last count there were thirty-five dogs in the Romero home. Indeed, animals play a large part in their lives, given that he also has a 200-hectare farm with horses, cattle and sheep. Though he was better off as a youngster than the children he helps, he hasn't forgotten how his father worked at the local Renault factory in the morning, before pursuing his craft as a golf professional in the afternoon. And how he himself caddied until he was sixteen, to try and contribute to the family income.

He spoke lovingly of his father. 'Before he die he tell me that it is much better you be good person than good player,' he said. 'Life for my father was very difficult, but golf give me everything and I say thank you very much to golf. And I thank my father because he give me a good example to be a good person. He was a very close friend of Roberto de Vicenzo. Oh yeah, they play together many times.' Glowing in his admiration for South America's greatest ever player, he continued, 'Roberto is like the Maradona of golf in my country. I play many times with him. We play five months ago and he play unbelievable. He still got a problem with the putter, but at eighty-two the swing is still fantastic.'

By way of illustration, he proceeds to swish with his hands. 'Unbelievable. Roberto don't teach me, but he say when you are under pressure in golf you must walk very slowly. And never look at your opponent in the face, just the ball and the green. That's all. When I first come to Europe in 1984 and I say I'm friend of Roberto, every door is open. He gave me more than fifty films about golf. Some of Ben Hogan. "Watch him," he tell me about Hogan. "This guy is not from this world. This guy is from the galaxy."' Typically Latin, he pointed animatedly to the sky while adding, 'I tell Roberto, "You come from the galaxy."' Interestingly, in the 1953 Open at Carnoustie, de Vicenzo was level with Hogan after fifty-four holes, only to slip five strokes adrift in the final round.

Roberto de Vicenzo urged Romero to play Royal Portrush – 'one of world's best courses' – where he had competed in the 1951 Open. And Romero did it in style last year when, in his first tournament as a senior, he was tied second with Tom Kite behind Pete Oakley in the Senior British Open. In the process, rounds of 69, 75, 74, 67 gave him a 3-under-par aggregate of 285.

'Roberto was right,' he said. No further comment was necessary.

On tour, Romero is probably best known for the helping hand he extended to Angel Cabrera, who has become a seriously good player in recent years (and won the US Open at Oakmont in 2007). 'Cabrera was very poor,' said his benefactor. 'When he was two years old, his mother left and he go to stay with his grand-mother with another brother. There were four of them. After a while, he caddie at Cordoba Golf Club and start to play. Then three members of Cordoba say they will sponsor him. He play in South America for a while and he do well. Then, after I win a few tournaments in Europe, starting with the Lancome in 1989, I tell Cabrera, "I want to talk with you." I will sponsor you I say. And he say he could thrash me at golf. And I think that's good. He got lots of spirit. But since I give him money, I can tell him he must practise.'

The upshot of it was that they agreed a ten-year contract, which ended in 2004, whereby Romero would underwrite Cabrera's travel, hotel and food expenses, in return for 10 per cent of his winnings. By his own estimation, it was a splendid deal, which brought him US $300,000 for an outlay of US $100,000. 'When he marry, his wife has four children from another marriage,' said Romero. 'Then they have two more, which mean they have six in all. I tell him I leave money in Cordoba for them while Cabrera is on tour. Not a lot of money. With 150 euro you could live for months in Argentina. It's cheap there.'

With eight tournament victories and official earnings of close on €9 million in Europe since joining the tour in 1984, Romero has clearly done well. However, having turned fifty in July 2004, he was looking to what he saw as a more challenging future on the US Champions Tour. He plans to continue competing for another ten years. In the meantime, his low-ball flight saw him revel in the chilly, windy conditions on the Montgomerie Course. After bring-ing in the third-placed team in the pro-am, he sank an eight-foot birdie putt on the last for a level-par opening round of 72.

'Great news,' he greeted me. 'The kid had a three-hour oper-ation yesterday and it's good. Fantastic. He soon go back to hospital in Cordoba.' I complimented him on his score. 'I play

OK,' he replied. 'But for the kid, this is a life. Fantastic.' And the smile was amazing.

Arnold and a priceless autograph

A stampeding crowd, showing what was described as 'a revolting disregard for stewards and police', closed in on the final pairing of Arnold Palmer and Kel Nagle. It was Troon 1962, when the charismatic American won the Open by six strokes from Nagle, so gaining sweet revenge for defeat by the Australian at St Andrews two years previously.

From reports of the chaos on the seventy-second hole, one can only speculate as to the problems a ten-year-old local lad named Ian Hay must have faced in attempting to get close to the final green. He needed to be there to get the autograph of this amazing American, who had shot a record aggregate of 276. And by way of illustrating the remarkable resourcefulness of children, young Hay succeeded in reaching Palmer's side in his moment of triumph by worming his way between adults' legs. And as evidence of Master Hay's success, the moment was captured in a photograph which appeared on the front page of the *Glasgow Evening Citizen*.

This charming incident was recalled to me by the player golf aficionados still call the King, when we met at The K Club in July 2001. 'After I was diagnosed with prostate cancer four years ago [1997], my wife and daughter went with me to the Mayo Clinic,' said Palmer. There, during a preparatory consultation, he noticed a familiar photograph on the wall of the doctor's surgery. Astonishingly, it was the photograph from the Glasgow newspaper of thirty-five years previously. And the same Ian Hay was now about to treat the man he had idolized.

'He became my quarter-back, that's a term I use,' said Palmer. 'If you go to a clinic it's nice to have a man who watches everything you do. And Ian got me to the right doctor and then watched what happened when I was there being operated on.' After surgery, Palmer made a full recovery. And Dr Hay's reward? 'I got Arnie to sign the picture,' he said. 'It's been wonderful being able to help my boyhood hero.'

Those who have come to admire Palmer over more than half a century would have seen it as a wonderfully appropriate dividend for someone who has always displayed a great love of people. Meanwhile, at The K Club, he said, 'I have an appointment with Ian in a couple of weeks at the Mayo Clinic. When I left there, he kept track of my progress with my local doctor. So I always say he's the best quarter-back in the league. He's an internal medicine man who knows the right people to treat your particular complaint. I had a check-up in May and I believe everything is OK. So my next meeting with Ian will be only routine, I hope.'

Palmer concluded: 'I believe that's part of why I have had so much good fortune in my life. Because I talk to people. I find if you're nice to people, it always comes back to you, one way or another.'

Ernie's quest for a quiet drink

It's not easy for a celebrated sportsman to have a quiet weekend in Dublin, especially if the time is November 2000 and Ireland are playing South Africa in a rugby international. And you happen to be Ernie Els. The situation becomes especially difficult, however, when a well-intentioned associate neglects to do his homework.

Els, of course, became a regular visitor to this country after his initial visit on a sponsor's invitation into the Irish Open at Killarney in 1992. That was when, as a not-so-callow youth of twenty-two, he shot a closing 77 on the Killeen Course to share sixty-fifth place with another invitee, Jody Fanagan, behind the champion, Nick Faldo.

So, having done the rounds on the Friday night, meeting with

South African players and officials before the rugby match that Sunday, he was hoping for a quiet spot where he could watch the telecast of England against Australia on Saturday afternoon, over a few drinks. His driver knew just the place. Absolutely. They wouldn't do better than Gleeson's licensed premises in Booterstown Avenue on the south side of Dublin. They'd be safe there.

Sure enough, on arrival in the lounge with his wife Liezl, a friend and his driver, the winner of two US Opens found everything as he had been promised. And he settled down to watch the match from Twickenham. That was when John Gleeson told him the news. 'I informed Ernie that a party of sixty, comprising all of the South African players and officials, were gathered only a short distance from him in the Willow Bar,' said Gleeson. 'They had booked it for the afternoon to watch the Twickenham match on the big screen and our instructions were to keep them well supplied with coffee and soft drinks.'

On hearing this, Els pleaded, 'Do me a favour. Don't tell them I'm here.' And Gleeson didn't. And while the active sportsmen of the weekend settled for non-alcoholic drinks on the eve of their battle with Ireland, Els savoured some pints of Guinness in glorious isolation. Then, when the Twickenham match was over and the South African party disappeared, he stayed on and posed for some photographs.

During the following week, I had a phone call from a golfing friend of mine. Because of what follows, he made me swear not to even hint at his identity, so let's just say he's from the Midlands. The conversation went something like this: 'You'll never guess who I was sitting beside for the Ireland–South Africa international at Lansdowne Road last Sunday? And given how friendly he's supposed to be, I was a little surprised at his decidedly frosty reaction when I asked him if he had heard whether Tiger Woods had won in Thailand [in the Johnnie Walker Classic earlier that day].'

The Midlander spake on: 'OK, so who was it?' 'It was Ernie Els,' I said. And I hadn't the heart to tell him it was one of the least inspired guesses I had ever made.

Irish Open memories from afar

When it's not healing wounds, time can allow old professionals to reveal some of their most closely guarded secrets. And as Ed Sneed illustrated in a fascinating chat at Gulf Harbour in November 1998, it is decidedly prudent to keep such incidents to oneself, if cherished, contemporary illusions are not to be shattered. Sadly for him, Sneed is remembered largely for missing a short putt on the seventy-second green which would have given him victory in the 1979 US Masters. His miss involved him in a three-way play-off with Fuzzy Zoeller and Tom Watson, which ultimately gave Zoeller the title.

Later that year, he and compatriot John Mahaffey came to Portmarnock to compete in what was then the Carrolls Irish Open. Neither player distinguished himself in the early stages of the event, Sneed carding an opening 75 to Mahaffey's 74. But the crowds were drawn by the warmth of a player who had suffered so acutely at Augusta. At Gulf Harbour, as a member of the Fox Sports TV commentary team covering the World Cup, Sneed took up the story: 'We still hadn't made a move after fifty-four holes on the Saturday. Anyway, with a few hours to kill before a dinner date that night, John suggested that we visit some of the local bars on the way back to our hotel in the city.'

So they went on a gentle pub-crawl, starting in Portmarnock and progressing to Baldoyle, having a beer in each and chatting to the locals. 'It wasn't serious drinking, but we had a few,' said Sneed. 'Later that evening we and our wives went to dinner in the Mirabeau with Pat Heneghan [of Carrolls]. There we had some exquisite wines and brandy with our meal, and the upshot of it was that I was in a terrible state the following morning. In fact, I was so sick out at the course that my caddie, Willie Aitchison, lay me down in the locker-room and applied cold towels to my face to try and bring me around.

'Eventually, when it was time to go to the first tee, I feared I couldn't make it. And I thought of the shame of having come all that way from the States at the sponsor's invitation. But somehow I made contact with the opening drive and thinned the ball down the fairway. I remember the first was playing downwind and was no more than a drive and a wedge, but I needed a seven iron. And when the ball landed on the green I could see there was a little blob of mud on it, but I was afraid to bend down to clean it. So I hit the putt and, remarkably, the ball went into the hole for a birdie.'

From there, Sneed proceeded to play one of the finest rounds ever witnessed at the famous North Dublin links. With a 7-under-par 65, he equalled Gary Player's course record and claimed second place, only a stroke behind the winner, Mark James. As he reflected, 'It was amazing. From a position of barely being able to play, I might have been Irish Open champion.'

As a footnote to our chat, he told me of his delight in meeting Harry Bradshaw and of the pleasure he still gets from playing tapes of Harry's stories. Immodestly, I explained that I was involved in producing the tapes in 1987 and we agreed, not for the first time, about the small world that golfers inhabit.

Goodbye to a colourful friend

They buried Peter Maguire on a weekend in March 2001, after fifty years of caddying and odd-jobbing at Portmarnock GC. His passing was marked by a large turn-out, including the club captain, Vincent Sex, who delivered a warm tribute at the funeral mass.

Colourful of speech and much loved of the members, Peter was the source of some marvellous stories. Like the one about the American visitor who, pointing to the pond on the short seventh, enquired: 'Peter, is that casual water?' To which the caddie replied: 'Oh no, sir. There's no f***ing way you can drink that water.'

Then there was the visitor who, after being instructed by Peter to slide his sandwedge under the ball, made several vain attempts at extricating it from the cavernous bunker fronting the green at the long sixth. Exasperated, the caddie demanded, 'Give me the club.' And when he, too, had smashed the ball into the face of the bunker, he remarked without batting an eyelid: 'That's what you're f***ing doing wrong.'

During the 1950s, in the whole of his health, it was no trouble to Peter to carry two bags at weekends, so he was understandably miffed when a regular client turned up with a new-fangled caddie-car. On the fourth, after carving his approach into uncharted territory, the man with the wheels enquired: 'Did you see that, Peter?' Whereupon the caddie turned directly to the caddie-car and repeated the question: 'Did you see that?' The contraption didn't reappear.

CHAPTER 4

* * * * * * * * * *

A Dip into History

'When he is in the right mood, he is probably the greatest
scorer in the game . . . possibly that the game has ever seen.'
BOBBY JONES IN PRAISE OF GENE SARAZEN

The first letter arrived on my desk in March 1993. Though I had
no reason to recognize the writing on the hand-addressed
envelope, there was no mistaking the sender. Towards the left-
hand side was a simple line-drawing of a familiar golfing figure in
plus-fours. And over it was printed: Gene Sarazen, PO Box 667,
Marco Island, Florida.

It was such a wonderful surprise that I couldn't wait to read the
contents, which began:

Dear Mr Dermont [sic].

Thank you for the nice article you wrote in *The Irish Times*. I
have a good friend who keeps me posted on what goes on in golf.
She used to write my script during the filming of the *Shell*
[*Wonderful World of Golf*] shows. I expect to visit Ireland this
year. Mr Donald Panoz, who has a home [there], invited me to
visit him after the British Open. Also I have been invited to be
Honoree at the Prince's Golf Club where I won the British Open
in 1932. I am looking forward to it. Mr Panoz is in the drug business, pharmaceutical business. Most of his manufacturing is in
Ireland. However, all these trips that I am about to make depend

on how I feel at the time. At ninety-one, you never know until you
wake up in the morning. As of this day, I feel I can make it.
Thank you again. Gene.

PS: Incidentally, Snead, Cathy Whitworth and myself consulted
on the new Legends Course at his [Panoz'] place in Braselton,
Georgia, called Chateau Elan. We each had to select four great
holes. I selected the seventh, twelfth, thirteenth and fifteenth from
Augusta National.

All I had done by way of earning such a generous response was
to note Sarazen's ninety-first birthday in my 'Golfing Log' in *The
Irish Times* on 2 February of that year. His letter was a reminder
of a gentler, more civilized age, when people did such things simply as an exercise in common courtesy.

Anyway, the trip was duly made, though it had a potentially
disastrous first leg. Setting out from his daughter's home in
Naples, Florida, Gene was on a commuter turbo-prop aircraft bound
for Orlando, when passengers were warned to take up crash positions: the brakes had failed. Arms were braced and heads bowed
by all but one passenger: like a daredevil schoolboy, the oldest passenger mischievously lifted his elbow and peeked out the window.
Fortunately, the plane landed safely, so sparing this remarkable
man for a sentimental journey back to Prince's, scene of his lone
Open Championship triumph, and on that particular trip, he lent a
delightful dimension to the Open climax at neighbouring
Sandwich, where he was treated, quite rightly, as golfing royalty.

Before his return to the US, I had the pleasure of meeting him
at a small dinner party at The K Club, where the guests included
the then Tanaiste Dick Spring, GUI president Ian Bamford, PGA
Irish Region secretary Michael McCummiskey and Sarazen's close
friend Panoz, chairman of the Elan Corporation in Athlone.

While reflecting on that potentially disastrous Orlando incident,
he gave one of his disarming smiles and said calmly, 'I was ready.'
Then, with a tinge of sadness, he added, 'At ninety-one, you go to
a tournament and you don't see anybody you know. They're all
gone; all the old friends. And you think, "Geez, what the hell am I
doing here?"' It was a totally superfluous question to those of us

who sat enthralled as this thoroughly charming and witty man recounted wonderful stories about his golfing career, the great players who were both friends and rivals of his, and the personalities he encountered from all walks of life. There was an obvious affection for contemporaries Bobby Jones and Walter Hagen, but a considerably cooler assessment of Ben Hogan. And he spoke of his friendship with Sam Snead and his admiration for the skills of the modern players, notably Jack Nicklaus, Arnold Palmer and Tom Watson. Listening to him was a pure delight.

The scope of the man's career was illustrated by a story he told of his meeting with the then US President, George Bush, in the Oval Office at the White House in 1992, on the occasion of his ninetieth birthday. Taking full advantage of the licence that comes with age, Sarazen said, 'Mr President, I'm delighted you invited me here: thank God you eventually recognized my accomplishments. The last time I was in this office, Warren G. Harding was sat behind that desk. And I notice they haven't even painted the place since then.'

For the record, Harding was president when Sarazen captured the US Open for the first time in 1922 and he was still there a year later when the then twenty-one-year-old travelled to Troon for his first challenge in the Open Championship. Which led him to talk about the two swings he most admired in golf. 'The best swing I've seen is Tom Watson's,' he declared. 'I think it's beautiful the way he hits the ball.' And it was difficult to avoid laughing out loud when he added, 'Next to Vardon.'

He knew the great Harry Vardon! 'Of course I knew Vardon,' he responded with mock anger. 'I played against him. When I went over in 1923, there were about four or five Americans practising at Troon and they said, "C'mon kid, let's go to Lytham and St Annes." But I replied that I had come to win the Open and I was staying in Troon. So Hagen and [Johnny] Farrell and a few others went to Lytham. And when they got there, they started calling me up on the phone and calling me all sorts of names. They got me so mad that when I hung up I said to the hotel porter, "How do I get to Lytham and St Annes?" He said I had to take an overnight train to Liverpool and drive from there. So he booked my ticket.

'Off I headed for Lytham and St Annes and when I got there I had a shower, practised and was ready for the tournament. It was the North of England Professional Championship, arranged for the week prior to the Open, and when I'm called to the first tee, who am I playing with? Only Vardon. Geez, I thought, this is really somethin'. Anyway, Vardon hits a beautiful baffy shot onto the first green [par three], about ten feet from the hole. It's blowin' hard and I take an iron and I try to steer it on the wind, but it never moves and finishes in the bunker. So I says to Vardon, "What sort of winds do you have over here?" And he replies, "The way you hit 'em son, they'll never move."

'I have never seen anybody putt as badly as Vardon. He was a terrible putter. Hagen was a great putter, right up to his last days. Jones was a great putter, but his stroke wouldn't have lasted. Too much backswing. You know I won that tournament and they were all there. I was the first player ever to come from America and win it. Then I went back to Troon thinking that there was nothing to the Open. But I couldn't understand the R and A putting me, the US Open and USPGA champion, out last on the first day and then first out the next day, when I hit a storm. I started eight, seven for an 85 and failed to qualify. But I vowed I would win it someday, even if I had to swim the Atlantic.' Which, of course, he did – win it, that is. And the R and A went some way towards rectifying the wrong of 1923 by extending a special invitation to Gene for the golden jubilee staging at Troon in 1973.

Despite its renowned difficulty, especially in high winds, the Ayrshire stretch has tended to look kindly on the more seasoned practitioners of the game. So it was that Sarazen grabbed the headlines on the opening day in 1973, when his five-iron tee-shot at the 126-yard eighth, the famous Postage Stamp, was perfectly on target for a hole in one. On that occasion, the celebrated American happened to be playing in the company of Ireland's Fred Daly, winner of the title at Hoylake in 1947. And Daly also witnessed another splendid effort from Sarazen in the second round, when the then seventy-one-year-old holed a bunker shot to make birdie there. All of which meant that in two rounds Sarazen had gained the remarkable distinction of negotiating the hole in a total of three strokes, without the need of his putter.

It was Sarazen who discovered Snead, and guided him on the road to fame and fortune. 'In the early thirties, I was on my way to Bel Air, right by Dunedin, when I dropped in on a tournament at the Augusta Country Club,' he recalled. 'My job at that time was to go around the country looking for good players who would sign up with the Wilson company. Anyway, this hillbilly from Virginia by the name of Snead won the tournament by eight or nine shots. I thought he was a helluva player. So I told Tom Wilson [president of the equipment company] that he was the best player I'd ever seen and that, from the cut of him, he'd take anything we had to offer. Later on, I discovered that Snead could tell the dirtiest stories you ever heard. When we were eating together at Augusta National this year [1993], I told [Jack] Stephens [club chairman] not to let Snead tell more than one story or I'd lose my dinner.'

What you saw with Snead was what you got. Sarazen, on the other hand, went through something of an identity crisis during his teenage years. He explained, 'I was born Eugenio Saraceni in Harrison, New York. I thought no more about my name until I made a hole in one on the public course near where I lived. They gave me the headline in the sports page the next day and when I saw it I said, "Oh Geez. That looks like a concert violinist. I need to change that quick."' Legally? 'No need. There was nothing legal about changing your name eighty years ago. Anyway, Sarazen sounded good and it can't be found in any telephone book.

'A lot of fellas change their names. That Mark Calcavecchia, he should change his. But maybe it's too late now. What the eye sees is important. And the newspapers were very important in my day. Wonderful writers like Bernard Darwin, Paul Gallico, Grantland Rice and Damon Runyon became great friends of mine. Darwin was the best of them. He did some beautiful golf reports.'

His affection for Bobby Jones was born from the heat of competition and nurtured through his association with Augusta National. In fact, Jones was among a small group of only twenty-three people who were positioned behind the fifteenth green during the final round of the 1935 US Masters when Sarazen had his famous albatross two. And, no doubt, he would have been among the first to be told about the advice Sarazen's caddie gave, while his master was standing over the 220-yard shot, which was heard around the world. 'Mister Gene,' said Stovepipe. 'You got to hit the three-wood if you want to clear that water.' Meanwhile, playing partner Hagen was urging, 'Hey, hurry up, Gene. I got a date tonight.'

The previous summer Sarazen made his first visit to this country. And it was a time when manic motorists returning from Carlow to Dublin had cause to be on the lookout for gardai, long before the M7 and M9 motorways were built. Indeed, the activities of one such driver significantly increased the loss incurred by Carlow GC, when Sarazen played Joe Kirkwood in an exhibition there on 15 July 1934. Details of the incident, and much more besides, are to be found in the richly illustrated history of Carlow GC – *From Gotham to Deerpark* – which was produced to mark the club's centenary.

As part of the Sarazen deal, apparently, the club would hire a taxi from Doyle's of Bachelors Walk, Dublin, to drive the players there and back, at a cost of three guineas. But the final bill was somewhat higher, due to the fact that the taxi driver, a certain D. Hunt, was fined £5 for dangerous driving after being stopped by gardai on the return journey. The fine was later reduced on appeal to £1, which the club were obliged to pay, along with legal costs of six shillings and eight pence. All of which had to be added to an official loss of £17.15s on the Sarazen exhibition.

As for his relationship with Jones, he explained that they were born two weeks apart; were married the same year; and both had wives named Mary. For his part, Gene claimed that he was 'looking for a girl who was well educated so that she could educate me'. Whatever his motive, the attraction was clearly mutual, given that they were together for sixty-two years until her death in 1988. Regarding married life, he took particular delight in a story dating back to 1934 when his Mary 'had been working hard on her [golf] game and was improving'. He went on, 'That was the year I played in the US Open at Merion and lost by a stroke to Olin Dutra. I took the train back to New York and Mary met me at the station.

Her first words were, "Shot an 84 yesterday." ' The memory of the moment caused him to laugh heartily, while he added good-naturedly, 'Here I'd lost the US Open by a stroke and she couldn't wait to tell me she'd shot the best round of her life. No sympathy for me.'

'Later on,' he continued, 'when Bob was confined to a wheelchair and I was doing the commentary for the *Shell Wonderful World of Golf* shows, I would write him a letter every show I did. And his wife Mary would say, "Keep writing, Gene, keep writing." He was a wonderful, wonderful man. I remember after winning the US Open at Stokie in 1922 I was real proud when I showed him the trophy. "What do you think of it?" I asked. "Well, you won it," he replied. Then he came back and won it for the first time a year later.

'Hagen had a different way about him. When he saw the trophy he offered to play me for it. I remember another time when I beat him in the USPGA in 1923, at Pelham, he claimed that my ball had gone through the window of a nearby house and that an Italian, who was inside eating spaghetti, threw it out. "Look at it," he said. "Look at the red on Wilson [the brand name]. That's spaghetti sauce." Hagen did a lot for golf in this part of the world with those four British Opens that he won.'

He went on, 'Talking about windows reminds me of the Ryder Cup at Scioto, Columbus, in 1931, when I played a guy called [Fred] Robson. I hit a shot right over the green and it went into a Coca-Cola stand. Robson was on the green about 35 feet from the hole and he called, "Are you there, Gene?" I says, "Wait a minute." I started moving boxes and all kinds of things, and then I hit the ball through the window and onto the green. And I won the match by 7 and 6. In 1930, I was playing behind Jones at Interlachen where he won the US Open for the third leg of his Grand Slam. I saw that shot he played on the ninth hole. Boy, oh boy! He hit the ball into a pond, but it came to rest on one of those big, big leaves, a lily pad. And he got four at the hole. He didn't like crowds, which was a bit strange really, given all the fame he had.'

And what of Hogan? 'I haven't seen him for 20 years. He wasn't as good a player as Nicklaus, who has got to be the best player of all time – a great hitter of the ball.' Better than Hogan? 'Oh yeah. Much better. More powerful swing. But the most miraculous player of all was Palmer. It's amazing he had so much success with that swing of his.' And dominant players of the early 1990s such as Nick Faldo? 'He's a fighter, but he's not as good a golfer as [Greg] Norman. We saw the proof of that at Sandwich in the British Open.'

Sarazen's association with the *Shell* show brought him into contact with an Irishwoman, Edna Forde, who was the script supervisor when segments were completed at Ardmore Studios in Bray, Co Wicklow. And as if to emphasize his constancy with those he has come to care about, he went to considerable trouble to get in touch with her on that 1993 visit to this country. Though he retained an undeniably sharp sense of humour, I remember looking at his kindly face and marvelling at his reputation as a tenacious little fighter who, at 5ft 5ins, overcame physical limitations to capture seven major titles – the US Open of 1922 and 1932, the USPGA of 1922, 1923 and 1933, the Open Championship of 1932 and the US Masters of 1935. More importantly, he became the first player to win all four major titles, a distinction that has since been matched only by Hogan, Nicklaus, Gary Player and Tiger Woods.

Before we parted that night, he asked me to be sure to send him a copy of the article I planned to write. Which I did. So it was that in early September 1993 I received my second letter from the man beloved in golf as 'the Squire'. And this time he got my name right. The letter read:

Dear Dermot.

Received your letter along with your story. You sure recorded the conversation right from the mouth. It's a very good story. I am forwarding it on to Mr Panoz. We had a delightful trip back [from Ireland], but two days later I came down with bronchitis and was sick for over two weeks. I stayed at My Daughter's house for over three weeks, but it left me in a weak condition. Now I am back home. It's very warm here, so this is what the doctor ordered. I enjoyed my trip to Ireland. Maybe the next time we will have more sunshine. Mr Panoz will open the Legends Course at Chateau Elan on 4 October next year [1994]. Some time in October we will have the World Championship and no doubt he will invite you over. Thank you again for everything. Looking forward to seeing you in the spring at Augusta, God willing. Sincerely, Gene.

Though I later saw him fulfil his role as an honorary starter of the US Masters, the last time I spoke to him was at breakfast in October 1996 at Chateau Elan, where he was attending the Sarazen World Open as guest of his great friend Donald Panoz. It was my first overseas assignment after undergoing heart bypass surgery at the end of August. The invitation to the World Open had come, just as Gene promised it would, and I went there with my wife, Kathy. My lasting memory of the occasion was the way the hotel staff delightedly fussed about their venerable guest. And by way of response, he was charming, witty and totally endearing.

The following April I happened to be walking down Washington Road, Augusta, Georgia, during a rather special week. 'Welcome Masters' proclaimed the sign in a shop window. It was a modest invitation which brought the owner of the shop a response he could never have imagined in his wildest dreams. In effect, it brought him face to face with one of the most celebrated figures in golf.

Situated 200 yards down from the main entrance to Augusta National, Golf Central boasted an impressive line in equipment. But in the context of that year's Masters, it was their expertise in club repairs and custom fitting which, ultimately, made my visit so memorable. I was in the shop browsing around when the owner, an elderly man with a modest knowledge of golf, began talking. 'See this photograph,' he said, pointing to a group shot of the competitors in the 1935 Masters. I told him I was familiar with it. In fact, I had a framed copy back home. 'But you don't have this one,' he added, triumphantly. With that, he pointed to a print which had been autographed by the winner, Gene Sarazen. 'He was in with me yesterday, hoping we could solve a problem with the grip of his driver,' the owner went on. 'He wanted to achieve a better feel and I'm happy to say we were able to do the job. As a thank you, he signed the photograph.'

Imagine it! At ninety-five, this winner of seven major championships, along with countless other tournaments, retained such pride in his craft that he wanted everything to be in order when he, Snead and Byron Nelson stepped up as ceremonial starters of the US Masters, sixty-two years after his memorable victory. At eight on the Thursday morning, I watched as this great old gentleman did the honours. On each hand he wore a white golf glove, which, with half the fingers cut away, looked more like mittens. And with the aid of what could be described as a bubble grip – a fattening where the right hand went on the club – he hit the ball arrow-straight up the middle of the first fairway. The crowd cheered his effort, as they had always done, but they couldn't have known about the trouble this wonderful old man had gone to in order to ensure that he got it just right.

For me, this experience of 1997 was further confirmation that the great players never take anything for granted in golf. Indeed, in 1999, the 16 April edition of the US magazine *Golf World* carried a picture of Gene and what had now become a bulky three wood. Wilson, with which he retained a remarkable relationship spanning more than sixty years, had resolved his concerns about the ceremonial tee-shot by building up the grip of a woman's three wood. And Gene also used copper bracelets to try and ease the discomfort from arthritis.

Something was certainly working insofar as he split the first fairway with his drive once more. 'These hands are ninety-seven years old,' he said aferwards, before heading off for Chateau Elan. 'All the meat is gone. They're all skin and bone.' Then he added, 'You know, this remains the hardest day of my life.' Why? 'Because when you don't play golf at all, you're afraid you're going to miss the ball and become the laughing stock of everybody,' he replied.

He would never have to face the ordeal again, in that a month later he passed away peacefully to join Hagen and Bobby Jones in those divot-free fairways in the great hereafter. As a competitor, he was admired as having the simplest method of all players. As one writer put it, 'He stood with both feet rooted to the ground, grasped the club firmly in both hands with a couple of inches showing at the top and gave the ball a tremendous, elementary thump.'

Four years after Gene's death, having fought successfully to have the lifetime exemption restored to the Masters, Arnold Palmer had no regrets about carding two 83s to miss the cut. It had to do with the discovery on his Masters debut that this was a different tournament from all the rest. 'I played with Gene Sarazen on my first Masters in 1955 and it was one of the greatest experiences of my life,' said Palmer. 'It was wonderful to have some conversation with him and I think the people in the galleries saw that. It was part of the tournament's great tradition and I think the people enjoy seeing it today.' Indeed they do.

Back in 1993, Gene had talked during his Irish visit about the departure of all his old friends and the feeling that the world was passing him by. He expressed similar views to Mark O'Meara, with whom he shared a locker in the champions' locker-room at Augusta National on his final appearance there, but he was wrong. Those who had the privilege of meeting him in his grand old age came away wonderfully enriched. He had a glow about him which seemed to light up a room. Perhaps it had to do with the elusive commodity which Hollywood describes as star quality. At a time when so-called legends, in common with many things, are not always what they seem, he was a very special exception.

Ireland's golfing diaspora

Eight months after claiming the European Order of Merit title, Ronan Rafferty restored an overdue Irish presence to the US Open on his debut at Medinah in 1990. By that stage, this country's link with the blue riband of American golf had become rather tenuous, to say the least, yet a very special bond existed with our US golfing brethren, going as far back as the beginning of the twentieth century and the formative years of tournament golf in the New World.

In truth, this shouldn't come as a surprise to us, given that the first 'home-bred' winner of that title was a player by the name of Johnny McDermott. And on the occasion of his triumph in 1911, one of those he beat in a three-way play-off was a certain Mike Brady. Then, when McDermott retained the title the following year, Tom MacNamara was runner-up and Brady finished third.

Where American observers were concerned, however, the first serious golfing Gael was Patrick Corcoran, who competed in the US Open at Chicago GC on 4 and 5 October 1900. As it happened, his challenge wasn't especially noteworthy, given that rounds of 101, 90, 96 and 90 for an aggregate of 377 left him no fewer than sixty-four strokes behind the winner, Harry Vardon. So it is hardly surprising that Corcoran has long since disappeared from the awareness of all but the more ardent American historians. Indeed, very little was ever heard of him after that particular event, yet in his own modest way he blazed a trail for more accomplished compatriots who would follow in his wake.

Notable among these was Chandler H. Egan, who came from a leading Irish-American family in Chicago and was clearly a golfer of some talent, given his US Amateur victories of 1904 and 1905. Born in 1884 of wealthy and socially prominent parents, he was also US Amateur runner-up in 1901 and 1909, and was victorious in the National Intercollegiate of 1902 and in the Western Amateur of 1902, 1904, 1905 and 1907.

However, there was also a notable defeat in 1904, which happened to have a decidedly ironic outcome. At the annual awards dinner of the Canadian Seniors' Championship, the rafters were raised by the strains of 'My Wild Irish Rose' as a tribute to an outstanding player from another era. This was the man who beat Egan to become the last Olympic gold medal winner for golf.

George Seymour Lyon, who was born in 1858 in a farming community south of Ottawa, was a seasoned forty-six-year-old when he beat the reigning US Amateur champion by 3 and 2 in the thirty-six-hole Olympic final at St Louis in 1904. Despite attempts to revive golf as an Oympic sport, with a proposed staging at Augusta National for the 1996 Atlanta games, his place in history remains secure.

As a latecomer to golf at thirty-eight, Lyon won the Canadian title within three years, recording drives of up to 280 yards, which was remarkable hitting with the equipment of 1898, especially for a man of 5ft 8ins and 12st 12lbs. And he is reputed to have had a wonderful temperament. He won the Canadian title on no fewer than eight occasions, the last of them in his native Ottawa in 1914 when he was fifty-six. And he might have won it again, but for the fact that the championship was then discontinued, because of the First World War. Still, the Olympics was unquestionably the high point of a wonderful sporting career.

After boarding a train from Toronto to St Louis in September 1904 for the Olympic competition at the 6,000-yard Glen Echo GC, he took his place in an original entry of eighty-six. Seasoned observers were seriously surprised at his progress through the strokeplay qualifying stage and then to the final of matchplay with what local newspapers described rather ungraciously as 'a coal-heaver's swing'. Stung by this, Lyon retorted, 'Whether I play like a sailor or a coal-heaver, I never said I was proud of my form. I only do the best I can.' As it happened, his best was good enough to beat the outstanding American of the time, and Lyon was so delighted by his win that he walked on his hands through the hordes of spectators and up to the clubhouse for the presentation ceremony.

He then received an Olympic gold medal and what he described as 'one of the finest, if not the finest, trophy ever given in a golf tournament'. The medal, incidentally, was replaced by the International Olympic Committee about ten years ago, at the request of his granddaughter, the original having been lost some time previously. And we are told that before the evening was out, he had the entire clubhouse singing his party piece, 'My Wild Irish Rose'. Lyon died a few months before his eightieth birthday, but is remembered each year through the strains of his favourite song.

Meanwhile, despite his disappointment at St Louis, Egan was

credited with having played a leading role in popularizing the game among high society in the American midwest. Shortly after his last Western Amateur triumph, Chandler moved to a remote area of Oregon, where further progress in the game was thwarted by the fact that the nearest golf course was three hundred miles away. Yet he returned to prominence in 1929 by reaching the semi-finals of the US Amateur. And five years on, aged fifty, he represented the US in the Walker Cup in 1934, when he shared in a foursomes win with Max Marston at St Andrews.

At professional level, we're told that the great Vardon was forced to cancel a booking on the maiden voyage of the SS *Titanic*, because of ill-health. Which, decades later, lent a fascinating dimension to the juxtaposition of illustrated stories about himself and a certain Patrick J. Doyle hanging in the hallway of Delgany GC. It seems that Doyle also planned to sail on the doomed liner in April 1912, but his train from Dublin was late arriving in Queenstown (now Cobh), with the result that the *Titanic* had already put to sea.

This was the young man who, in August 1908, became the first professional at Delgany, where he was also expected to do additional greenkeeping duties, all for a wage of twenty shillings per week. He was there in September 1909, when crowds travelled from Dublin and Greystones to see Vardon play a thirty-six-hole exhibition match against the reigning Irish Professional champion, Michael 'Dyke' Moran, which the great man won by 3 and 2.

As a twenty-three-year-old, Doyle decided to emigrate to the US and, after missing the *Titanic*, he boarded another ship for the transatlantic trip. Some time after arriving in the US, he met up with Vardon again. This time it was in the 1913 US Open at Brookline, where the Channel Islander was famously beaten in a play-off by Francis Ouimet. Seven strokes back, Doyle's tenth-place finish stood for eleven years as the best performance by an Irish-born player in the US Open. In 1919, he challenged again when the championship returned to Massachusetts and was tied eighteenth with Ouimet at Brae Burn, behind the victorious Walter Hagen.

So, it is clear that Doyle settled successfully in the US, where he

became a highly respected teaching professional. Among his pupils were the first golfing US President, William Howard Taft, along with another leading politician, Joseph Kennedy, and world heavyweight boxing champions Jack Dempsey and Joe Louis. After a long, full life, he died at the age of ninety-two. And by way of emphasizing the value of sporting genes, he happened to be the great-uncle of Eamonn Darcy.

Even Doyle would have readily acknowledged, however, that the real story of the 1913 US Open was not about him, but of the astonishing breakthrough by Ouimet. The American's achievement in becoming the first amateur to win the US Open led to Mark Frost's remarkable book *The Greatest Game Ever Played*, recently turned into a delightful movie which I happened to catch on American television.

There was also the fascinating role played by a Boston lad named J. H. Sullivan. Five years prior to his historic exploits of 1913, Ouimet was beaten by Sullivan in the opening round of the Greater Boston Interscholastic Championship of 1908 – his first tournament appearance. But later he was to gain rich compensation by winning the hand of Sullivan's sister in marriage. By that stage, a native-born Irish player, who happened to be a woman, had taken the US by storm. In the autumn of 1903, as the reigning British Women's champion, Rhona Adair accepted an invitation to the US from the parents of Pansy Griscom, the US Women's Amateur champion of 1900.

Born in Cookstown, Co Tyrone, Ms Adair was reported to have been overwhelmed by American and Canadian hospitality and 'somewhat abashed by their publicity'. Her hosts were especially impressed by the Irishwoman's power, notably her feat of driving a ball across the 170-yard expanse of a river. She made tournament appearances in Boston, Toronto, Montreal and Quebec, and for the duration of the tour was beaten only once. As her great rival, May Hezlet, observed, 'No other lady golfer in the world could have performed such wonders or given the American people such a splendid exhibition of fine play. The visit made a tremendous sensation over the water and will probably have the effect of arousing fresh interest in the game of golf and enlisting many new members into the already large ranks of enthusiasts.'

In terms of national impact in America, however, nothing compared with the victories of McDermott in the US Opens of 1911 and 1912, after he had lost in a play-off to Alex Smith in 1910. Yet his successes came as no surprise to those who had witnessed the rise of the Irish-American professionals. McDermott was born in Philadelphia on 12 August 1891 and came into golf as a caddie. And a distinctly Irish flavour was lent to the 1912 championship by the fact that runner-up MacNamara was Boston-born of Irish parents. With a final round of 69, he gained the distinction of becoming the first player to break 70 in the history of the championship.

The Irish were noted as particularly keen competitors and acknowledged American experts of the period were of the view that the greatest golfer not to win the US Open was Brady, the son of Irish parents who emigrated to Boston. As the registered professional at the Commonwealth GC, Boston, he made his US Open debut in 1905. Apart from a play-off defeat by McDermott in 1911, Brady also had winning chances in the US Opens of 1912 (tied third), 1914 (tied fifth), 1915 (sixth), 1916 (tied ninth), 1919 (second) and 1925 (seventh). In 1919 he tied with Hagen, only to lose the play-off by a stroke.

That was a time when a professional's primary role was to take care of his club job, which meant that tournaments became something of a busman's holiday. In the event, from the early days of Corcoran and McDermott, Irish-American ranks were swollen by illustrious names such as J. J. O'Brien, Tom and George Kerrigan, Willie Maguire, Tom Boyd, Eugene McCarthy, Doyle, Tom Mulgrew, John Shea, Johnny Farrell, Frank and Tom Walsh, and by the O'Hare brothers, Peter and Pat.

One could imagine researchers of the O'Hares' activities in American tournaments becoming decidedly frustrated at finding no record of them under their given surname. It could have been a simple spelling mistake. Either way, the Americans insisted on calling them O'Hara, which had a more fetching lilt about it. And this is how their names appear in the annals of US golf. The brothers, Peter, Pat and Jimmy, who hailed from 4 Anglesey

Terrace in Greenore, Co Louth, all became professional golfers, but whereas Jimmy remained at home and was the resident professional at Skerries when he won the Irish Professional Championship of 1914 at Royal Co Down, Peter and Pat emigrated to the US. There they made such an impact that Greenore Golf Club, to which each of them had been attached at various stages, instituted the O'Hare Memorial Perpetual Cup, which had its inaugural staging in August 2007.

For all the successes of these early Irish-Americans, victories in the US by Irish-born players have been decidedly thin on the ground. One thinks of the World Seniors' win by Christy O'Connor Snr in 1977; of Claire Dowling's success in the 1983 South Atlantic tournament; of the two Champions' Tour wins each by Christy O'Connor Jnr and Des Smyth; and the two World Golf Championship wins by Darren Clarke, in the 2000 Accenture World Matchplay at La Costa and the 2003 Bridgestone Invitational at Firestone. Most recently, Padraig Harrington won the Honda Classic and the Barclay's Classic, both in 2005.

However, long before the current generation of golfers thought to look west for fresh fields to conquer, an Irish trailblazer had his greatest triumph on 1 April 1922. That was when Pat O'Hare captured the North and South Professional Open at Pinehurst in what became the only staging of the event over fifty-four holes after Donald Ross, the course designer, decided that the second round should be abandoned because of torrential rain. After winning the Irish Professional Championship of 1919 while attached to Dundalk, Pat joined his brother in the US as resident professional at the Richmond County CC in Staten Island, New York. His Pinehurst triumph came three years later, when he had the distinction of beating such luminaries as Gene Sarazen, Jock Hutchison and Hagen.

The North and South Amateur was inaugurated at Pinehurst in 1901, and two years later the North Carolina resort also launched the North and South Open and the North and South Women's Championship. The professional event, in which Ross became a popular inaugural winner, went on to become one of the leading tournaments on the US scene. Indeed, its importance can be gauged from victories by Hagen in 1923 and 1924, and by Byron Nelson in 1939. It then gave Ben Hogan his breakthrough tour victory in 1940. Tommy Bolt, who would go on to capture the 1958 US Open at Southern Hills, won the final staging of the North and South in 1951.

In the 1922 staging, Pat O'Hare spreadeagled the field to lead by six strokes after a superb second round of 69. Then, when the round was declared void because of the weather, outraged friends tried to persuade him to withdraw in protest at what they considered to be a terrible wrong. However, he replied, 'Not me. I beat them today and I'll go out and beat them again tomorrow.' And he was as good as his word, carding rounds of 75 and 72 for a fifty-four-hole aggregate of 220, to win by four strokes from his closest challenger, Clarence Hackney of Atlantic City. Hutchison, the reigning Open champion, shot 78 and 81 to finish on 229.

American newspapers gave extensive coverage to Pat's victory, which was also reported in the *PGA of America* magazine. And in January 1923 the win was noted in the *New York Tribune*, which also carried a photograph of Pat alongside Sarazen. As it happened, he had finished thirty-fifth behind Sarazen in the 1922 US Open at Stokie CC where, incidentally, Brady was tied eighth. Pat then returned home to Ireland, ostensibly for a two-week holiday, but he never went back to the US. Instead, he settled into the easy pace of life in Greenore, punctuating golf lessons with some quiet refreshments. His enduring skills remained very much in evidence, however, in 1927 at Royal Dublin where he won the Irish Professional title for a second time with an aggregate of 301.

Peter O'Hare, the eldest of the brothers, was professional at Greenore from 1903 to 1907 before moving south to Cork, where he became the first professional at Monkstown GC on its inauguration in 1908. He stayed there for six years, during which time he had a considerable input, along with David Brown, the Scots-born professional at Little Island, into the construction of the original nine-hole course of 2,500 yards, laid out in the grounds of Monkstown Castle.

We're told that, in 1909, Vardon played an exhibition match at Little Island, having travelled there from Delgany. Also in the fourball was Willie McNamara and a fourth unnamed professional, who could, conceivably, have been Peter O'Hare. In the event, O'Hare emigrated in 1914 to the US where, typically for the time, he worked as a club professional and made infrequent tournament appearances. His first impact in a major championship came in the USPGA at Flossmoor CC in Chicago in 1920, when he reached the quarter-finals. His brother Pat also played in that event and lost in the first round. Four years later, Peter's finest achievement on American soil came in the 1924 US Open at Oakland Hills, where he was tied seventh behind Cyril Walker. Remarkably, Brady was also in the top ten on that occasion, finishing in a share of ninth place, while another full-blooded Irishman, Doyle, failed to make the third round cut after carding 82, 81 and 83.

A measure of Peter O'Hare's performance on that occasion was that it remained the best US Open finish by an Irish-born player for seventy-six years, until Padraig Harrington claimed a share of fifth place behind Tiger Woods in the 2000 championship at Pebble Beach. And it was also the best by an Irishman in any American major championship, until David Feherty matched it in 1991, when he was tied seventh behind John Daly in the USPGA Championship at Crooked Stick.

Enduring skills were later in evidence from O'Hare in the 1931 USPGA at Wannamoisett, Rhode Island, where he beat no less a figure than five-time winner Hagen by 4 and 3 in the first round, before losing to the eventual winner, Tom Creavy. This, incidentally, was to be the last appearance by an Irish player in the PGA as a matchplay event before the current strokeplay format was adopted in 1958. As a fascinating aside, Jimmy O'Hare, who went on to win a second Irish Professional Championship in 1920, was reputed to have been the first owner of a motorbike in Skerries, where he served as professional before the First World War. A humorous man and a splendid teacher, he later returned to live in Greenore where he was in great demand for lessons.

Meanwhile, players of Irish extraction maintained their impact on the US scene where they were a real force in the 1925 US Open at Worcester, Massachusetts. Following the pattern of the period, Brady was once again in the top ten, finishing seventh behind Willie

McFarlane. And further down the order were Tom Kerrigan, Doyle, Jack O'Connor and Martin O'Loughlin.

So we can see that the first three decades of the last century formed what was truly a golden age for Irish-American golf – some time, incidentally, after the great-grandfather of 1998 US Masters and Open Championship winner Mark O'Meara had emigrated from these shores. And it is fascinating to note that by a happy coincidence, Bobby Jones was born on 17 March, St Patrick's Day, in 1902. It is equally fascinating that when winning the first of his four US Open titles, Jones finished bogey, bogey, double-bogey at Inwood CC, New York, in 1923, which prompted him to make the famous admission: 'I didn't finish like a champion, I finished like a yellow dog.'

By the time the Canada Cup was staged at Portmarnock in 1960, Jones had not played golf for twelve years, which invested a message he sent to the organizers with inescapable poignancy. It read: 'Because of the winning of this event two years ago by Harry Bradshaw and Christy O'Connor, the holding of it this year in Ireland is most appropriate. It was for a long time, years ago, my ambition to play the Portmarnock links. I envy those who will have this privilege. I might add that since I was born on St Patrick's Day (albeit in Atlanta, Georgia), it is mandatory that I should pull for a victory for Ireland. With best wishes to all. Most sincerely, [signed] Robert T. Jones Jr.'

Ireland's fine legacy to US Golf had not been forgotten by the greatest amateur the game has known.

A century in the Open

When the guns on the Western Front fell silent at the eleventh hour of the eleventh day of the eleventh month in 1918, the estimated 35,000 Irish who perished in the First World War included the country's finest golfer. But it was 14 December of that year before his family were notified of the death of Michael Moran, the first Irishman to win prize money in the Open Championship.

Moran had been mortally wounded in Germany's desperate offensive in the spring of that year and, according to *Irish Life* magazine, he died on 10 April at the War Hospital Le Chateau, which was in German hands at the time. Only eight months previously the wonderfully gifted player, who first saw the light in a modest abode in the heart of the Royal Dublin links (between the present third and thirteenth holes), displayed his skills here for the last time. He had returned on a visit from Seaham Harbour GC in Co Durham, where he took up a prestige appointment as professional early in 1914.

It was a memorable occasion. Using borrowed clubs and attired in British army uniform, right down to spurs, Moran played exhibition matches at Hermitage and Clontarf in August 1917. Sadly, Royal Dublin was out of commission during the war years when it was used as a musketry range, so there was no opportunity of a farewell trip around the beloved links he knew so well. At Clontarf, a few of the members put together a set of odd clubs for their celebrated guest. Then, attired in his 'ammunition' boots, puttees and a cap, Moran played the nine holes at Mount Temple in a remarkable 32 strokes – three under par.

It was also a nine-hole score which captured the imagination of spectators at Royal Liverpool, Hoylake, on the afternoon of Monday, 23 June 1913. With a superb homeward 33 in the second round of the Open, he had become an improbable hero, even allowing for five successive Irish Professional Championships, starting in 1909. Then, with a halfway total of 150, he was placed third, only three strokes behind the holder, Ted Ray, and two adrift of the incomparable J. H. Taylor.

According to *The Irish Times*, the slightly built twenty-seven-year-old drove the ball 'with great power' and his only slip while recording the lowest nine holes of the championship was to three-putt the short eleventh, more commonly known as the Alps. Almost incredibly, Moran was a serious challenger for golf's greatest prize when he stood on the first tee for the third round the following morning. After a fitful night, however, his dream was shattered within minutes. In high winds and driving rain, he knocked his second shot at the opening hole out of bounds and later took four from a pot bunker to run up a disastrous 10 and a front nine of 48.

The London *Times* the following morning was highly critical of the manner in which he handled the crisis. 'Moran very quickly fulfilled my prophesy as to his Celtic temperament,' their man reported. '. . . if he had played with discretion [from the bunker], he could still have holed out in seven, but in his impetuosity he went for the green and this sealed his fate. Four times he lashed at the ball before getting it out.' But the writer went on to acknowledge: 'Moran's performance in going round in 74 strokes (in the fourth round) after his most ruinous start of the morning was really a splendid one. At present, he seems fated to have one bad round and 'til he is a little more the master of himself, he probably always will. If he could school himself to take things rather more quietly, he might easily win, for he has grand golf in him.'

The Irish Times reported: 'After a good five at the second, Moran found the bunker guarding the third green off his cleek and, although he got well out, he took three putts and a seven was recorded. Battling against the storm, the little Irishman now played brilliantly. At the short fourth he got a three, while at the next a good five was the outcome.' Thoroughly soaked by the hostile weather and with the clubs frequently slipping in his hands, Moran battled on and carded an inward 41 for a thoroughly dispiriting 89, compared with an 81 from Ray and a remarkable 77 from Taylor.

As it happened, a final round of 74, which included a birdie two at the eleventh, gave Moran an aggregate of 313 for a share of third place with the legendary Harry Vardon. Meanwhile, Taylor, with closing rounds of 77 and 74 for an aggregate of 304, regained the title which he had won at Sandwich in 1894, at St Andrews in 1895 and at Royal Cinque Ports in 1909. His reward was the famous claret jug, a gold medal and £50. Ray, the runner-up on 312, received £25, while Moran and Vardon each received £12.10s. This was to be the first prize money to be won by an Irishman in the Open Championship.

Incidentally, the so-called *Greatest Game ever Played*, in which the local amateur Francis Ouimet beat Ray and Vardon in a play-off for the US Open title, took place at Brookline, Massachusetts, on 18 to 20 September of that year. An Irishman also had a fairly prominent role on that occasion. As indicated elsewhere in this book, Pat Doyle, who was Delgany's first club professional before emigrating to the US, finished tenth for prize money of US $30.

When Moran was born, in 1886, the Dublin Golf Club were planning a move from their original home in the Phoenix Park to a new location at Cush Point, Sutton. In a modest little house in the centre of the North Bull Island at Dollymount, his forebears had lived for several generations, close to a well-known landmark called Curley's Yard, named after Moran's maternal grandfather, Patrick Curley, who was something of a celebrity in the area.

It can be assumed that one of Moran's earliest sights as a toddler was members of the Dublin Club enjoying golf at their splendid new home. And, no doubt, he would also have learned of the club's elevation to Royal status on 14 May 1891. Historians later wrote of him 'roaming the links, knocking a ball about with an old, discarded iron'. In the natural way of things, he progressed to the role of caddie and made such excellent progress as a player during his teenage years as to earn an appointment to Dundalk GC as a twenty-year-old in 1906. Then, by June of the following year, he had become an assistant at Royal Dublin, prompting a correspondent with *Golf Illustrated* to predict, 'I am convinced that Moran is one of the most consistently brilliant players I have seen on the Royal Dublin course.'

Quite apart from his skill as a player, Moran had also become well known in Irish golfing circles through the appendage 'Dyke', which we associate with him to this day. Though it is not clear how the sobriquet came about, the common belief is that it had to do with his penchant for scoring twos, presumably at short holes. Hence a birdie two in current parlance became a dyke. Others claimed that the appellation derived from the familiar sight of Moran bounding over the many ditches and drains – or dykes – on the Royal Dublin links as he made his way from Curley's Yard to the clubhouse. Either way, he was responsible for adding the word 'dyke' to the Irish golfing lexicon.

Early in 1914 he was appointed professional at Seaham Harbour, which had been founded in 1911 at Dawdon, six miles south of Sunderland. And little more than a year later, Moran, like thousands of his fellow countrymen, enlisted in the South of Irish Horse Regiment of the British Army and was posted to France, where he transferred to the Royal Irish Regiment. He was only thirty-two when he died, an age when most golfers are approaching their prime. And a measure of the esteem in which he was held in the game here was that within four years a competition was instituted in his memory. It was to become one of the major events on the professional calendar in the Republic of Ireland and was won on a record twelve occasions by Harry Bradshaw, between 1940 and 1960.

If Moran was the first Irish professional to claim prize money in the Open, devotees will not need to be reminded that the country's first winner of the title was Fred Daly, the champion of 1947. And it would be sixty years before the title eventually returned here through the skills of Padraig Harrington.

Daly burst onto the home tournament scene when the Irish Professional Championship was staged at Little Island, Cork, in 1940. On firm, fast fairways he achieved the appropriate control of club and ball to compile an aggregate of 305 for a one-stroke victory over another player of considerable potential. Indeed, by 1945 Harry Bradshaw would be attempting to emulate Moran's achievement by capturing the native title for a fifth successive year.

J. P. Rooney, the then golf correspondent of *The Irish Times*, calculated that 'The Brad' had returned the remarkable figures of 33 under fours, or an average of 68.7 strokes per round, for ten rounds played in GUI and club competitions during the 1945 season. But to Harry's disappointment, victory at Newlands went to John McKenna, the Douglas professional. A year later Daly set his heart on another target, that of becoming the first player to achieve the treble of Ulster, Irish Open and Irish Professional titles. The first two were already safely secured when he went to Clandeboye, where a course record 64 in the opening round set him en route to his ambitious target. In recognition of his course record, incidentally, the Clandeboye members presented him with a special bonus of £200, which brought into focus the poor prize money in the Open Championship in the years following the Second World War.

Were it possible to have Roddy Doyle's character Jimmy Rabbitte transported forward a couple of decades and dragged away from soul music matters with the Commitments, we could imagine him enquiring, 'What was the difference in the winner's cheque, Terry?' '£749,850, Jimmy.' 'So I suppose Harrington got £800,000 and Daly got £50,150.' 'No, Jimmy. Padraig got £750,000 and poor old Fred had to settle for a measly £150.' 'Jaysus, Terry. That's unbelievable.'

It is indeed difficult to fathom an inflation factor of such proportions, even over a period of sixty years. In truth, the disparity has more to do with the huge difference in the money available in the professional game. If we take it that a medium-sized house could have been bought in Dublin in 1947 for £1,000 and that the same house today would be valued at around £500,000, then Daly should have received £1,500 relative to Harrington's Open Championship haul in July 2007. But rewards were far more modest in the immediate aftermath of the Second World War, even though competitors were required to play the final thirty-six holes on the same day.

As the Portrush man observed years later, 'There were no Mark McCormacks around then. Let's just say I was born too soon. And how many of the great players of my time, come to that, could say exactly the same thing?' But, he added, 'One of the very, very few things I would change if I had it all to do again would be to think very seriously about going to the US.' For what it's worth, Jimmy Demaret received US $2,500 for winning the 1947 US Masters and Lew Worsham got US $2,000 as US Open champion that year, while USPGA champion Jim Ferrier collected US $2,500 from a prize fund of US $17,000. So the difference was significant, even allowing for the fact that prior to the devaluation of September 1949, Stg£1 equalled US $4.03.

On his way to capturing the title at Royal Liverpool GC, Hoylake, Daly joined England's Sam King in the fifth pairing to start Saturday's play at eight forty in the morning for the third round, and at eleven ten for the last round. He covered the thirty-six holes in 150 strokes (78, 72) to win by a stroke from Reg Horne and the American amateur Frank Stranahan in a tie for second place. We are informed, incidentally, that the official programme carried the warning: 'Bicycles must not be brought onto the links.'

Victory came on 4 July when the doughty little fighter from Portrush made an indelible mark on golfing history, certainly from an Irish perspective. He travelled to Hoylake with Max Faulkner and his good friend Bradshaw, and they stayed together in the same lodging house. Sixty years later, Padraig Harrington rented a private house at Carnoustie for championship week and among those who stayed with him were Dr Bob Rotella, the noted American sports psychologist.

Meanwhile, Daly still stands apart among all Open Championship winners as the only one to earn a mention in *Hansard*, the official record of exchanges in the British House of Commons. It happened in the week after his Open triumph, during a debate on the India Bill. Complaining about too much handshaking over India, Sir Walter Smiles MP was reported in *Hansard* as saying, 'The situation reminds me of Fred Daly, who won the Open Championship at Hoylake the other day and went over to Northern Ireland to compete in the championship [Irish Open] there and was beaten. He said he lost because too many people had shaken him by the hand . . . I think Lord Mountbatten might lose in the final round because we are all too busy shaking him by the hand.'

When informed of the comment, the bold Fred responded, 'I have hit some long tee-shots in my time, but I never expected to hit *Hansard* from Hoylake. It's true my hand was not in the best of order after all the hearty shakes, but I was pleased to get them.' For the record (golfing rather than parliamentary) there were 263 entries for the 1947 Open, of whom a hundred – ninety-two professionals and eight amateurs – qualified for the championship proper on a score of 155 or better. The thirty-six-hole cut was 156 on which forty players – thirty-eight professionals and two amateurs – got through. Daly shot 73, 70, 78 and 72 for an aggregate of 293 to win by a stroke.

In a playing sense there was never the chance of the paths of Ireland's two Open winners crossing, insofar as the Northerner died in November 1990, only two months after Harrington had made his debut in the Amateur Home Internationals. And whereas the Dubliner's career has achieved unbroken progress from those early years, Daly lost much of his golfing prime to the Second World War, though he captured the Irish Professional title in 1940 and won both the Irish Professional and Irish Open titles in 1946.

To fully appreciate Daly's enormous talent one need not look beyond his Open Championship performances over a relatively short period of seven years. When the ending of hostilities in Europe paved the way for the resumption of the championship in 1946, he finished eighth behind the great Sam Snead at St Andrews, where he shot rounds of 77, 71, 76 and 74 for an aggregate of 298, eight strokes adrift of the American. And for those who might have regarded his Hoylake performance as something of a fluke, Daly's refutation could not have been more emphatic. He was runner-up to Henry Cotton at Muirfield in 1948; tied third behind Bobby Locke at Troon in 1950; tied fourth to Faulkner at his beloved Royal Portrush in 1951; and was third behind Locke at Royal Lytham in 1952.

Indeed, his great affection for the event never waned and he had the considerable pleasure of sharing in a rather special incident in 1973 at Troon, where he played on a special invitation from the Royal and Ancient. So it was that he happened to be standing on the tee when Gene Sarazen, the 1932 champion, holed-in-one at the famous Postage Stamp eighth hole. And he was also present when the Squire holed out of a bunker for a birdie there the following day. As for the merit of their respective triumphs, both men beat the best players around at their particular time – and one can't ask for more.

When I was writing Bradshaw's biography, he chuckled at the memory of Hoylake in 1947 and the money he had made from bookmakers by backing his friend to win the Open. It was probably as much as he himself would have collected as the runner-up two years later at Sandwich, in a challenge which will always be remembered for his altercation with a broken bottle.

In carrying out their periodic review of the *Rules of Golf* in 1946, the Royal and Ancient made no major changes. So the *Rules*, which were aimed essentially at matchplay at that stage, remained decidedly vague in two crucial areas. Rule 6 stated: 'A ball must be played wherever it lies, or the hole be given up, except as otherwise provided for in the *Rules*.' And Rule 11, which dealt with the removal of obstructions, stated: 'Any flagstick, guide post, implement, vehicle, bridge, bridge planking, seat, hut, shelter or similar obstructions may be removed. A ball moved in the removal of such obstructions shall be lifted and dealt with as provided for in Rule 8, without penalty.'

It was generally accepted at the time that a ball could be deemed to be unplayable only if the player could not make a stroke at it and dislodge it into a playable position. Nowadays, under Rule 28, a player is entitled to declare a ball unplayable at any place on the course, except in a hazard. In fact, he or she is the sole judge as to whether the ball is unplayable. Meanwhile, as can be seen from Rule 11, no clear distinction was made between a movable and immovable obstruction, and the vague nature of the *Rules* in general caused golfers to adopt the safe dictum of 'play it as it lies', except in the most dire circumstances.

In the autumn of 1949, the authorities added a clause to Rule 11, whereby a ball could be removed from 'any artificial object, placed or left on the course'. This crucial addition came too late, however, to avert one of the most controversial incidents in the history of the game.

During the early summer of 1949, the Brad was playing excellent golf; by his own estimation, the best since he turned professional. His putting had never been sharper, a fact which prompted Henry Cotton to remark, 'I always thought of Harry Bradshaw's putting slogan of "hitting and harking" as one of the best I ever heard. The genial Irishman is certainly a perfect example of not taking the eyes, or the head, from over the spot where the ball is until it arrives at the hole or is heard to rattle in the cup. On his best days, he is a superb putter.'

Royal St George's was new to Bradshaw, who arrived there virtually unnoticed. 'I didn't expect anything else, particularly with such great and famous players as Bobby Locke, Arthur Lees, Roberto de Vicenzo, Sam King and the marvellous Jimmy Adams in the field,' he later recalled. 'They were the big names: I was small fry by comparison.' Of these challengers, he had the greatest admiration for Locke, whom he had met for the first time at Portmarnock in 1946, when the South African was runner-up to Daly in the Irish Open.

As it happened, the Brad's opening qualifying round at Sandwich was a sparkling 67, four strokes better than Locke. And when the line-up of qualifiers was completed by Tuesday evening, 5 July, Bradshaw was in the clubhouse as leader on 139 while the later-finishing Locke and American Johnny Bulla challenged him without success. The leading qualifiers were: 139 Bradshaw 67, 72; 140 Locke 71, 69; 141 J. Bulla (US) 72, 69; 142 R. W. Horne (UK) 69, 73; 143 A. Murray (New Zealand) 71, 72; M. Faulkner (UK) 72, 71; J. Panton (UK) 72, 71; K. Bousfield (UK) 69, 74.

In the tournament proper, an opening 68, which contained a superb outward journey of 31, left the Brad a stroke behind Adams. His playing partner for what was to prove to be a fateful second round on the Thursday was Henry Osborne, an English professional from Newquay. In the event, Harry had no cause for concern when he covered the opening four holes in 4, 4, 3, 5 – two strokes more than he had taken the previous day. 'Then the thing happened', he recalled to me almost forty years later, when I was writing his biography. 'There was a strong breeze and my second shot to the fifth was slightly off line, but was still a reasonably good shot.'

The fifth, 422 yards back then, is a sharpish dog-leg to the left where the drive is played through a gap in the sand dunes. There's a lot of featureless ground between the dunes and the green, with a view of the sea and the cliffs of Ramsgate on the far side of Pegwell Bay. 'How is my ball?' he asked his caddie anxiously. 'All right,' came the reply. 'It won't be difficult to reach the green.' As he walked over to the ball, the Brad had a quick look towards the green. 'This should be easy enough,' he mused. Suddenly, he stopped dead in his tracks. Speechless. The drive had been pushed into the rough on the right where it lay near the road which separates the course from the shore . . . in a broken bottle.

Much fiction has been written about the nature of that infamous bottle. At the time, it added an appropriately ironic touch for scribes to report that an Irish golfer had sent his ball into a Guinness bottle. The truth is that nobody, including Harry, had an idea of the type of bottle it was. Asking the Kilcroney man to identify it was like asking a drowning man if the water was polluted. The walking scorekeeper, along with Osborne, the respective caddies and a handful of followers from Kilcroney, came to stare in amazement at the Brad's predicament. Someone made the tasteless comment, 'You won't play that shot from memory.' The English professional advised, 'For your own safety, that's a shot that'll take careful hitting.' Bradshaw saw the danger. As soon as he hit the glass, the splinters would fly in all directions. The shot might cost him an eye.

'Looking back on it now, I feel I could have put the championship committee in a quandary,' he said four decades later. But it wasn't easy at the time to get a ruling on the course. There were no walkie-talkies or golf buggies. After considering his position for between ten and fifteen minutes, Harry took out a nine iron, had a few practice swings, closed his eyes, turned his head away from the ball, and gave ball and bottle all he had with a blind swing. Contact was good in that the top part of the bottle was smashed into little pieces and the neck, which had been stuck in the sand, flew several yards in front of him. But the ball travelled only about 20 yards and, after taking a further two strokes to reach the green, Bradshaw ran up a double-bogey six.

So what were his options? When I discussed the matter with John Glover in his capacity as Rules Secretary of the R and A, he sent me an extract from a paper prepared by a predecessor of his on the incident. It read: 'If he (Bradshaw) declared it unplayable, he could (under the *Rules* at the time) go back to the tee (penalty, loss of distance only), or drop a ball not more than two club-lengths from where the ball lies, but not nearer the hole (penalty, one stroke). But was the ball unplayable? This was understood as being "if the player considers he cannot make a stroke at it and dislodge it into a playable position." It was not until later that the player became the sole judge as to whether his ball is playable or unplayable.

'Bradshaw, a delightfully quick player, decided to play the ball, perhaps because he believed in the basic principle that "a ball should be played where it lies", or maybe he was afraid of being disqualified. The *Rules* at that time were not clear on the distinction between movable and immovable obstructions, and even officials were not certain of precisely what could be done. Today, of course, the *Rules* are clear and Bradshaw would have been in no doubt as to the procedure and the free relief available.'

Under the current *Rules*, the bottle would have been treated as a movable obstruction. And if there were any doubt about the matter, the player could drop a ball (Rule 3-3), complete the hole with both balls – playing one of them from where it lay in the bottle – and then report the entire incident to the organizing committee afterwards. This, however, was not permitted under the *Rules* as they applied in 1949.

It is also important to note that had Harry taken a drop to which he was not entitled after separating ball from bottle, he would have been disqualified. According to Glover, 'Harry could have been fortunate to find an official who decided on a generous interpretation of Rule 11, covering obstructions. The problem as I see it, however, is that certain objects were listed in the rule. It would be very difficult to consider a broken bottle as being similar to a hut, bridge, seat or shelter. There was also the point, as Harry proved, that it was possible to dislodge the ball into a playable position. Taking these points into consideration, I believe that it would have been very difficult for an official to grant him relief under the *Rules* of the time.'

A month later, in the August edition of *Irish Golf*, the noted Scottish journalist Frank Moran, who was president of the Association of Golf Writers at the time, wrote an article under the heading 'Should Bradshaw have played that ball in the bottle?' It read:

It might have been: the saddest words of tongue or pen, the poet called them, and with Harry Bradshaw at Sandwich fresh in my mind, how right the poet was. Not to many, even once in a lifetime, does the greatest honour in the golfing world come so close. Bradshaw's brilliant failure will go down to posterity as one of the nearest misses ever. He built himself the professional's ultimate dream right to the brink of reality with a wonderful week's golf . . . Had all six rounds, including the thirty-six holes qualifying, been counted, Bradshaw would have beaten Bobby Locke by a stroke. Even over the four counting rounds, he set up the 283 aggregate which has been spectacularly sufficient in three other years to win the Championship, by five stokes in two cases, four in the other.

In the end, Locke could only tie with it and the South African looked as if he had thrown away his chance by taking four for the seventeenth hole – the short sixteenth – when he had to do the last three holes in the strictest par. That dramatic error left him to cover the last two holes – stiff par fours – in seven strokes, and you know he picked up his lifeline three at the seventy-first hole. It was preciously near Bradshaw's title round about that time. His own putt on the home green needed only two or three more rolls and there would have been no tie.

Now I must refer to what will be historically known as the Bradshaw bottle incident. Without hesitation, I enter upon the controversial subject in the knowledge that angels in their sense of fairness would not dare to tread. There were those at Sandwich who pooh-poohed the idea that Bradshaw's lost title should be pinned down to that accident. Locke, they pointed out, had a seven at the fourteenth hole. But you must get behind the figures for a just comparison. After all, Locke took his seven entirely by his own hand and without any extraneous interference with his play. He drove out of bounds. Bradshaw, on the other hand, was a victim of circumstances absolutely outside his own control.

In what I have written, I have tried to take a judicial view of the affair and in the same vein I must add that Locke is the superior golfer. His technique is better; he has a great command of the shots to the flag, long or short; and he gave himself more chances to hole the first putt than the Irish player did. Against the South African's masterly exhibition in the play-off, Bradshaw was like a caged man; he could not find a loop-hole anywhere, even when he was in fighting trim in the early phases of the duel. Yet Bradshaw is entitled to echo the sad words of a famous Scottish golfer, beaten in the Amateur Championship final on the thirty-sixth green. 'It's hard to get so near and have to start all over again.'

Locke, who is a grand sportsman as well as a great golfer, would be the first to acknowledge that he had had big advantages that have not, of course, been available to Bradshaw, whose *proxime accessit* is all the more meritorious for that fact.

In the play-off, Locke shot 67 and 68 to Bradshaw's 74 and 73 to win by twelve strokes. And there was further disappointment for the Kilcroney player when he learned he wasn't considered for the Ryder Cup at Ganton in September 1949, because of his extraordinary status as 'an overseas player' under British PGA rules. For his part, Locke was suitably generous in victory, saying of Harry, 'He is a grand fellow to play with, always first to congratulate you on a good shot. But I'm afraid he did not have a chance in the play-off. I never made a slip.'

A few days later, in a rather optimistic attempt at exorcising the ball-in-the-bottle incident from his golfing consciousness, Harry presented a Kilcroney friend of his with a souvenir. He decided to part company with the ball which had been the source of so much grief. 'Funny thing about it,' he reflected, 'is that it was a number two and I always played with a number one.'

In praise of a natural

When tournament colleagues from the fifties got together during the week of the Ryder Cup at The Belfry in 2002, John Jacobs could hardly credit that Christy O'Connor was still swinging the club so well. They met at Kilworth GC, about forty miles south-east of The Belfry, where a number of Ryder Cup old boys came together for a charity pro-am. 'One of the great joys of the occasion, for me, was seeing Christy, *the* Christy,' said Jacobs. 'I'm almost afraid to describe him as the best natural hitter of a golf ball I've ever seen, knowing the way he protests about the amount of practice he did. But it's true just the same.'

The man they describe as 'Dr Golf' because of his status as one of the finest tutors the game has known, went on, 'I could watch Christy hit golf balls for ever. People often criticized him for letting the club go at the back of the backswing, but it would have killed Christy to hang onto the club with the last three fingers. Happily, the Lord took over and what we saw from there on was absolute perfection. Not only does his swing look right to me, it remains correct in every key, technical sense. Which is truly remarkable for a man of seventy-seven.'

Comments of this nature tended to heighten the sense of bafflement at O'Connor's failure to win the game's greatest prize. From his first appearance at Royal Portrush in 1951, to his last, at Royal Lytham in 1979, he played in twenty-six Opens. The closest he came to victory was second place behind Peter Thomson in 1965 at Royal Birkdale, though he was only a stroke outside a play-off with Thomson and Dave Thomas at Lytham seven years previously. His amazing longevity is reflected in a share of seventh place behind Tom Weiskopf at Royal Troon in 1973 and he finished thirty-fifth on his swansong as a fifty-four-year-old in 1979.

The Brad, who knew him better than most, expressed the view to me that, deep down, O'Connor was afraid that winning the Open Championship would change him into an international player, so dragging him away from the native patch he loved so well. For this reason he didn't seem to produce of his best down the finishing stretch as he did in other tournaments. And it could also explain why he declined to play in the US Masters, where there was an open invitation to him from 1955 to 1973, as a current Ryder Cup player.

As to whether he felt his career was diminished by not winning an Open, O'Connor responded, 'No, I don't believe so. If you talked to the top guys, they viewed it as a pension. That's what they said. It didn't kill me that I never became Open champion. It just didn't seem that important to me, though when I think of it now and consider all the publicity I would get as a former Open champion, I regret I didn't win it. I tried to qualify for the US Open once and failed. I never played the Masters, though I could have done so about twenty times.' And he made only limited appearances on the Seniors Tour in the US, most notably in the Legends, which he graced on four occasions between 1979 and 1986. His last appearance was as a partner to Doug Sanders, the so-called 'Peacock of the Fairways', who famously remarked to a woman accidentally blocking his backswing, 'I hate to bother you, madam, but would you please move. I have a lot of alimony to pay.'

Though O'Connor never got as close as Bradshaw to lifting the Open title, the quality of the Galwayman's challenges gained rich emphasis through subsequent decades, when the nearest any Irish player got to the elusive prize was in 1985 at Royal St George's, where Christy O'Connor Jnr, his nephew, was tied third behind Sandy Lyle. As it happened, a frustrating gap dating back to Daly wasn't bridged until July 2007 at Carnoustie, where Padraig Harrington finally captured the title in extraordinary circumstances.

With the intrusive eye of the television camera picking up every wince and wobble, we had the deeply disturbing spectacle of a decent, dignified man being stripped bare before Carnoustie and the world. Yet the unremitting trauma of the seventy-second hole was the price Harrington had to pay in pursuit of the 136th Open. In the process, fresh relevance was lent to the words of Shakespeare, who might have had Harrington in mind when he wrote, 'You gods will give us some faults to make us men.'

With two balls in the clear, menacing waters of the Barry Burn, he was made to suffer the most cruel humiliation, before producing a recovery of such raw heroism as to be unrivalled in the rich history of the Championship. In a sense, he couldn't have done it any other way. Revealing himself as a very complex individual, he once admitted, 'I think far too much for my own good, which generally results in making things difficult for myself. There are players who seem to have the confidence to do what's expected of them, but not me. Nothing in golf has ever come easy to me. I've always taken the difficult route.'

Inevitably, those gripping scenes evoked chilling images of Jean Van de Velde's collapse in similar circumstances in 1999, when I was pleased to note that there is no word for 'choker' in the French language. This American invention has become such an accepted part of the sporting lexicon, however, that it is impossible to ignore, much as one might dislike its connotations. And it was typical of Harrington's admirable honesty that when his list of second-place finishes was growing at a disquieting rate, he said, 'Talk of choking doesn't bother me. In fact Caroline [his wife] keeps telling me that the winner of a golf tournament is often the guy who chokes least.'

In terms of competitive steel it wasn't the sort of performance one would associate with Jack Nicklaus or Tiger Woods. But courage can take different forms and by pulling himself back from the brink of disaster, Harrington won a victory for all of us mortals. In the process, observers witnessed a level of drama which is the very essence of professional sport. Triumph and disaster had never been closer. 'This was the ultimate in putting my neck on the line and imagine what the story would have been had I lost,' reflected Harrington. 'Having put myself right out there under public scrutiny, I would have had great difficulty in facing the future. That's why I felt embarrassed by hitting it in the water.'

He went on, 'Things were outside of my control when Sergio [Garcia] was hitting his putt on the last green. Had that gone in, there wouldn't have been all these interviews. I'd have been behind a closed door, saying through a shutter, "Go away! I'm not talking today." There would have been a lot of pain.' As it happened, less dramatic blunders were the undoing of the Spaniard, who saw potentially decisive putts slip tantalizingly past the target.

So it was that almost exactly two years after the death of his beloved father, Harrington climbed golf's highest peak, while becoming the first European winner of a major title since Paul Lawrie succeeded at the same venue eight years previously. And there was the charming bonus of seeing eighteen-year-old Rory McIlroy take the silver medal as the leading amateur. And now that the breakthrough had been achieved, we hoped for similar success from McIlroy, while feeling optimistic about further 'major' achievements from the Dubliner, simply because it is in the nature of Harrington to become the best he can possibly be, even if he has to endure further anguish along the way.

Late on a Sunday afternoon at Carnoustie, Ireland found a new golfing hero. Dating back to Michael Moran at Hoylake in 1913, it was as if a protracted chapter of spirited, if largely unavailing challenges for a coveted crown, had reached a thrilling conclusion in another century. We were more than happy to settle for the fact that Daly's achievement had finally been matched. But a modest champion, who readily acknowledged frailty among his undoubted strengths, had set his sights on further glory, without ever imagining it would happen so soon.

In early autumn 1983, a twelve-year-old lad with a shock of black hair darted among the 700-odd crowd at Stackstown, hardly aware of the golfing giants who were plying their craft to mark a special occasion for the club. 'As a prelude to our first invitation Open Week being held to celebrate the official opening of the course and clubhouse, an exhibition was held on Sunday, 11 September between two of the most renowned and respected names in world golf.' These words were written in a commemorative booklet by the honorary greens officer, Paddy Harrington, who happened to have acted as match referee.

Paddy's son found it difficult to remember the occasion, by the time he had embarked on a professional career. 'I imagine I was more interested in chasing rabbits,' Padraig recalled. 'Though I was aware of Christy's prominence in Irish golf at the time, I knew nothing of Peter Thomson.' So he would have been blissfully unaware of the key role Royal Birkdale played in the career of the great Australian, who won his first and fifth Open titles there. Nor of the fact that O'Connor had been tied second behind Thomson on this majestic strip of Lancashire duneland in 1965, before going on to produce sparkling golf as a partner for Peter Alliss in the Ryder Cup the same year. Nor would he have known anything of the marvellous two-iron approach shot of 213 yards which Tom Watson had hit to Birkdale's eighteenth green on the way to victory in the Open, two months before those celebrations at Stackstown.

Twenty years on, the occasion took on a fascinating, fresh relevance in the wake of Harrington's play-off triumph in the Deutsche Bank Open in Hamburg. Among other things, it brought delighted surprise to Thomson. It being May, he had yet to move to his summer residence in St Andrews, so I phoned him at his Melbourne home and thought it best not to remind him of the outcome of the exhibition in which he was soundly whipped 82-75 by Himself on a wild, windy day which became almost typical of Stackstown. We spoke instead about that young observer, who by this stage in 2003 was occupying eighth place in the world rankings.

Thomson, who had seen Harrington get within a shot of a play-off for the Open title at Muirfield in July of the previous year, had noted the player's progress since then and was fully aware of the victory in Germany. 'That was a fine win, but unless a player can distinguish himself on a really big occasion, he can't claim to have reached the top of the tree,' he said. 'And if Padraig is looking to win a major title, he can gain confidence from the knowledge that the opposition are now no better than he is. With his athletic build and warm smile, I believe he would be a popular, saleable champion. I like players who aren't afraid to smile.'

On the Tuesday of Open week at Birkdale 2008 – a world removed from the Open Week for the modest handicappers at Stackstown – the Association of Golf Writers held their annual dinner in the R and A marquee. And during the course of the evening, they presented their annual award to a player who had distinguished himself on a really big occasion. As the Open champion of 2007, Harrington became only the fourth Irishman after Joe Carr, Harry Bradshaw and Christy O'Connor Snr to be so honoured by the scribes. And by a charming coincidence, the man the AGW chose to present the award was none other than Thomson. On reflection, one could be forgiven for thinking that strange forces were at work.

Meanwhile, the winds that sweep over Stackstown, on its hilly perch to the south-west of Dublin City, had played a crucial part in shaping Harrington for the test which lay ahead. And while he was coming to terms with an injured right wrist while planning his assault on a second, successive Open title, other words of Thomson's came to mind. 'To win the Open,' he said, 'you don't have to be perfect. You just have to be a little better than the rest of the field over four specific rounds. But there is no easy way of finding out whether you have what it takes. In my experience, it demands determination and a pretty smart brain. A fellow must know what he's doing all the time. You could describe it as a combination of brain power and muscle power.'

Late on the Sunday evening at Birkdale, when the crowds were departing one of the most absorbing Opens in recent memory, I stood beside the 72nd green speaking to Harrington's mental coach, Dr Bob Rotella. And he spoke with obvious affection and admiration for a player who wasn't afraid to test himself. A player who met Thomson's requirements as 'a good learner'. And Rotella added, 'He's incredibly honest with himself and with me.'

As we talked, I became aware of how cool and calm the weather had become under a bright, blue sky, as if nature were mocking those hapless challengers who had been overwhelmed by conditions which ranged from punishingly difficult to downright horrific, over four days. There were glorious memories of an event in which Greg Norman had us thinking that it just might be possible for a player to win a major championship at the venerable age of fifty-three. But, of course, we remembered Harrington most of all, and his execution of what came to be known as the perfect shot on the 572-yard seventy-first hole.

With a helping wind, the yardage of 272 was perfect. The club, a favourite of the player's, was also perfect for a situation of extreme pressure. And, most remarkably, the downhill lie was perfect in that it would send the ball on a low trajectory which would cheat the wind. In such circumstances, the fact that he made perfect contact illustrated the heights to which Harrington had risen as a master of his craft.

When the ball came to rest three feet behind the pin, the defending champion rolled in the downhill putt for a glorious eagle. In that instant, we knew we had witnessed something quite special; a memory which would live down through the years. And when the Dubliner went on to become the first European to retain the title since James Braid in 1906, there was an awareness of Ireland now having a world-class sportsman of rare vision and determination.

Carnoustie had been only a stepping stone.

Bullets fly in Connemara

Confronted by an acute shortage of transport in a rural area, it seemed like a splendid idea to commandeer the finest car available. In which case, the Lanchester had few rivals. But the mistake the Old IRA made in purloining such a vehicle in a remote part of County Galway in 1922 was that it belonged to an extremely formidable owner. In short, you crossed John Talbot Clifton, the Squire of Lytham, at your peril.

Born in Lytham, Lancashire, in 1868, he became a celebrated figure in such scattered places as San Francisco, the barren reaches of northern Canada, parts of Africa, the wildest areas of Siberia and throughout these islands. His name is commemorated in Blackpool in Clifton Square and Talbot Road, and in Clifton Street and Talbot Terrace in Lytham. And he was once the owner of Kylemore House in Connemara.

Meanwhile, by way of illustrating how splendidly the car fit the man, the Lanchester held the distinction of being Britain's oldest marque, dating back to 1895. It was the brainchild of Fredrick William Lanchester, who was born in 1868, the same year as Clifton, and who formed the Lanchester Engine Company with the help of his brothers. Given my own weakness for cars, I was fascinated to discover that a chief feature of early Lanchesters was their 'vibrationless' engine. Lanchester was also the first British company to manufacture left-hand-drive models, which led to no less a figure than Henry Ford becoming a customer. Rated more highly than the Rolls Royce, surviving models have appeared from time to time in period television pieces, notably *Jeeves and Wooster*.

Against this background, we can imagine Talbot Clifton's concern when a group of armed members of the Old IRA declined the offer of his Ford and appropriated the Lanchester with the promise that it would be returned 'in a day or so'. But it wasn't. And Talbot received reports of it being driven all over Galway, appearing at markets and sometimes filled with young women. Seething with anger, he decided to set up an ambush to recover his car, vowing, 'I may be killed, but they shall not make a fool of me.'

As things turned out, he only half succeeded – and in remarkable circumstances.

I first learned of Clifton from Dr Steven Reid, the 1996 captain of Royal Lytham and St Annes GC, who gave me access to biographical details from the admirable book *The Clifton Chronicle*, by John Kennedy (Carnegie Publishing). Initially, my interest concerned his fascinating golf exploits, but there would be an intriguing postscript involving two Irishmen, eighty years after his death in 1928.

His reputation among the Lytham caddies was notorious. 'He was a hell of a big fellow and a bad bugger,' one of them remarked, with feeling. 'If he drove into the rough, in his rage he grabbed you and shaked you like a rabbit.' There was an occasion when, after hitting his ball into a pond, he ordered his caddie to 'Go in and get it.' But the boy was wearing a new suit and, quite reasonably, refused. After the round, all the caddies were called to the pond and ordered to get the ball. Showing solidarity with he of the Sunday suit, they declined, whereupon a handful of sovereigns were flung into the water. As might be expected, this did the trick.

It was said that at the sight of Talbot Clifton driving his Lanchester over St Thomas's Bridge, caddies would hide in the bushes for fear of being hired. This was the Squire, a 6ft 4in giant of a man who was president of the Lytham and St Annes GC from 1890 until his death. He converted to Catholicism as a young man and while it has been suggested in certain quarters that this was the reason he was never titled, it is an improbable thesis. The truth is that as someone who clearly enjoyed bucking the system, he was never material for a knighthood and seemed to enjoy the role of outsider, even among the aristocracy.

We can see from the marvellous stories told about him, mostly of an hilarious nature, that he was a truly extraordinary man. Profligate in the extreme, he dissipated a great fortune with seeming equanimity, while his various escapades around the world would suggest someone either admirably brave or somewhat unhinged; a few cards short of a full deck, you might say. Both were probably applicable, though we may be drawn towards the latter conclusion by the assessment of author Evelyn Waugh who, after being a guest at Lytham Hall in June 1935, observed in a letter to Katherine Asquith that all the Cliftons were 'tearing mad'.

If so, it was a charming madness insofar as Talbot had an affair with Lillie Langtry, the so-called Jersey Lily, who, though sixteen years older than him, wrote the Squire a number of passionate love letters around the turn of the last century. On his departure to the US, she sent a passionate *billet-doux* from her residence at 18 Pont Street, London. It read: 'My darling Talbot, I was so sorry to say goodbye and to feel that we had wasted the last three days in quarrelling. Will you be glad to see me if I come out to America? I feel that I must see you again soon. I was so pitiful to see the poor coach left behind – I wept all the way back and feel so blue. Do be a good boy and don't drink too many brandies and sodas, you will kill yourself if you do. And write to me from Queenstown (Cobh) to say you care for me, my own darling. And telegraph the address that will find you in America. I suppose you will go to the Brevoort House in New York. God bless you, my darling boy. Love you – L.'

The story in Kennedy's book which probably characterized Clifton's nature better than any other concerned the occasion when, on arriving in London and finding himself strapped for cash, he telegraphed his estate office with the message, 'Send me five thousand pounds.' When the office replied, 'Regret no funds available,' he responded, 'Sell Lytham.' Since rent week was only a few days away, however, a mollified Talbot decided to return to Lytham and, as a gesture to impress his estate officer, he would travel third class rather than first. *The Clifton Chronicle* takes up the story: 'Upon arrival at Euston, however, it occurred to him that he had never seen a third-class compartment in his life, so, buying a platform ticket, he went through the barrier and peered into the carriages of the waiting train. Having satisfied himself that, after all, they were not so bad, he returned to the booking office and purchased third-class tickets for himself and his valet. But upon reaching the barrier again, he found to his fury that the train had gone. So he booked a special!' So much for fiscal rectitude.

He had a great love of music, which he described as the most companionable of all the arts, and his baggage always included a silver flute to play on his travels, while a gold one was left at home. His favourite instrument, however, was a full concert organ, the pipes from which ran all over Lytham Hall. We're told that when he played it, the house vibrated with the cacophony. And the fact that the stops were, in some cases, placed under the beds in guest-rooms, effectively gave him control over how long an unwelcome guest might stay. In the middle of one particular night, he played 'Nearer my God to Thee' at full blast on the trumpet stop, with the result that an unwanted guest was lifted not just from his sleep but virtually out of his bed, as the sacred music soared from beneath his mattress. We're told that he departed the following morning, pale and shaken.

Talbot Clifton's run-in with the Old IRA occurred some time after his move into Kylemore House. This, incidentally, is now being run as a bed and breakfast, and is notable for a large extension to one side. Apparently, one of Clifton's daughters had an upcoming birthday and as the house did not have a room large enough for the celebration, the Squire did what he considered to be the obvious thing and had an extension specially built. Meanwhile, as a commissioned lieutenant in the RNVR in 1917, he wore naval uniform while patrolling the west coast of Ireland in his own ocean-going yacht, on the lookout for German submarines during the First World War.

By that stage he had married a woman who was almost as eccentric as himself. Though his maturity was open to question, the Squire was aged thirty-nine when taking Violet Mary Beauclerk as his wife, having met her in Peru, of all places. Initially, they lived more or less permanently at Lytham for several years, entertaining lavishly. By the time of their move to Connemara, they had five children. But they were to leave Ireland in extraordinary circumstances. *The Clifton Chronicle* informs us: '. . . one evening, the Lanchester was seen heading on the way to Letterfrack with two men and a woman. He made his preparations to ambush them on their return journey.' Despite the daring of Talbot's night-time escapade, however, the car remained in Irish hands, but not before he had shot one of its occupants, an IRA man by the name of Eugene Gilen. When Clifton's wife expressed horror at such a

Radio ham!

Above: A Laureate on the links. Samuel Beckett with friends, 1920s.

Below: With Greg Norman, Doonbeg GC, on the occasion of a press briefing on the eve of opening.

Left: Getting it all on record with Nick Faldo.

Below: 'The Shamrock Shoot-Out': the Old Head of Kinsale in July 1999. (*Left to right*): Mark O'Meara, Tiger Woods, me in background, caddie David Duval, Lee Janzen.

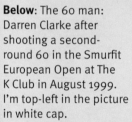

Below: The 60 man: Darren Clarke after shooting a second-round 60 in the Smurfit European Open at The K Club in August 1999. I'm top-left in the picture in white cap.

Left: Gene Sarazen with his friend and mentor Donald Panoz in the background in maroon blazer.

Right and below: A letter from the Squire, Gene Sarazen, 1993.

Sept 6-199
GENE SARAZEN
P.O. BOX 667
MARCO ISLAND, FLORIDA 33969

Dear Dermot
 Received your letter also with your Story, You have recorded the Conversation right from the mouth, a Very good Story I am forwarding on to Mr Pan
 We had a delightful trip back, But two Days later I came down with Bronchitis, was sick for over two weeks, I stayed

GENE SARAZEN
P.O. BOX 667
MARCO ISLAND, FLORIDA 33969

FT MYERS FL 339
PM
7 SEP
1993

USA 50
Chester W. Nimitz

Dermot Gilleece
The Irish Times
P.O. Box 74 - 10-16 D'olier St
Dublin, Ireland

Above: The King: Arnold Palmer at The K Club, 2001.

Below: Dinner in West Palm Beach, Florida, January 2006. (*Left to right*): me, my wife Kathy, Barbara Nicklaus, Jack Nicklaus.

Above: A gathering at The K Club in 1993. (*Left to right*): Dick Spring, Donald Panoz, Gene Sarazen, Ian Bamford (President of the Golfing Union of Ireland), Ray Carroll (Chief Executive of The K Club), me.

Below: With Joe Carr at Sutton GC in 2002.

Above: With Christy O'Connor Snr. My wife, Kathy, takes an overview.

Below: George Hook, Adhamhnan O'Sullivan, me and Paul Kimmage.

Padraig Harrington, the Claret Jug, and me, after Padraig's second victory at Royal Birkdale in 2008.

happening, the Squire replied, 'I don't shoot at a fellow without hitting him and it would have been more awful if he had shot me in the back.'

On 14 April 1922, Violet Clifton received the following letter signed by Michael Kilroy, GOC 4th Western Division IRA: 'On the night of 12 April 1922, your husband, Talbot Clifton, with others who are known to me, lay in ambush at a point on the main road between Kylemore and Leenaun, and fired at officers of this division who were proceeding to Castlebar. As a result of the shots fired, Captain Eugene Gilen of the Irish Republican Army is now hovering between life and death in Mr McKeown's Hotel, Leenaun. I am satisfied, from information received, that you also participated in the ambush, and this is to notify you that an armed guard will be placed on your premises and that you, Mrs Clifton, are to leave Connemara before noon, Monday 17th, 1922. Otherwise, other steps will be taken. If you desire to make any statement, it will be necessary for you to come to Castlebar and I promise you a safe conduct.'

When I made reference to these events in a piece in the *Sunday Independent* in January 2008, a remarkable thing happened. A phone message was received in the office from a man called Sean Connolly in Ennis, saying that he had information which might interest me. When I eagerly contacted him, he told me a fascinating story.

In 1992, a fellow member of Lahinch GC, a Dr Tom Fitzpatrick, phoned Connolly, enquiring if he would play a game of golf there with a Dr Joe O'Donoghue, a friend of his since their student days at University College Cork. As a resident of Lytham, Dr O'Donoghue had learned of the friendship between Talbot Clifton and Oliver St John Gogarty and how, in gratitude for Gogarty's assistance when he himself had to flee Connemara, he gave the writer sanctuary at Lytham Hall. Indeed, the Squire received very honourable mention in Gogarty's *As I was Going Down Sackville Street*, in which the author described how, 'I gazed at him [Talbot Clifton] as he sat in scarlet at the head of his table in the great dining hall hung with old rose velvet and gold. Golden candelabra expanded all around. He sat magnificent and munificent. And for all its arbitrariness, the uniform in which he was attired was not bizarre. It well became the scene.'

Arising from this link, Dr O'Donoghue had promised himself a trip some day to Renvyle House Hotel in Connemara, thinking it was Gogarty's former home. He would learn later that this had been burned down during the Civil War and that the hotel was actually built on its site. He recalled of that particular trip, 'My wife, Kay, and I went from there to a medical meeting in Waterford via Ennis. That's how I happened to stop off at Lahinch, where I played golf with Sean Connolly.'

Dr O'Donoghue was born in Cork City in August 1938 and was twenty-four when he went to Lytham 'to get some money so that I could head for the west of Ireland with my classmates'. That was in 1962 and he has been there ever since. The move wasn't as strange as it might seem, insofar as an uncle on his mother's side, Dr John Glynn, had established a practice there in 1947. He, too, was a graduate of UCC where the celebrated Kerryman Dr Billy O'Sullivan was a classmate. In fact, Dr O'Donoghue believes that during his uncle's student days his uncle won the Captain's prize, which was presented by Billy O'Sullivan's father at Killarney. Dr Glynn later became a great friend of Joe Carr.

'When I came to work in Lytham, my uncle used to look after Violet Clifton,' recalled Dr O'Donoghue, when we talked early in 2008. 'He also looked after the Squire's other son, Michael, and would have had one or two meetings with another son, Harry, the chap who squandered what was left of the money. Harry travelled extensively and, to my knowledge, spent some considerable time in Dublin, and lived for a period in the Shelbourne Hotel. Though Harry used to phone all these psychics and the like, there was a famous story about Uncle John being summoned to Lytham Hall to treat a sore throat.

'It happened to be a morning call and Uncle John had trouble getting up, with the result that he arrived a little late. As a sort of punishment, the patient kept him waiting. Later, when Harry wanted to settle the account, Uncle John indicated that he usually sent a bill. Whereupon Harry opened a drawer and took out a handful of old, white five-pound notes. Uncle John nodded gratefully, saying, "I think that should cover it." And it was only on his way down the avenue, out of sight of the house, that he counted 150 fivers, which was a very considerable sum of money in those days.'

Dr O'Donoghue, who was looking towards his seventieth birthday in August 2008, once played off six and is a former council member of Royal Lytham. 'We still go up to see the [Lytham] Hall, which is now owned by a local trust,' he said. 'The townspeople bought it and the long gallery is still there. I used to take care of one of the Cliftons' old retainers, named Lizzie Taylor [the nursery governess]. She looked after Talbot's children when they were living in Connemara and she gave me some books signed by Violet Clifton, who wrote about the car being stolen and how they left Ireland.'

He went on, 'On that trip to the west in 1992, we [he and his wife] had a lovely time at Renvyle. And we went to see Kylemore Abbey, where one of my cousins, who is now in Canada, went to school. It being early in the morning, we didn't go in. Nor did we visit Kylemore House [a relatively short distance away on the Leenaun side of the Abbey]. I understand that during his time in Ireland, Talbot kept his yacht in Killary Harbour, where the Guinness family kept their boats. The Cliftons were fabulously wealthy and the fact that they were a Catholic family is why they didn't get a title. Violet was Catholic, so the children were brought up Catholic. For his part, Talbot was a great hunter and traveller, and Connemara would have attracted him for its Atlantic sailing.'

When he and Sean Connolly had their fateful round of golf together at Lahinch, there was the customary chat afterwards at the nineteenth. That was when Dr O'Donoghue talked of his life at Lytham St Annes, the Cliftons, how the old Squire once lived in Connemara and how he and his family had to get out of Ireland. This was when Connolly volunteered information about the ambush which totally surprised him, including the fact that the 'Sinn Feiner' who was shot actually survived. It was a situation in which Connolly also played a key role, albeit unwittingly.

Connolly told me, 'When Dr O'Donoghue started relating the story of Clifton, my reaction was, "That's strange, now. Because my father was the IRA commander in charge of that episode and

was driving the car, the Lanchester, on the night in question." '
Allowing this dramatic piece of information to sink in, Connolly
went on to explain that when Eugene Gilen from Carraroe was
shot by the Squire he remained sufficiently mobile to escape into
the hills. 'Covered in blood, he made his way down to my grandmother's house [Molly Kerrigan's] in the early hours of the
morning,' he said. 'And on seeing a light on, probably from a
candle or a paraffin lamp, he knocked and asked for help. But he
was told this wouldn't be possible because there was a woman
inside having a baby. The woman was my mother and the baby was
me. And the upshot of it was that he had to struggle on for another
mile before receiving help in a hotel in Leenaun.'

He went on, 'Clifden, Co Galway, had been my only home until
I moved to Clare. My father was the brigadier in charge of the local
IRA during the Civil War and a man called Kilroy was the area
commander. It was my father who originally asked for the
Lanchester. So they commandeered it. But it was only on meeting
Dr O'Donoghue that I learned about the Clifton side of the
ambush. He told me he had a book written by Violet Clifton and
that he would send me a photocopy of the relevant part. Which he
did – and I still have it.

'In the book [*The Book of Talbot*] she described everything that
happened, including my father and his men calling to the house the
following day. Apparently they were very kind to her, and she
packed all her belongings and was allowed to proceed to Recess,
where she took the train to leave Ireland. The incident was always
called the Bluebridge Ambush and when I heard about it as a
young lad from my grandmother, I thought the Clifton family
name was spelt the same as the town in which I was born, until I
saw it in Violet's book. My father never mentioned it, but it
happened on the night I was born, in 1922.'

Dr Steven Reid, who has become something of an expert on the
Squire, did considerable research, including details of the ambush,
which he has put together in a most illuminating talk. The car was
appropriated while the Squire completed a break of 57 at billiards
and within a few days a servant, apparently, came in with word
that the Lanchester would be returning along a nearby road that

evening. Talbot's plan was to put two cars on a bend in the road and, at a signal, his servants would use the headlights of both vehicles to dazzle the oncoming Lanchester. 'I will do the rest,' he declared. Violet insisted on accompanying her husband and brought a rope to bind Connolly, who was expected to be alone or with no more than one or two others. She also brought pepper to throw in their eyes and took the precaution not to wear any jewellery, in case it might go astray in the event of a scuffle.

Clifton's first problem, however, was that it happened to be a bright, moonlit night, which effectively ruined the dazzle factor as the approaching Lanchester screeched to a halt on the car-blocked road. The second misfortune was that the car contained not one or two but six armed Old IRA men, along with another man they had taken prisoner. Yet when Talbot ordered them to 'Get out of my car and leave your rifles in it,' they complied, though danger still lurked from hidden hands. When one of the men ran off down the road, Talbot reasoned it was with the intention of approaching him from behind. So he opened fire, whereupon Connolly was heard to call out, 'Gilen, are you behind Mr Clifton? Are you covering him with your revolver?' Silence was followed by a stand-off lasting several minutes, during which Talbot's gun remained raised and Connolly's revolver was at the ready. Then, out of concern for the injured Gilen and believing he had won his point anyway, Talbot allowed Connolly to have the car for one more day. Whereupon they disappeared into the night.

Some hours later, acting upon the advice of Conroy, the skipper of his yacht, Talbot took the decision to flee the area and return to England, via Belfast. It proved to be an astute move, for by the next day, with watches placed on all likely ports, the Old IRA went to Kylemore House seeking revenge for their fallen comrade, Gilen, only to discover the Squire was gone.

Later, in what remained of the Civil War, two of the IRA men were killed in a fight with 'Free Staters'. Ironically, they died on the running board of the Lanchester. And when the country was finally at peace, Connolly wrote to Clifton stating, 'All the people here spoke for you – your goods (including the Lanchester) shall be returned. The people want you to stand as a member for Galway.' Which was a reflection of Clifton's remarkable charisma, given everything that had happened. In fact, he returned as a guest of the Irish Free State in 1924, when he attended the Tailteann Games with the celebrated men of letters, G. K. Chesterton and Hilaire Belloc.

Meanwhile, on being reunited with his beloved green Lanchester, the squire treated it as something of a trophy. So it was that Dick Williamson, a long-time member of Royal Lytham, where he worked as a caddie when he was ten, remembered him driving away from the club in the car with two Alsatian dogs chained in the back and bullet-holes in both sides of the bodywork from its adventures in Connemara.

As for Violet, we're told that by way of complying with the order from the Old IRA, she departed Connemara with the help of nuns the day after the ambush and returned to England. And the wonderfully resourceful Squire bought the Kildalton Estate of no fewer than 16,000 acres on the Isle of Islay in Scotland and made it his main residence. Gilen not only survived, but bore the Squire no grudge. In fact, as a further illustration of Clifton's astonishing appeal, Gilen wrote to him some time later to the effect that if the Squire ever needed a faithful servant, he was his man. The offer was never taken up.

Finally, after some time on his massive Scottish estate, Clifton succumbed to wanderlust once more and embarked on what proved to be a final trip to Africa. This time the primary objective was not to explore, but to travel to Timbuktu. Though beset by health problems, he stubbornly drove on, vowing to the long-suffering Violet, 'We will not go back.' So it was that in January 1928 the seemingly indestructible Squire fell seriously ill in Dakar. He never reached Timbuktu, which, for all we know, may have represented his Valhalla. Instead, his last journey was home to Britain, where he was buried on his Scottish estate.

At sixty, he had lived as full a life as even the most ardent adventurer might have wished for, from the time of his first visit to America as a twenty-two-year-old. And the reaction of acquaintances at Lytham and adversaries in Connemara leads us to believe that those who made his acquaintance were greatly enriched by the experience.

Is your fescue bent?

What was it that Andy Warhol said about everybody being entitled to fifteen minutes of fame? Well, I had mine during the presentation ceremony for the 1996 Open Championship at Royal Lytham. It was there for the whole world to see on TV, as Steven Reid, captain of the host club, presented the famous claret jug to Tom Lehman.

Of course you're confused, so let me explain. Dressed in a sports shirt and slacks, I had arrived at the clubhouse earlier in the day to apologize to the captain for being unable to attend a formal lunch party. With Irish players in strong, challenging positions, I felt I couldn't afford the time. Without replying, Dr Reid excused himself and dashed upstairs. No more than two or three minutes later, he returned with a shirt, tie and blazer, which he handed to me while insisting, 'Now you'll have no problem in joining us.' Which I did.

After lunch, I changed back into my own glad rags and returned the apparel to the captain who, it has to be said, appeared to be enjoying the week enormously. 'Just think of it,' he mused. 'You have just worn the blazer I'll be wearing when I present the trophy to the winner later today.' Now, if that doesn't qualify as fifteen minutes of fame . . .

Steven Reid was born in England of Irish parents and educated in Dublin. An enduring love of County Sligo GC is evident in his charming book *Get to the Point*. Over the time I've known him, I've concluded that his remarkable equilibrium may be attributed in no small way to a particularly wicked sense of humour, evidence of which is to be found in the Royal Lytham yearbooks. In the Open Championship issue, he turned his attention to grass. No, not that stuff – Reid happens to be a respected medical man. Rather he was concerned at fielding questions like 'Is your fescue bent?' which can be disconcerting 'even if a glance downwards assures you that your attire is not in a state of disarray'.

He went on, 'I remember the first time I found myself in the presence of grassmen. I came in on the end of a conversation as a large Gin-and-Tonic asked: "When did you ever see a Yorkshire

Fog like that?" A silence fell that I quickly realized was going to last for ever unless I chipped in. Before my brain knew what my mouth was doing, I was trilling away. "Last week I was coming back from Harrogate and it was so dense that day the visibility must have been less than ten yards."

'My voice tailed into nothingness as I was pierced by a quiver of steely glances. Then, as one body, the several owners of the eyes arose and drifted away. As he passed me, the last member of the group paused, gently rested a hand on my slumped shoulder and murmured, "We were talking grass, old boy." ' After some deliberation, Dr Reid decided that the only solution was to face such coves armed with mysterious Latin names for hybrid grasses like Agrostis Capillaris and Poa Cratensis. He suggests that the latter name may equally be applied to the grassman himself. In the meantime, he wishes the world of grassmen 'close cuttings'.

A Nobel Laureate fails to master putting

It's not often that a humble handicap golfer gains the distinction of making significant contributions to the centenary histories of two clubs, but this has been achieved by the remarkable Billy Cunningham, whose membership of Carrickmines spanned no fewer than eighty years at the time of his death in August 2004. Back, in fact, to his times there with Samuel Beckett.

To mark the club's centenary in 2000, they produced a charming book titled *On Carrickmines Hill*, which they kindly sent me. And it had me looking back to the 1993 centenary history of Foxrock GC, where Beckett and his brother Frank were also members. In it, Cunningham recalled how Beckett carried few clubs and putted with a two iron.

There is considerably greater detail in the Carrickmines book, splendidly compiled by Marcus Webb and John Briggs. In the event, Cunningham could trace his membership of the club back to 1924 when he and Beckett, among other Dublin University undergraduates, were granted special junior status at the knockdown subscription of a guinea a year.

In a delightful chapter, Cunningham recalled playing with Beckett on one particular afternoon, when the prospective Nobel Laureate missed a putt: 'He then made a skelp at the ball with his putter, took a divot and hit the ball into heavy rough. Neither of us could find the ball and an elderly gentleman, Grove White, arriving on the green, enquired, "Are you looking for your putt?" He then gave us a dressing-down for disgraceful behaviour, tramped off with his walking-stick and reported us to the Secretary, who was playing on an adjoining fairway. J. H. Carnegie was a man of foresight. We heard nothing further about the incident.'

The then oldest member continued, 'Sam Beckett and I played together for Carrickmines in the Barton Cup. We lost a match on one occasion against Royal Dublin at the twentieth hole. Our opponents were a stockbroker named Nicky Manly and a Captain Jameson. [In fact Manly and J. F. Jameson were members of the Royal Dublin teams which completed the double of the Senior Cup and Barton Shield in 1924.]

'Beckett, who incidentally played cricket for Trinity 1st XI, was a fine natural golfer, a proficient iron player and a splendid companion, with a good sense of humour. I enjoyed my golf with him at Carrickmines. Money was scarce and we contributed little to the bar receipts. We might perhaps have a glass of ginger beer on a hot day or even a glass of beer. From time to time we might combine to play against James Barrett.'

This, of course, was the celebrated club professional from 1908 to 1950 when his son, Jimmy, took over the role which he filled until his retirement in 1984. In the history of the game in these islands, it is doubtful if any club enjoyed such long and distinguished service from a father and son.

Among Jimmy Barrett's exhortations to his pupils were, 'Don't mind where it goes so long as you hit it properly.' 'Harness the wind.' 'If you hook the ball, you can play golf.' A grateful club granted him honorary status in 1994.

Meanwhile, Billy Cunningham informed us that 'When Sam

[Beckett] went off on his literary career, his father found himself without a successor in his firm of quantity surveyors. Frank returned to Dublin to fill the gap. I enjoyed many games with him. Frank told me that they had to send food parcels to Sam during the Second World War when he was living in occupied France.'

Another delightful contribution to the book on this much-loved institution was made by Vere Wynne-Jones, who, sadly, has also gone from us since the centenary celebrations.

CHAPTER 5

● ● ● ● ● ● ● ● ●

Team Golf, the Irish Way

'It doesn't matter how many Open championships or titles
you may have won, when you stand on the tee in a Ryder
Cup match and play for your country, your stomach rumbles
like a kid turning up for his first tournament.'

ARNOLD PALMER

Philip Walton had a rather special interest in the January 1999
announcement of the successful venue for an Irish staging of the
Ryder Cup. Apart from having scored the winning point at Oak
Hill, Walton represented the Jefferson Smurfit Group, owners of
The K Club, on the European Tour. Any sentimental attachment to
the 1995 matches in Rochester, however, stopped short of a
reflective look at the official video.

'I'm scared of being reminded of what might have happened,'
explained the player who, in the second-last of the twelve singles,
secured a nerve-tingling, one-hole victory over Jay Haas, having
been dormie three earlier on that memorable afternoon. 'It
probably sounds crazy, but I don't want to think about my
experience at Oak Hill,' Walton insisted. 'I know it's three and a
half years ago, but any time it comes into my mind I get this shiver
down my spine as I imagine myself having a seven instead of a five
at the last hole.'

When considering the Ryder Cup's development in recent years,
I believe that the importance of the Oak Hill staging cannot be

overstated. Though Europe had made the breakthrough in 1985, to be followed by their first victory on American soil at Muirfield Village two years later, it looked by the mid-1990s as if the Americans had regained control. They tied at The Belfry in 1989; achieved a dramatic, if controversial victory at Kiawah Island in 1991; and won again under the captaincy of Tom Watson at The Belfry two years later. Another American victory in 1995 would have seriously undermined European morale.

American scribes clearly believed another win was on the cards, particularly when they thrashed their hapless European counterparts by 11½ to 2½ in what we viewed as the major happening on the Tuesday at Oak Hill. There was a fine trophy at stake and the match took place in the afternoon at a fine course called the Blue Heron on the outskirts of Rochester. Having partaken well, if not wisely, of a liquid lunch, the demise of our fine team was not unexpected.

None of us was prepared, however, for what happened on the Thursday afternoon. The press conference given by US captain Lanny Wadkins that day was almost like a rallying cry to his troops before battle was engaged. And in the middle of it, the captain of the victorious American golf writers' team stood up and held aloft the trophy from Tuesday's match. He then proceeded to talk of the admirable lead the nation's scribes had given their Ryder Cup players, before walking up to Wadkins and presenting him with the trophy which, he believed, would inspire the American team.

This nauseating sycophancy was very much in my mind when I walked the front nine with Walton the following Sunday afternoon, before returning to the media centre to bring myself up to speed on happenings elsewhere on the course. Later, with Walton heading towards the fourteenth, I set about returning to the scene of battle. As I walked past the desk of the US writers' golf captain, I stopped and shouted to a colleague that I was heading back onto the course to watch an Irishman win the Ryder Cup for Europe. It was a delicious moment.

Notwithstanding the more important happenings of that memorable afternoon, Bernard Gallacher later admitted that he had made one serious blunder. And it concerned Walton. The European skipper confessed, 'I told the players it was my fault and that's all there is to it.' This referred to his decision not to play either Walton or Ian Woosnam on the opening day. It was a miscalculation compounded by the fact that in the last fourball of the afternoon, the rain-drenched and mentally exhausted pairing of Bernhard Langer and Per-Ulrik Johansson were crushed 6 and 4 by Corey Pavin and Phil Mickelson.

When he was left out of action both morning and afternoon on the Friday, I went in search of Walton and tracked him down on the fifth fairway where, two holes behind the last of the fourball matches, he was practising with Mark James and Woosnam. There was no need to ask the Dubliner if he were disappointed: his expression said it all. 'This is supposed to be a team event,' he said. 'All the Americans are in action today yet myself and Woosie have been left out in the cold. I know I didn't do well in foursomes practice, but I honestly felt I would get a run in the fourballs.'

Ironically, while we were having that chat Gallacher had already decided to put Walton and Woosnam into action the following morning. It was a rum-looking partnership for foursomes, yet they managed to take Loren Roberts and Peter Jacobsen to the eighteenth before losing. This would be Walton's only match before the singles, which Europe faced with a 9–7 deficit.

The crisp, overcast morning of Sunday, 24 September could have been borrowed from autumn at Wentworth. Around the sylvan setting, the air was redolent with the tension of impending battle as spectators supporting the American cause prepared for what they believed would be a glorious celebration. All that remained to be decided was the eventual margin of a home triumph.

One felt an acute sense of history on seeing the great Byron Nelson on the first tee being introduced to players from both sides, on this the golden jubilee of his famous 'streak' of eleven successive tournament wins. Haas, playing at number 11 for the US, felt moved to rub his right hand over Nelson's back in the hope of extracting some of the magic for his match against Walton.

Seve Ballesteros was to lead Europe into battle at number one against Tom Lehman. Though desperately at odds with his game, the wounded conquistador was still happy to respond to the urging of his skipper. 'I'm sending you out first because you cannot lose us the Ryder Cup from that position,' said Gallacher, who believed he had arranged an order capable of an unprecedented comeback. As things turned out, he read the mind of his counterpart, Wadkins, to perfection, while turning a predicted American procession into a memorable European victory. At number four came the meeting of Woosnam and Couples in a repeat of their clash at The Belfry two years previously, which ended in a half. Number five brought another repeat of a match from 1993, with Costantino Rocca and Davis Love doing battle once more, though one suspected the Italian would be a vastly different proposition this time around.

Moving downwards, eyes lingered on the pairing at number eight. Now, this was something to savour: Nick Faldo had been drawn against Curtis Strange in a repeat of their play-off clash for the US Open at Brookline in 1988, when the American captured the first of his two successive titles. NBC commentator Johnny Miller described the confrontation as 'watching two glaciers at work'. Strange observed, 'There's nobody in the world I would rather go head-to-head with than Nick, because I admire him as a player, especially his work ethic. You always want to beat one of the best in the world.' The icemen cometh!

At the bottom of the order, Europe's two rookies were in action, Walton against Haas and former Arizona State University room-mates Per-Ulrik Johansson against Phil Mickelson in the anchor match. 'I saw the players from three to eight [James, Woosnam, Rocca, David Gilford, Colin Montgomerie and Faldo] as the main part of my team,' said Gallacher. 'But I still had a job trying to convince myself that Philip and Per-Ulrik wouldn't have too much pressure on them.'

A badly pulled three wood from Ballesteros off the first tee gave promise of a quick and relatively painless execution. But, typically, the Spaniard delivered one of the most remarkable performances of his career. 'Seve kept getting the clubface shut at the top of the backswing,' Lehman remarked afterwards. 'As a result, the ball was liable to go anywhere – and it generally did. In the circumstances, I find it hard to believe that he took me to the fifteenth. If any other player in the world had been playing Seve's second shots, I'd have beaten him 8 and 7.'

Even in defeat, the Spaniard's unconquerable spirit became something of a rallying cry for his European colleagues, though from the twelfth green spectator shouts sounded more like jeering than cheering. It later transpired that Ballesteros had incensed the home crowd by having Lehman replace a 12-inch putt, which the American assumed had been conceded. With the Spaniard two-down at that stage, cynics might have been tempted to suspect that with plan A apparently doomed, it was time to introduce plan B.

From an overall European standpoint, however, things were looking decidedly bright by noon. And as if to order, Concorde, like a sleek bird of prey, was just then in the process of completing its descent into Rochester Airport in preparation for Europe's flight home the following morning. 'Now that's a plane!' enthused an American spectator, looking upwards from the fifth fairway. Everything seemed to be coming together beautifully. Good heavens! The unthinkable could happen and Europe might actually win!

Wild dreams were, indeed, beginning to adopt a sense of reality when even the rookies whom Gallacher was anxious to protect seemed to be doing quite well for themselves. Walton had regained an early two-hole lead over Haas, while Johansson had achieved the same supremacy over Mickelson. Whatever else might lie in store on an eventful afternoon, a pulsating climax was clearly in prospect. And as players fought for control of individual battles, there were certain developments which turned the tide inexorably in Europe's favour.

The first of these came in the second match, in which Howard Clark holed in one at the 192-yard eleventh to draw level once more with the tenacious Jacobsen. 'It was a six iron, just about the sweetest shot I hit in my life,' the Yorkshireman reflected afterwards. It proved to be the trigger for a determined surge, which delivered victory for Clark on the eighteenth. Which meant the overnight gap had been closed to one point, in view of James's decisive win over Jeff Maggert at number three.

By that stage the formidable eighteenth had become the scene of some breathtaking drama – as in Woosnam's struggle with Couples, in which the Welshman appeared to be in a winning position at one up with two to play. But Couples squared the match with an exemplary birdie on the seventeenth, a fearsome 458-yard par four which he reduced to a 300-yard drive and an eight-iron approach to 15 feet. So, they were all square playing the last and I can still picture Woosnam's agonized look as a downhill, 20-footer for the match slipped tantalizingly over the right lip. 'I can't get that putt out of my mind,' he said days afterwards. 'It was so disappointing, especially when it meant I had still to win my first Ryder Cup singles.'

In a blistering stretch of holes from the seventh to the eleventh of his match with Rocca, Love went birdie, birdie, par, birdie, birdie. From all square, the Italian was four down without making a major error. In the overall scheme of things, however, this became no more than a minor setback when Gilford stepped into the spotlight on the fateful eighteenth. Dormie one against Brad Faxon, Gilford needed only to halve the final hole for Europe's fourth singles point, given that Montgomerie was taking care of Ben Crenshaw's challenge further down the order. In the event, wayward approach shots from Gilford and Faxon betrayed the tension of the occasion, with one going into the grandstand and the other, Faxon's, ending in a greenside trap. After taking relief, Gilford was faced with a nasty recovery over greenside rough. Aware of the player's weakness with this particular shot, Ballesteros, crouching anxiously beside the opposite fringe, urged Gallacher to advise Gilford how to play it. But the captain refused, the attempted chip didn't reach the putting surface and, almost predictably, with his next attempt Gilford ran the ball 10 feet past the hole.

It meant that if Faxon holed a six-footer for par, the Americans would gain a precious half. Much to his credit, however, Gilford regained composure to sink the 10-footer for a creditable bogey and, with the hole now having shrunk to the size of a thimble, Faxon missed.

Montgomerie became only the second player to birdie the seventeenth when beating Crenshaw. 'I had been struggling up to then, but it's nice to know I can get the birdies when they're needed these days,' said the Scot. In the process, the reigning US Masters champion had crashed to his eighth defeat in twelve Ryder Cup matches. Which brought us to Faldo and the point that made a European triumph possible. After a superb pitch, his battle with Strange came down to a four-foot par putt on the eighteenth. It would break down the green from the left lip and as Faldo studied the line, Gallacher and seven European players crouched anxiously, hardly daring to breathe. If he missed it, the US would probably retain the Cup. But if he holed . . .

Reflecting on his feelings in those dramatic moments, the winner of five major championships said afterwards, 'It was a terrible feeling. Everything was shaking but the putter.' Yet Europe could not have had a more capable candidate for such crushing responsibility. Even the Americans sensed that, whatever else might go wrong, Faldo's nerve wouldn't fail him. And it didn't, much to the delight of Ballesteros, who leapt to grab his colleague in a tearful embrace.

Two holes earlier, the advantage lay very much with the Americans, as Strange held a one-hole lead which he had maintained since holing a 15-footer for a winning birdie on the short eleventh. But the player who had successfully defended the US Open on this course six years previously finished bogey, bogey, bogey, missing a seven-footer on the last. By keeping faith with his old Wake Forest college-mate rather than the in-form Lee Janzen as a wild-card choice, Wadkins was blinded to the reality that if Strange were still capable of sinking those sort of putts, he wouldn't have been without a tournament win in the US since 1989. 'It was terrible for me to finish the way I did,' said Strange afterwards. 'I had Nick going and I should have beaten him. I could have been the hero; now I'll be the goat.'

Then the envelope man of 1993 made his expected delivery. By holing a 10-foot birdie putt to win the sixteenth, Torrance went dormie two against Roberts and sealed victory on the next. Suddenly images returned of the Scot with his arms raised in glory at The Belfry in 1985. Langer, meanwhile, was going to lose to the doughty Pavin, but Walton was firmly in control against Haas, having secured an unbeatable position when a six iron to four feet at the 184-yard fifteenth left him three up with three to play.

Which was just as well, given developments in the bottom match, where birdies at the tenth, eleventh and twelfth paved the way for a Mickelson win. So it all depended on Walton, who expected the match to end on the sixteenth, where he lay two feet from the hole in three. But in an instant, everything changed. With a bunker recovery that seemed likely to overshoot the green, the American's ball hit the flagstick and dropped in for a winning birdie. 'Oh God!' thought Walton. 'This is all I need.'

With another chance to seal the match on the seventeenth, he missed from four feet. Now he knew the worst – or would it become the opportunity for a hero? Faldo had turned it around. 'Oh Jaysus,' groaned Walton, 'I can't believe this. Everything is down to me.' As Gallacher was to admit afterwards with a wry smile, 'I had every confidence it wouldn't get down to Philip . . . and I was nearly right.'

Still, salvation appeared to be at hand for Walton in the form of a badly pulled drive by Haas which had him blocked out by trees on the left. 'He's dead,' declared Gallacher while urging his man to one final effort. Walton, meanwhile, had pushed his own drive into light rough on the right. Woosnam, his foursomes partner of the previous day, came running up the fairway. 'It's a good lie, perfect for a five wood, if he has a five wood in his bag,' he said. I told him Walton carried a five wood. 'Good.'

Then Walton and his caddie, Bryan McLauchlan, waited . . . and waited. What was Haas doing behind that tree? By his own admission, the former Lancashire taxi-driver who came late to caddying 'couldn't stop shaking'. McLauchlan recalled, 'When we get up to the green, I can see that our five wood, which I thought would get us up all the way, has caught the front and dropped back into the grassy bank. The ball's nestled down and we have an uphill shot. When I say nestled down, that's an understatement. It was so badly buried we nearly stood on the ball while looking for it.

'Philip got a tip from Woosie, though, on how to play out of rough like this, especially the rough near the green. Having finished second in the US Open at Oak Hill, he had plenty of experience of it, whereas Philip hadn't. In fact, the tip had paid off all day, but this was the big one. It had to be perfect. Short and he's still in; long and he's got a frightening putt down the slope. He just nicked it out perfectly.

'The ball ran to about twelve feet below the hole. I whispered to him that the putt was going to come off the left. He took a deep breath and told me: "Bryan, I've got two putts for it. I think I'll take them." And that's what he did.' When Haas conceded the second putt, Walton stood bemused as Gallacher gave a huge leap into the air.

Amid pandemonium on and around the eighteenth green, we had all forgotten about Johansson in the final match, which didn't really matter since the magic target of $14\frac{1}{2}$ points had been reached. But it mattered to the Swede, who was about to lose on the seventeenth. 'The image that will stay with me for the rest of my life is of Per-Ulrik's face when word got back to us that Philip had halved the eighteenth to win the Ryder Cup,' said Johansson's caddie, Tim King. 'I never saw that look before on anyone's face. It was like every possible emotion rolled into one.'

All the emotions were certainly in evidence around the eighteenth, where I had never before witnessed such unbridled joy among a group of sportsmen. Tears flowed freely, especially from Ballesteros and Rocca. 'You must be very proud of Philip,' the Spaniard insisted to me. 'The whole of Ireland must be proud of Philip.' For his own part, Walton was stunned, unable to grasp the enormity of the situation. He shook his head as if somehow enlightenment would come. Faldo was in tears; so was Torrance. Wives and partners wept with the joy of what their men had achieved.

Unlike Walton, Gilford's emotions had had more time to adjust. He just stood there, not a tear in sight, only what appeared to be a whimsical smile. Perhaps he was contemplating what a crazy old game this was; a game that had reduced him to near-despair at Kiawah Island four years previously and was now bestowing emotional enrichment beyond belief.

The Americans looked on, dazed. Gradually, players from both teams began to move away from the green and in the direction of the locker-room. Ballesteros had a magnum of champagne. 'There's nothing wrong with your swing,' Walton kept assuring him. 'Your only problem is lack of confidence.' To which the Spaniard replied, 'Don't worry about my swing. Here, have a drink.' Then Wadkins, whom I had decided was an exemplary captain, came over and warmly congratulated the man from Malahide. 'I can't believe it,' Walton kept repeating. Spoken congratulations from Jacobsen; an embrace from Crenshaw. 'These are great guys,' said Walton as an inner warmth replaced the crippling stress of battle.

Though all of those present readily acknowledged the immense contribution of Faldo, there was also genuine pleasure in how Walton had found the courage to overcome his stumble on the seventeenth green and go on to ultimate victory. We knew that the crucial blow had been struck on the short fifteenth, where his winning birdie had delivered a priceless lead.

When Mark O'Meara was asked prior to Oak Hill what he thought of the pressure in this uniquely demanding event, he replied, 'I've been on a winning Ryder Cup team, a losing one and the team that tied in 1989, and to tell you the truth I didn't have fun in any of them.' And any pleasure he would later get from the American victory at Brookline in 1999 was dampened for him by a singles defeat against Padraig Harrington.

Truth to tell, there wasn't much fun for Americans on that fateful Sunday evening at Oak Hill. 'It's heartbreaking,' said Haas. 'We had them; we had a chance. Our matches, mine and Phil Mickelson's, were supposed to be the icing on the cake. It wasn't supposed to end like this.' Strange highlighted American shock when he said, 'I really didn't think they would win. I honestly thought we were too good. But that's what makes the Ryder Cup so exciting.'

Gallacher, meanwhile, had cause for immense gratification. After being the target of much abuse as a beaten leader in 1991 and 1993, he had now been thoroughly vindicated. As his wife, Lesley, put it, 'It had been a tough few years and I prepared myself for another failure, so that I could cope if it happened again. Not having to deal with that is such a relief. Now we can get on with the rest of our lives with a certain contentment. You just feel grateful, really. But Bernard has deserved this.'

He certainly did. And his first contact with a grateful European public was when Concorde landed at Dublin Airport on the evening of Monday, 25 September, so as to bring the players to the inaugural Smurfit European Open at The K Club later that week. Local wits considered it appropriate that the victorious team should be ushered into the North Terminal, which was little used at that time except for pilgrimages to Lourdes. Hadn't these players produced something akin to a golfing miracle?

Acknowledging his surroundings and the enthusiasm of 5,000 spectators, Gallacher spoke about Walton's contribution, before adding, 'Philip obviously played a special role, but this was essentially a team effort. Perhaps more of a team effort than any previous occasion, because every player won a point and could feel they had really contributed to the win. As for myself, I tried to keep them as happy as I could. I tried to make them positive, to feel the sort of confidence I felt about our chances of winning. Though I didn't really shout it from the rooftops, I felt all along that we could do it. And we did it together. I listened to the players and I put out what I considered to be the best team based on their views. Looking at the outcome, there can't be much wrong with that sort of captaincy.'

Though the visit to Dublin Airport was a short one, there was still sufficient time to lower some of the local brew while raising the Ryder Cup in triumph. Which was entirely appropriate, given that no fewer than half the Oak Hill team had competed in the event for the last time. Faldo, Montgomerie, Woosnam, Rocca, Langer and Johansson would be back in action at Valderrama two years later. But 1995 proved to be the swansong of Ballesteros, Torrance, James, Clark, Gilford and Walton.

An extraordinary year for Walton, easily his best in golf, included the Smurfit Irish Professional Championship at Belvoir Park, where he captured the title after a head-to-head with Paul McGinley over the final day. After winning the Catalan Open on

17 April by a three-stroke margin over Andrew Coltart, he beat another Scot, the mighty Monty, to capture the English Open after a play-off at the Forest of Arden, where, incidentally, he also earned a rebuke from Vijay Singh. That was when he played a typical kamikaze second-shot with a driver at the second play-off hole (the long seventeenth), which cleared the water fronting the green by barely a yard.

As the Malahide man recalled, 'When I met Vijay a couple of weeks later, he called me aside, said he had watched the play-off on TV and that he wanted to know what in God's name I was doing with a driver in my hand. I agreed it was crazy, but that's me.' In another footnote to that event, it was responsible for one of the greatest quotes I've ever heard delivered. It happened on the night of his English Open win, in the Dunraven Arms Hotel in Adare, where he had arrived directly from the Forest of Arden in preparation for the J. P. McManus Pro-Am starting at Limerick GC the following day. Late in the evening, I came upon Philip surrounded by an apparently endless stream of well-wishers. 'How are you?' I asked the newly crowned champion. 'I've a pain in me bollix being happy,' came the deadpan reply.

It was some years later before Walton revealed to me one of the most charming stories in the wake of Oak Hill. It had to do with Concorde's arrival in Dublin and the general agreement among all on board that the Irish hero should be the one to hold the trophy aloft as they emerged from the plane. Walton stubbornly rejected all their entreaties, however, before eventually relenting to a rather special member of the party. 'You must do it, Philip,' urged HRH Prince Andrew, who had travelled with the team. And so he did.

Phone calls from Faldo

Enthusiasts in these islands were still revelling in the aftermath of events at Oak Hill when a phone call from Nick Faldo was taken by a member of the staff of Our Lady's Hospital for Sick Children in Dublin. 'I'm sorry, but Paul died this morning,' the golfer was informed. That was Tuesday, 3 October 1995, when the light went out on the young life of Paul Conaty.

Among other things, it meant a sad adjustment for his many friends at Clontarf Golf Club. No longer would the familiar figure of the eighteen-year-old with the baseball cap be seen hitting balls out on the course, whatever the weather. Gone, too, was the mischievous banter of the professional shop, which became a sort of second home for the lad.

'He was a little gem, one of the best kids I've ever had,' said Joe Craddock, his golfing mentor. 'He would come down here just about every day and was always trying to build up strength he didn't have. Golf was a wonderful outlet for him and never once did I hear him complain about his illness.'

Paul had been ill with cancer for six years and it was Craddock who suggested to his parents, Tom and Lily, that they should take him from school so that he could play golf whenever he liked. Which is what happened. And he developed skills to become a very useful six-handicapper and a member of the Clontarf team which beat Bodenstown in a dramatic final to the Metropolitan Trophy in 1994.

His ultimate ambition was to become a professional, just like his hero, Faldo. Indeed, such was his admiration for the British player that while attempting to copy his swing, he would also try to imitate his mannerisms. Then, through the Make a Wish Foundation, Faldo was made aware of the youngster's plight. All of which led to the first of two phone calls to Our Lady's Hospital.

'On the Friday before Paul died, Nick Faldo rang him at the hospital and they chatted for about half an hour,' said Tom Conaty. 'It was five days after the Ryder Cup, so I'm sure Paul had plenty of questions. He watched the closing stages on television and, sick and all as he was, he still managed to get up in the bed when Philip Walton was striking that putt on the eighteenth.'

Faldo had promised he would phone again and, on hearing the youngster had died, he had a funeral wreath delivered to the parents in Paul's memory. 'I've never met Nick Faldo and have never had anything to do with the man, but I deeply appreciate his gesture to Paul, who idolized him,' added the father. 'It meant a huge amount to Lily and myself.' Walton, another hero of Oak Hill, also sent a wreath.

There was a disarming irreverence about the youngster. Like the occasion he played nine holes with one of the club's older high-handicappers. 'You weren't at your best today, Paul,' he was chided. 'You're right,' came the chirpy response. 'My father often said that if you play with rubbish you'll play rubbish.' A potentially hurtful remark was delivered in such a manner as to provoke only laughter.

I wrote at the time that we had reason to be grateful to Paul for helping us adjust our attitude towards others. And the story didn't end there. Some members of Clontarf decided to hold a charity day to acknowledge the marvellous work done by Our Lady's Hospital and in early July 1996 the club played host to the Paul Conaty Memorial Tournament. When arrangements were being finalized, it was suggested that I might find out if Faldo wished to be associated with the occasion, perhaps through some items that could be auctioned.

When I put it to him during the Benson and Hedges International at The Oxfordshire in May of that year, his response was entirely positive. All I had to do was remind him during the Volvo PGA Championship the following week. Which I did. Then, prior to the US Open at Oakland Hills in June, Faldo came into the media centre for a practice-day interview. Before a word was spoken, he turned to me and said, 'That stuff is winging its way to you.' And when I arrived home from the US the following Tuesday, there it was.

A large package contained one of the player's XXL shirts, with his signature across the front of it. There was also a signed golf ball, an official bound chronicle of his 1989 US Masters triumph, signed, and some signed photographs. When told of these items, Paul's father, Tom, determined he would have them at any cost. And he succeeded, but not before the bidding had gone to €2,860 (IR£2,250). As a bonus to the tournament fund, €635 (IR£500) was bid for the navy Ryder Cup slipover which Walton wore on the

Saturday at Oak Hill. The total fund exceeded €16,500 (IR£13,000).

It was a memorable occasion, sprinkled with joyous memories of a young man who was both a fine golfer and a delightfully mischievous character. And Faldo was very much a part of it all, though he had never met the parents. As it happened, that, too, was to change. In 1997, at a time when *The English Patient* had been scooping up Hollywood Oscars, a famously patient Englishman returned to the Irish Open after an absence of two years.

As a three-time winner of the title, it came as no surprise that Faldo distinguished himself at Druids Glen, breaking 70 in all four rounds to finish third behind the winner, Colin Montgomerie. One imagined the spirit of Paul Conaty witnessing it all. Especially those special moments on practice day, when his hero, Faldo, eventually came face to face with Tom and Lily Conaty. And graciously accepted their heartfelt thanks.

Aces over Niagara

There is an enduring, if improbable, connection for me between Niagara Falls and the short sixth at Oak Hill. It has to do with the Saturday of the US Open in 1989, when I made the two-hour journey on a Greyhound Bus from Rochester to see one of the Wonders of the World. In the process, I inadvertently finished on the Canadian side, without my passport.

The upshot was that I was summarily dispatched back the one-mile distance to the US border post in a taxi, courtesy of the Canadian authorities. Then came the problem of gaining re-entry into the US without a passport. After I had explained the nature of my business, a US official eventually said, 'Something very special occurred at Oak Hill yesterday. What was it?'

With a heartfelt sigh of relief, I explained that in a period of one hour and fifty minutes on the previous (Friday) morning, four players in separate groups – Doug Weaver, Mark Wiebe, Jerry Pate and Nick Price – each scored a hole in one on the sixth, using a seven iron. 'Welcome to the United States,' the official beamed.

Himself and The Brad in Mexico City

Harry Bradshaw was such a marvellous storyteller that it seemed a pity to have facts interfere with his captivating flow, but this was to present serious problems for me in 1988 when I worked with him on *The Brad*, two years before his death. The project, which owed much to the enthusiastic support of the late Paddy Wright, who sponsored it under the Smurfit banner, comprised two audio tapes and a little book, all presented in a specially designed plastic container.

In terms of the book, problems arose for me when information which I had established as fact was given decidedly imaginative treatment by Harry. Like for the Canada Cup of 1958, when, apparently, he made a creditable bogey at a par three on the second day after a recovery played from a shallow, fast-running stream beside the green. One could picture the Brad, surrounded by a rapt audience at Portmarnock, describing how, with water lapping around his ankles, he was about to play a daunting recovery when, 'This Mexican opened a sluice gate at the top of the hill and I had to hit the ball before this huge flood came splashing down on me.'

Though it made for a marvellous yarn, the notion of such a happening in the middle of a tournament round seemed decidedly far-fetched to me, but when I suggested as much to Harry he seemed deeply hurt by my scepticism. 'Ask Christy,' he said. And when I talked to his Canada Cup partner, Christy O'Connor Snr, he smiled and said gently, 'I think Harry's memory is playing tricks on him.' In other chats with O'Connor, it became clear that he had enormous respect for his Canada Cup partner. As he recalled,

'Myself and the Brad were great old pals. They talk about modern players with great short games: Harry used to pitch the ball into the hole three or four times a round. On a regular basis. "You were lucky there," I'd say to him. Then, by way of response, he'd do it again.'

O'Connor went on, 'The Brad was very much his own man, who did things his way. You wouldn't bend him. He was a great competitor and I would get annoyed with people who referred to his agricultural swing. In his younger days, his swing was upright and very effective. It was only when he began to put on weight, later in life, that his swing flattened. I really enjoyed the times we played together in the Canada Cup and obviously Mexico City was a particular thrill. But it was only when we arrived back at Shannon that we realized the impact our performance had had in this country. We discovered we had done something very special.'

Meanwhile, the Brad bowed to O'Connor's recollection of the short fifth. As a consequence, the amended version of the story which went on the tapes was: 'In the second round I hit trouble at the fifth hole, just like at Sandwich in the 1949 British Open. This time it was a par three of about 215 yards. I played a four wood and, though it wasn't a bad shot, the ball missed the green by six feet on the left, hit a slope and went down into this water. And after myself and Christy had looked at the situation I said, "Christy I'm going to play it." There were trees on the top of the hill between me and the green, but I saw an opening of about four or five feet. So, as I'm playing it, Christy turns his back and walks away as much as to say, "The best of luck to you."

'Water splashed everywhere, but the ball went through the opening and when I got up there it was only four feet from the hole. I was so excited, you know, I didn't even try for the putt. It could have cost me anything. There we had two fifth holes, both of them in the second round. In one, there was glass everywhere and in the other there was water everywhere.'

The Irish pair were among the last teams to arrive in Mexico City, along with the Germans and the Dutch. Bradshaw recalled, 'On the airport tarmac, a local Golf Federation official approached myself and Christy and said, "We thought you were not coming."

It was around twenty to four in the afternoon their time and I looked at him – he was a huge man of about 6ft 6ins – and told him we had a very old saying back in Ireland. "What would that be?" And I said, "The last shall be first." Of course we won it. And when it was all over, the same official came to me and tapped me on the shoulder and said, "Do you remember what you said to me when you arrived on the tarmac at the airport?" I had forgotten all about it.'

With tree-lined fairways and an overall length of 7,216 yards, Club de Golf Mexico was a long, demanding course, especially given the golf equipment of the time. Indeed, Peter Alliss was moved to remark afterwards, 'I must say I was surprised by Harry Bradshaw's marvellous show. I wouldn't have picked this course to suit him, but he handled it like a master, keeping the ball straight and putting amazingly well.' Ben Hogan, who continued after his partner, Sam Snead, withdrew injured at the halfway stage, compiled an aggregate of 291, which was five strokes higher than the Brad's. 'I gave it all I had,' said the bone-weary Hawk. 'I don't see how anybody should be expected to play golf at this altitude.'

In his build-up to Mexico, Bradshaw reckoned the only way to beat the Americans was to prepare their way. 'That meant long hours of practice, paying huge attention to chipping and putting,' he said. He also received priceless advice from the brilliant Irish amateur, Dr J. D. McCormack, a distinguished member of Hermitage. 'I used to play every Tuesday with him and he had been out in Mexico the year before at a doctors' conference,' said the Brad. 'He told me, "Harry, I played the course where they're going to play the Canada Cup and it's right up your street. But you have to do three things." "What's that?" says I. "Bring a shooting stick, eat very little – which hurt a wee bit – and talk very little, because it's easy to get exhausted in the altitude." So I passed this on to Christy and it seemed to work for us. It certainly worked for me.'

The good doctor clearly knew his man, because Bradshaw saw the course as a shorter version of Hermitage, where he won the local Pro-Am Foursomes on no fewer than six occasions with Joe Carr. And in hot, sticky conditions the shooting stick was invaluable. Over the opening two rounds, he carded two 70s while O'Connor shot two 73s to lift Ireland to the top of the leaderboard, two strokes clear of the US at the halfway stage. The gap remained the same at the end of the third day, but now, after Snead's withdrawal, the Scottish pair of Eric Brown and John Panton had moved into second place, while Spain's Miguel brothers, Sebastian and Angel, were a further two strokes back in third place.

Alliss, who was representing England with Bernard Hunt, reported the closing stages for the *Daily Express* and the cutting found its way into Harry's scrapbook. It read, 'I had just finished my round for England and I was there at the dramatic climax. It was pretty tense, I can tell you. The excitement was over the amazing battle for the individual trophy between Harry Bradshaw and Angel Miguel. Sadly, I have to report that our "Brad" was beaten by the Spaniard in a sudden-death play-off.

'. . . hole by hole, Miguel did 4, 4, 2; Bradshaw shot 4, 4, 3. Bradshaw pitched to two inches from 80 yards at the second tie hole, but Miguel holed a five-yard putt for a half. At the next, Harry was 12 inches short with an eight-yarder and the twenty-six-year-old Spaniard clinched it by holing out from six yards. But nothing can take away from the glory of Bradshaw and O'Connor bringing this great trophy to the British Isles for the first time since the tournament began six years ago. Bradshaw's personal tragedy was that he took five on the seventy-second hole, while Angel Miguel, playing in the same fourball, got a four that enabled him to tie.'

As the Brad remembered it, his heart wasn't in the play-off. 'I'd love to have won it, to bring off the double, but it wasn't to be,' he said. 'I won the PGA Championship before going to Mexico, and before that I won the Dunlop Masters twice and the Irish Open twice. But winning the Canada Cup was the biggest moment in my golfing life.' Among other things, the victory was notable for debunking some decidedly unfair impressions here about Henry Longhurst being anti-Irish, simply because he had once described Bradshaw's swing as 'agricultural'. Reflecting on the Canada Cup, Longhurst wrote, 'While others were sinking exhausted in the locker-room, he [the Brad] was ready with affable conversation.

As for the fears of dysentery – "I drink the water out of the tap. If you're going to get it, you'll get it anyway." '

His article concluded, 'My colleagues are due shortly to elect a Golfer of the Year who has "done most for British golf". Had they seen him in Mexico, they would look no further than Harry Bradshaw – and never mind what part of Ireland he comes from!' Suffice to say that the Brad got the award a few weeks later, making him the second Irish recipient after Joe Carr in 1953. O'Connor Snr received the award in 1977 and Padraig Harrington became the country's fourth recipient in 2007, to honour his Open triumph.

On Tuesday, 25 November 1958, the triumphant duo were accorded a tumultuous welcome on their arrival into Shannon Airport. Television and newsreel lighting illuminated the gloom of a dull winter's morning. Shannon had not witnessed the like since Ronnie Delany had returned home in triumph two years previously from Melbourne, where he captured an Olympic gold medal for Ireland in the 1,500 metres. By a remarkable coincidence, the plane from which Bradshaw and O'Connor disembarked was the same Swissair craft which had carried Delany home in glory.

Hundreds of golfers, led by Golfing Union of Ireland president Bob Davitt and including the captains of Portmarnock and Killarney, had spent the night at the airport, awaiting the arrival of golfing heroes whom they cheered to the echo. But there was also a note of disappointment. The gold trophy remained in Mexico. 'We fought hard with promoter Frank Pace but he explained that the cup was too delicate and too valuable to be allowed out of the possession of the promoters,' said Bradshaw.

While O'Connor travelled south to Killarney, where he remained as professional only until the following April, when he moved to Royal Dublin, Bradshaw flew on to Dublin where another large crowd was waiting. Amid shouts of 'Good old Harry', the hero's wife, Elizabeth, claimed she had never been so excited. With O'Connor in his prime and having an apparently indestructible partner, observers could never have imagined a lapse of thirty-nine years before similar scenes would be witnessed again.

Bridging a gap at Kiawah

The 2007 PGA Championship took place at Southern Hills only three weeks after Padraig Harrington had captured the Open Championship, so, predictably, the focus of most interviews from an Irish perspective centred on the Dubliner. And that included a chat with his long-time World Cup partner Paul McGinley. Typically forthright, McGinley said, 'Everybody talks about how Nick Faldo restructured his game, but it was nothing compared to what Padraig did. Yet nobody talks about that. The truth is that even when we won the World Cup at Kiawah Island, he didn't have a game. He couldn't flight the ball. He would hit a low fade and when I played with him in the Walker Cup he couldn't get the ball properly airborne.'

McGinley went on, 'Before he started working with Bob Torrance [in 1998] he wasn't the ball-striker we know him as today. He was a chipper and putter who got it around. By his own admission he couldn't strike the golf ball. In terms of being a success, however, I'd much prefer to have a brilliant short game than a brilliant long game. When it comes to the meat of scoring and winning golf tournaments, the short game is far more important. And Padraig was born with an unbelievable talent. As long as I've known him, he could chip and putt, and when he started going to Bob he addressed the weak parts of his game to become the very good ball-striker he is now, with a big, high draw where there was once a low fade.'

Confidence in his short game was evident in Harrington's attitude towards Kiawah and his second appearance in the World Cup. He wanted the course to be tough, claiming that he simply loved the challenge of difficult venues. As he put it afterwards, 'The tougher the better, preferably with the wind blowing. In that way, I was sure Paul and I would have a great chance. Call it crazy, but that's the way I am.'

He had probably heard the story of the shattered quartet who comforted each other with the shared conviction that 'the pros would never agree to play strokes around here'. That was Kiawah Island on Monday, 30 September 1991, the morning after the

Ryder Cup in which matchplay had masked much of the horror inflicted by a brutally relentless course. Former Ryder Cup representative and Portmarnock professional Peter Townsend, European Tour referee John Paramor, Irish international John Carr and former Connacht interprovincial Bill Thompson availed of the opportunity of playing it as a fourball.

The outcome? Paramor, a two-handicapper, scored best with an 82; Townsend carded 84; Carr shot 87; and Thompson, then a five-handicapper, carded a 91. There wasn't even the comfort for Townsend of collecting on bets he had struck with two English friends. 'They were six- and eight-handicappers and I wagered that they wouldn't break 100,' he recalled later. 'I was nearly right: they shot 97 and 99.'

At about two in the afternoon on another Monday, six years later, Harrington and McGinley played Kiawah for the first time: a quick eighteen holes. Given the experience of Townsend et al and other horror stories from 1991, the Irish pair were somewhat surprised by their initial experience of the Pete Dye creation. Playing it blind, McGinley shot 70, with two three-putts, and Harrington had a 72. And their build-up to the tournament remained smooth, despite the non-arrival of McGinley's regular caddie, 'Edinburgh' Jimmy Rae.

The wonderfully resourceful John O'Reilly, Harrington's caddie, had already arranged a replacement. 'Through a problem with flights, Jimmy told me he couldn't get here until Wednesday,' recalled McGinley. 'In the circumstances, I told him not to bother, at that stage of the week.' The player's decision was greatly helped by the fact that O'Reilly's substitute, a 6ft 4in Corkman named Alan Kelly, was waiting in the wings. Kelly, who hailed from Bantry and had spent three years caddying on the European Tour, met up with O'Reilly in Florida the previous week. 'I told him to look out for work for me at Kiawah,' said the Corkman. And O'Reilly obliged, in spades.

After Ireland's latest triumphant duo returned to Dublin as champions, these were Harrington's recollections of a memorable four days:

Day 1

We decided on Tuesday that Paul would hit first off every tee, because he's solid and straight. But it didn't work out that way. When setting off in the pro-am on the Wednesday, he wasn't ready to hit, so I did. And like a good fourball combination, we kept the order for the next five days. The greens were superb; medium-paced and very true. Still, I had a battle to keep my game together and I was really thrilled that Paul shot 66 to my opening 71.

Though we were seven strokes behind Sweden at that stage, I preferred to think that we were seven under on our own cards. Then I thought about the Swedes and how inconsistent they were as a group. So focused are they on playing well that they don't seem to have the ability to grind it out when the ball isn't running for them. Joakim Haeggman won a tournament this year [1997], but must have missed ten cuts. Look at Per-Ulrik Johansson: he won twice this year yet was behind me in eleventh position in the final Order of Merit. He would have missed eight cuts whereas I missed only two. Yet they were still to be feared when their tails were up and it was obviously very unfortunate for the team that Johansson got sick and was eventually forced to withdraw.

Day 2

Going to the course the second morning, my feeling was that four 7-under-par aggregates would do us nicely. Then I reminded myself of how Paul had described it as a marathon not a sprint. There were six rounds to go.

While working on my putting the previous night I found something and the result was that I hadn't felt as comfortable on the greens since my win in the Spanish Open, more than eighteen months previously. Basically, I needed to slow down the pace of my stroke, but I couldn't afford to think about it over the ball. I needed something that would work without having to think about it.

I shot 67, which was really important. Apart from lifting my confidence I felt it lessened the pressure on Paul, who would have been challenging for the individual lead had he shot a comparable score, instead of a 70. Though we had become the balanced partnership everyone had been predicting, we continued to play as individuals and I was determined to be more aggressive. I had counted exactly thirty-two players ahead of me after the opening day and that simply wasn't good enough. It wasn't that I should have been leading the tournament, but I knew I could do better than that. And the answer was to attack. So, rather than play for the middle of the greens, I began to go for the pins in earnest, with the result that it became my low-putting round of the tournament: 27 putts.

Day 3

Though I now thought of us as favourites, I was also aware that all of the leading teams would be aiming to move forward in the third round. And we proceeded to make a cardinal error by spending the first nine holes watching our playing partners, the Americans. Our thinking was that if we managed to stay with Justin Leonard and Davis Love, we must finish the day in a strong position. After all, they had been shown the way by countrymen Fred Couples and Love, who had dominated the event in recent years.

At the turn, we didn't discuss the situation; we didn't have to. Having let teams like Germany and England get into the frame, Paul and I knew our strategy was wrong. We were defending when we should have been attacking. By looking over our shoulders at the Americans, we were losing touch. Instinctively, our mood changed on the homeward journey, particularly on the scoring stretch from the tenth to the thirteenth, before we turned back into the wind. I got two birdies on those holes and Paul got one. We were back on track and by the end of play we'd each shot 68. More importantly, we had moved to 22 under par to be second on our own, two strokes behind Germany and two ahead of Scotland.

I remember wondering if Alex Cejka could keep up his phenomenal scoring for the Germans, while aware that his partner, Sven Struver, was a bit erratic. Later, determined not to lie awake thinking of the golf, I stayed up until eleven thirty watching Andrew Coltart on TV on his way to victory in the Australian PGA Championship.

Day 4

I knew that to think about winning would be to tempt fate. I wanted to stay in the present, because I had learned that once a tournament player starts daydreaming he's into dangerous projection. But I couldn't blank my mind. Eventually I decided to try and make up the four strokes that separated me from Ignacio Garrido in the individual event.

In the car on the way to the course, I told Paul about how I coped with my nervousness and that I now had a positive focus on the day's challenge. I would try and shoot at least 68 to catch Garrido. Meanwhile, my caddie, John O'Reilly, became a very positive influence on both of us, while calling some very good clubs. For instance, I was about to hit a seven iron third shot to the long eleventh when he advised me to hit an eight. Which I did – and left the ball stone dead for my second successive birdie and my last of the tournament.

Though we led the tournament for the first time after three holes of the final round, the leaderboard told me we couldn't relax, what with the Scots and Americans in challenging positions, not to mention the Germans. Then came the scoreboard at the ninth, where we discovered that the Scots [Colin Montgomerie and Raymond Russell] had committed suicide. That was a terrific boost in view of the threat Monty could have presented. It was also the first time I allowed myself to think we were in a position to win. We controlled the tournament and, bar serious mistakes, we were going to deliver a famous Irish victory. Things became even better when I birdied 10 and 11 to leave us 28 under. Now I began bailing out, because for the first time in the tournament we had something to defend.

With the last five holes playing downwind, I figured there was going to be a last-ditch charge from our opponents, so we needed to make a few more birdies. And the way Paul and I were playing I was confident we could get them. I wasn't a bit bothered that it happened to be Paul who delivered with birdies on the fifteenth, sixteenth and seventeenth. At the short seventeenth, which was always going to be a dangerous hole, I aimed for the B in the middle of the CBS sign at the back of the green and hit a really nice six iron exactly as I wanted to. Then I relaxed. When Paul chipped in for a birdie, it became a tremendous bonus. A few minutes later we had got our drives away on the eighteenth and I knew the job was effectively done.

Granted, Tiger Woods wasn't there. Nor was Greg Norman nor Nick Faldo. But the fact remained that a country could enter only two players and I honestly believe we would have won, irrespective of who was put in against us. Even Tiger. When it's your week to win, nobody can take it away from you. In the meantime, there was much to celebrate. Of course I knew about Christy and the Brad in the Canada Cup in 1958. And I also knew that this tournament had been won by legendary players such as Jack Nicklaus, Johnny Miller, Arnold Palmer, Ben Hogan and Sam Snead. All of this would be very special to me in the years ahead. Much to celebrate. And I was getting married to Caroline the Saturday after the tournament.

Indeed the future Mrs Harrington was pressed enthusiastically against the spectator ropes at Kiawah, alongside Allison, McGinley's wife of eleven months. Then there was the support of David Feherty, who had known Kiawah in a meaner mood when he competed there in the Ryder Cup in 1991. He had returned as a supposedly neutral CBS commentator, but was unashamedly biased towards the Irish cause. He even saw fit to keep spirits high with typical banter. Like on the fifteenth fairway, where Harrington's caddie, O'Reilly, attempted to tell a bar-room joke which fell somewhat flat. Feherty piped up, 'Heard about the tin of beans which went into a bar and the barman said to him, "Sorry, we don't serve food in here."'

As the winning duo walked off the final green, Harrington captured the essence of the moment with typical understatement when he said, 'Paul and I were good company for each other this week.' Indeed they were, while earning prize money of US $200,000 for each other with a record aggregate of 31 under par. There was an additional US $15,000 for McGinley (272) as fourth leading individual behind Montgomerie (266), while Harrington, in fifth place, received a bonus of US $10,000. But he didn't achieve his last-round objective of beating Garrido, who was third.

Meanwhile, a personal memory for me was the sight of the Irish pair walking up the seventy-second fairway with a five-stroke lead and a gentle breeze on their backs, and Harrington turning to myself and fellow scribes and, with a grin from ear to ear, remarking mischievously, 'Isn't it a pity, lads, that the wind didn't blow.'

Where Alliss had acted as a stand-in scribe in 1958 to relay the glad tidings from Mexico City to these islands, Harrington and McGinley told the world's electronic and print media at Kiawah about the inspirational impact O'Connor had had on their golfing careers. 'We play with Christy in Links Society outings during the winter months,' explained Harrington to American writers, who were anxious to hear more. And they were especially pleased when McGinley singled out Tom Watson as his favourite golfer, a highly appopriate choice as it happened, given Watson's win in the Dunlop Phoenix Open in Japan that weekend.

And I remember thinking that, from an Irish perspective, the tournament's significance went way beyond the success of Bradshaw and O'Connor thirty-nine years previously. In fact, the Canada Cup/World Cup could be seen as largely responsible for the way golf in Ireland has prospered over the last fifty years. When the event came to this country in 1960 crowds flocked to Portmarnock to watch Sam Snead and Arnold Palmer capture the trophy for the US. It was a magical occasion which had the effect of prompting an extraordinary expansion in the game at club level here.

As for the caddies, O'Reilly positively beamed at the thought of his percentage of his master's winnings, but there was disappointment for 'Edinburgh' Jimmy, whose percentage, an estimated £13,000, went to a stand-in from Bantry as an extremely welcome Christmas gift, while making this particular World Cup triumph an exclusively Irish affair.

Shortly after the players returned home they were accorded a Government reception in Dublin and among the attendance was a familiar-looking figure, who established a fascinating link with 1958. 'I was only nine when the Cup was won in Mexico City, but I was given cause to remember it with particular affection,' said Harry Bradshaw Jnr, a sound recordist with RTE who had been responsible for the audio tapes we did with his famous father.

'When the old man came back from Mexico, he said, "I have a present for you,"' said Harry. 'With that, he produced this wonderful new watch and strapped it to my wrist. My first watch.' Smiling at the memory, he then pulled up his left cuff. 'There it is,' he proclaimed proudly. 'Thirty-nine years on, it has had three or four new winders, four new glass faces and about twenty straps, but it still works perfectly.'

A record slips away at Waterville

On the mean, unforgiving fairways of Waterville in October 1986, Christy O'Connor Snr made one final heroic attempt at reaching a milestone which had been stubbornly elusive. That was when he carded rounds of 73, 69, 74, 73 for a one-over-par aggregate of 289 in the Irish Professional Championship, which he and Harry Bradshaw had each won on ten occasions.

In the event, it was good enough only for second place behind Des Smyth, who was then at the peak of his powers. Though naturally disappointed by the realization that he would never again have such a chance to win the title for a record eleventh time, I can remember Himself being genuinely pleased to hand the baton over to Des. This was his last hurrah and, typically, he carried it off beautifully – two months short of his sixty-second birthday.

His legacy has been enormous. One has only to think of Padraig Harrington, who kept a picture of O'Connor in his parents' home in Rathfarnham, and who first met and played golf with him as an eager fifteen-year-old. And the winner of three major championships retains vivid memories of a blustery winter's day some years later, when he ventured out to Royal Dublin to watch Himself hit practice balls. It was January and a bitter wind was whipping sand from the shore around Dollymount's marram grasses.

'Most people wouldn't have let their dog out,' Harrington

recalled, 'yet Christy was there in the Garden, hitting shots. And they were beautiful shots. That's what was fascinating to me. I figured at the time that nobody in the world could play this one particular shot – a six iron of maybe 140 yards, which he was holding onto the wind with a low draw. One after the other. Again and again. Then he hit a few fades. And I don't think anybody could have played them as well. It was just spectacular. Here was a man in his sixties at the time, who still had the will to go out in that weather and hit shots.'

In his seventies, O'Connor's appeal was undiminished, as I discovered at The K Club in late June 2000. It was one thirty in the morning and a long day of golf, food and drink had passed into the wee small hours. In the normal way of things, people had broken into little groups when my attention was caught by a trio of distinguished golfers whose various achievements included a combined twenty-nine Ryder Cup appearances. There was Himself, resplendent in dinner wear and swishing his outstretched hands in a simulation of the golf swing, full shoulder turn and all. Even more interesting was the look of rapt attention on the faces of Ian Woosnam and Peter Baker.

Meanwhile, in the background, former Irish international Noel Fogarty, who has known O'Connor as a friend and golfing colleague for about forty-five years, took it all in with a quiet smile. 'Christy learned his swing from old Bob Wallace in Galway and it has never changed in all these years,' he said.

First it was Woosnam who moved centre-stage in this O'Connor masterclass. Himself shook his head. This is the way, he indicated, raising the player's hands noticeably at address.

Then it was the turn of Baker, who had been the outstanding home player in the Ryder Cup defeat of 1993 at The Belfry. This time O'Connor was more demonstrative, slapping him repeatedly on the outside of his left thigh. 'Isn't golf a wonderful game,' remarked Fogarty. 'There you have players from different generations, totally absorbed in the wonder of it all. And you know Christy is a terrific teacher, a far better teacher than most people imagine.'

When I met up with Baker a few days later at Ballybunion for the Irish Open, he agreed wholeheartedly. 'Christy got chatting with Woosie and told him he had seen something wrong with his swing, from watching him on television,' he said. 'And since I was in the company I wasn't about to turn down the chance of a chat with Himself. I have a tendency to tilt, which becomes a reverse pivot, and Christy told me that it couldn't happen if I kept my left knee inside when starting the backswing. That's why he kept slapping me. I have watched him play on a few occasions and he still has a wonderful swing. He must have been a fantastic player in his prime.'

Quite properly, enduring recognition of those skills extend beyond these shores. Tune into a golf telecast from the BBC and you're likely to hear reminiscences about a four-wood recovery from rough or a driver smacked confidently off a tight fairway lie. Whatever the circumstance, there can be no doubting the affection in the acknowledged voice of golf, as viewers are told about the daring deeds of 'my old pal, Christy O'Connor'.

Peter Alliss seems to reserve his most glowing tributes for commentaries from Wentworth. This has to do in no small measure with O'Connor's marvellous achievements there, notably in setting an aggregate record of 274 for the famous West Course, when capturing the Daks Tournament of 1959. Then there was the majesty of his play with the big American ball, in his Martini Tournament triumph of 1964, when Alliss, incidentally, finished third.

The year 1959 retains a special resonance for Alliss for another hugely significant happening. It was when he and O'Connor came together for the first time as Ryder Cup partners, for the matches against the US at Eldorado Country Club in California. That was when the British and Irish team survived what became known as 'The Long Drop', as the charter aircraft in which they were travelling the 150 miles from Los Angeles to Palm Springs dropped like a stone from 13,000 to 9,000 feet, scaring the players half out of their wits.

Later, for reasons that were never fully explained, skipper Dai Rees decided to team Alliss and O'Connor together for the first time as foursomes partners. Now, five decades on, I wondered if they had responded in the manner advocated by the celebrated American psychologist Dr Bob Rotella, who has advised Ryder Cup partners, 'Before you start, you've got to turn to the guy you're playing with and say, "Look, I love you; I'm going to support you out there." '

When I spoke with Alliss about one of the greatest duos in the history of the Ryder Cup, he gave a quiet smile at the notion of such overt togetherness. 'As far as that's concerned,' he said, 'I remember on one of our early holes, I hit the ball into bushes and turned to Christy saying, "Oh, I'm so sorry." To which Christy replied, "Are you doing your best?" And when I assured him I was, he looked me in the eyes and said, "Well, never apologize to me again." And I never did.'

Rees knew he had uncovered some magic when O'Connor and Alliss shot 63 in practice for the 1959 matches. And the little Welshman was fully vindicated when the Anglo-Irish partnership beat the reigning US Masters champion, Art Wall, and the 1957 Augusta winner, Doug Ford, by 3 and 2 over 36 holes. 'It seemed that destiny had decided we were a partnership for the long haul,' Alliss went on. 'They didn't have player-power in those days, so there was no question of the two of us informing the captain that we'd like to play together. You were told what to do and you simply got on with it, despite being terrified of coming up against such American legends as Sam Snead.

'Anyway, who would have thought of pairing chalk with cheese? Because that's what we were. Though we've broken bread together, Christy and I have never dined in each other's homes. We've never done anything that might prompt people to suggest, "Oh, they'd make a great partnership; they're like blood brothers." Chalk and bloody cheese. In those days, Christy was what you might describe as a little bit rebellious, a bit of a smoking gun. And I suppose, in a quiet English way, I could have been considered a sort of wayward catapult. Anyway, fate threw us together and I know I always did my very, very best for Christy and, God knows, he did his very best for me.

'I just had the most amazing confidence in him. Neither of us were good putters, yet we holed putts when it mattered. We gave

confidence to each other to the extent that we became a very solid partnership. All the while, a wonderful golfing friendship developed over the years. And I love Mary [Christy's wife] to death. I've always thought of her as a great lady.' In successive Ryder Cups from 1959 to 1969, after which Alliss retired from tournament golf, they played twelve matches together, winning five, losing six and halving one. Other notable partnerships from this side of the Atlantic were Nick Faldo and Ian Woosnam (played ten, won five, lost three, halved two), and Bernard Gallacher and Brian Barnes (played ten, won five, lost four, halved one).

But in terms of matches played, Alliss and O'Connor reigned supreme, until the so-called Spanish Armada of Seve Ballesteros and Jose-Maria Olazabal was launched at Muirfield Village in 1987. Their record, which is unlikely to be beaten, is played fifteen, won eleven, lost two, halved two.

Meanwhile, it should be noted that the Anglo-Irish pair started by playing thirty-six-hole matches in 1959 before eighteen holes became the norm at Royal Lytham two years later, by which stage O'Connor was acknowledged as being at the forefront of European golf. 'I would have been among those who considered Christy to be in the genius class as a striker of the ball, despite relaxing his right-hand fingers at the top of the backswing,' said Alliss. 'He had all the shots except one – the putt. He won numerous tournaments with a flicky putting stroke. God knows how many more he would have won had he the putting skills of even a modest player of today. Anyway, I had been doing some good things myself when the Americans recognized what a wonderful player Christy was. So we were respected and feared for a variety of reasons.

'Dave Marr [1965 USPGA champion] once told me that the Americans all wanted to get at me first, because they thought I was a toffee-nosed if quite an elegant player. A bit snobby, having served my apprenticeship in Ryder Cups going back to 1953 at Wentworth, while my father [Percy] was in the winning team at Southport and Ainsdale, twenty years previously. And, of course, Christy and I were both part of the wonderful 1957 victory at Lindrick.'

Which was their stronger discipline? 'It didn't matter to us whether it was foursomes or fourballs, though I suspect we were better at foursomes,' Alliss replied. 'Better than the record books would suggest. I know I concentrated more on foursomes. You know the thing: if it was my tee-shot I had to get Christy on the fairway, or if it was an approach-iron I had to get him on the green. And I gave similar care to putting. I concentrated on getting him closer than four feet from the hole, if I could.'

He went on: 'Outside of the Ryder Cup, possibly in the Joy Cup [against the Continental professionals], or in matches against the Walker Cup amateurs, I remember partnering John Panton. He and I were also very different people. And John was a very good putter who never seemed to miss a fairway, which made him a comforting partner. But we never quite hit it off like Christy and myself. I remember one particular occasion when we were about 235 yards from the green and Christy was faced with a downhill lie into a left-to-right wind, with out of bounds on the right. And I heard him telling his caddie that he'd take the driver. I have to admit I was terrified by the idea, but as players it wasn't in our nature to have conversations about such matters.

'We were two up with three to play and our opponents were in trouble. And I wanted to say that the driver was a little bit ambitious, but all that came out was a stammered "I-I-I . . ." Then Christy said casually, "I'll just nick it . . ." This prompted a sharp intake of breath from me, which must have sounded like a punctured bellows. Next thing I knew it was going like a bullet for the green, where it landed, naturally. And we won with ease.'

He continued, 'I especially remember Royal Birkdale in 1965, where Christy and I won two games out of four. We played some terrific golf in the foursomes on the opening afternoon [they reached the turn in 31, yet were only one up] when beating Billy Casper and Gene Littler. But the following morning we got a terrible hammering by 6 and 4 in the fourballs against Arnold [Palmer] and Dave [Marr]. That was a very unusual occurrence for us and, by way of proving it, we went on to beat the same pair on the eighteenth in the afternoon. I tell you, over the years O'Connor and me had the ability to surprise the best that America could throw at us.'

As with all matters of team selection, their partnership was not thought of as sacrosanct. But the renowned, mellifluous tones acquired a perceptible edge as Alliss recalled how skipper John Fallon had considered it appropriate to split them at East Lake in 1963. That was when Alliss played with compatriot Bernard Hunt and O'Connor partnered Neil Coles. 'They soon put us back together again,' he said with obvious satisfaction. 'Our last match was in the opening foursomes at Birkdale in 1969, when we halved with Casper and Frank Beard. That was when I decided to retire at the ripe old age of thirty-nine.

'Later on, it became obvious that Seve and Ollie were going to beat our record of appearances together, and we couldn't have bowed to a more wonderful pair. The interesting thing to me was that Ollie was the strong man in that partnership, which was not generally recognized. While Seve produced the flamboyance, Ollie was the anchor. And together they wrought unbelievable magic. Absolutely majestic.

'Nor does it surprise me that Bernhard Langer has had the most partners in Ryder Cup history. [The German's twelve partners were Manuel Pinero, Faldo, Jose Maria Canizares, Sandy Lyle, Ken Brown, Ronan Rafferty, Mark James, Colin Montgomerie, Woosnam, Barry Lane, Per-Ulrik Johansson and David Gilford.] Apart from having the ability to keep the ball in play, there was always a wonderful calmness about him and you knew instinctively he was doing his very best. That's how it was with Christy and me. In fact, the day I discovered Christy O'Connor as a partner was one of the happiest of my golfing life.'

Meanwhile, by way of explaining the skills that Alliss admired so much, the man himself claimed that he never hit a practice shot without a specific target to aim at or a clear idea as to what type of shot he wanted to execute. And it was always that way, from the time when, as a youngster at Galway GC, he would stand some distance back from a tree with a five iron in his hand and proceed to hit balls around the left side of it, then the right and then over it.

As a great devotee of practice, did O'Connor believe that Ben Hogan could have found something special in the dirt. A secret? 'I don't think so,' he replied, when I spoke with him on the occasion of his eightieth birthday, 'but when I played with him in the Carling Caledonian Tournament I saw a man who had mastered the art of hitting a golf ball better than anybody else, in my experience. Everything was fired at the stick. I tried to copy the way he controlled the ball and I nearly got it. Then it would go again.'

He went on, 'I have always loved the game; being out there with nature in the fresh air; getting a little exercise. The roar of the crowd is gone and, believe me, it was magnificent. Now my enjoyment is in playing the odd game with friends and having a laugh. And even after all these years, I'll still be looking for something different.'

In the porch of O'Connor's house in the Clontarf suburb of Dublin there's a black and white photograph from the 1985 Irish Open at Royal Dublin, in which Ballesteros, Langer and Lee Trevino are watching Himself driving off. As I gazed at it admiringly, the voice over my shoulder said softly, 'That position: that's as good as I could do. See how the right shoulder is completely through the shot.'

And one could imagine his inner glow at re-living the special feel of a perfectly executed golf shot.

Dunhill delight on the double

Wild, chilling winds whipping in from the North Sea carried the threat of seriously challenging conditions on the Old Course for the Alfred Dunhill Cup. Yet the weather couldn't be blamed for a decidedly sombre mood as the teams prepared for battle in mid-October of millennium year. As far as the local *cognoscenti* were concerned, the corpse of an event which held a special place in Irish hearts had already been laid out: only the obsequies remained.

Suspicions deepened with the staging of a firework display on the Saturday evening and, sure enough, hardly had the cheers for a Spanish victory died down than it was announced that this much-loved team tournament was being replaced by a Pebble Beach-style celebrity pro-am to be played over the Old Course, Carnoustie, and the new high-profile Kingsbarns links, situated about two miles from the Auld Grey Toon.

Des Smyth, a delighted replacement for Darren Clarke, who was then the world's eleventh ranked player, was honoured with the captaincy of the 2000 Irish side by way of marking his return to action after an absence of twelve years. In joining colleagues Padraig Harrington and Paul McGinley, it was Smyth's first time to play the Old Course since the Open Championship of 1990. 'Obviously I've got some wonderful memories of this place, especially our win here in 1988,' he said on the eve of battle.

The Dunhill Cup became a wonderful adventure for a select group of Irish golfers, right from April 1985 when the qualifying stage of the inaugural event was held at the Italian resort of Albarella, near Venice. That was where the trio of Smyth, Eamonn Darcy and Ronan Rafferty qualified for the tournament proper, six months later, along with Wales and France. It was also a memorable occasion for me, in that having travelled to Italy to cover the qualifying for *The Irish Times*, I rounded off the week by managing to convince Darcy to part with a rather fetching Dunhill sweater in exchange for a silk tie. Few items of apparel have ever felt so good.

Three years later, after undistinguished Irish performances in the intervening events, Darcy and I got together at St Andrews on 12 October 1988, the final practice day before the fourth staging of the Dunhill Cup. And it has to be said that local bookmakers didn't share the confidence of the Irish skipper. 'I believe we are strong enough to think realistically about going all the way and winning this,' said Darcy. Yet himself, Smyth and Rafferty were still on offer at odds of 12/1, some way adrift of 5/2 favourites Spain, who were represented by the Ryder Cup trio of Seve Ballesteros, Jose-Rivero and Jose-Maria Olazabal. Indeed, Ballesteros was also the reigning Open champion at the time.

As Smyth prepared for the 2000 staging, he could take a more detached view of the events of 1988. 'What memories!' he enthused. 'It remains the most exciting event of my golfing life – by miles. We were rank outsiders and we had to beat all the top teams to secure the trophy. It was as if we were destined to triumph against all the odds.' It was an occasion when Darcy beat the reigning US Open champion, Curtis Strange, and when Rafferty crushed former USPGA and US Open champion David Graham. But most memorably it was when Smyth gained an extraordinary semi-final win over Nick Faldo before going on to an equally dramatic victory over Rodger Davis in the final.

When it was all over, at the end of a long day's journey into glorious night, a grateful nation toasted Ireland's greatest team victory in golf since Harry Bradshaw and Christy O'Connor had captured the Canada Cup in Mexico City in 1958. Yet, typically, when I spoke with him in the wake of the event, the Brad generously suggested that such comparisons only diluted the achievement of the Dunhill trio. 'The pressure at St Andrews was far greater, for two important reasons,' he said. 'The three Irish boys stood man to man against the finest players in the world and they were constantly aware of what they had to do. Christy and myself had no such pressure.

'There were no leaderboards on the course in Mexico City and, being four rounds of strokeplay, we kept plugging away without really knowing how the opposition were doing. Indeed, I didn't really know we had the title within our grasp until Dai Rees told me so on the long seventeenth – our seventy-first hole. These boys stood up to the pressure like heroes. And what impressed me most was the quality of their putting. You know it was almost as good as mine – at my best!' While those last few words were uttered with a mischievous grin, praise never came higher.

When I reflected with Smyth on those heady days it struck me how little everything had changed for him, even with the benefit of hindsight. He had sportingly insisted at the time that Faldo was correct in refusing to finish their match in the fog of the Saturday evening and he retained that view. He also stuck to his view that it was only when an Irish victory was secure, and he saw me walking towards the great old clubhouse with tears streaming down my face, that he realized the significance of what the three of them had done.

'If Nick was just out there for himself he probably would have played the shot, but he was the English captain, with two other players to think about,' said Smyth. 'He did the right thing in refusing to finish the eighteenth until the Sunday morning, though it made for a fairly tense wait for me.'

After beating Canada by 2–1 in the opening round, Ireland went on to overcome the mighty Americans by 2½ to ½ on the Friday. Rafferty beat Mark McCumber 71–72 in the top match, Smyth halved with Chip Beck on 71–71 and Darcy secured a wonderful victory over Strange by 66–68. 'It normally takes the whole of Europe to beat the Americans,' joked the captain, who had played a key role in the historic Ryder Cup triumph at Muirfield Village, Ohio, a year previously.

So it was that Ireland met the holders, England, in Saturday's semi-finals. In the other clash, Greg Norman led by example when his 67 against a 69 from Ballesteros pointed Australia towards a 2–1 win over Spain. But, ominously, play had been delayed for three hours as the Old Course became shrouded in a Scottish haar – a dense fog sweeping off the North Sea. Early concerns proved to be well founded when, as late starters, Ireland's victory surge against England came to a controversial halt late in the day. Smyth had slotted a superb putt for a par on the seventeenth to draw a stroke clear of Faldo, but after the Drogheda man had played his approach shot to about 18 yards behind the flag at the last, Faldo refused to hit his pitch of 78 yards. 'Visibility was down to 30 or 40 yards when we crossed the Swilcan Bridge and with two other guys to consider [Barry Lane and Mark James] I couldn't risk the shot,' explained Faldo.

During a subsequent delay of thirty minutes, the Englishman remained steadfast in his refusal to continue, with the result that play was abandoned for the day. It meant an official measurement of Smyth's ball on the eighteenth green, where a marker would be left overnight: it was 54 feet 4½ inches above the hole, which was located just beyond the Valley of Sin. There were those who took the view that Faldo was guilty of gamesmanship. Indeed, students in the university building directly behind the eighteenth green hung banners from the windows taunting the Englishman with such messages as 'Can you see this, Nick?' Others were of the opinion that Smyth had acted impetuously by playing his wedge-shot through the fog. Either way, he had to endure an anxious night. 'Though I went to bed early, I kept my mind off things by watching television until my eyelids eventually began to close,' he recalled.

Play resumed at eighty thirty on a Sunday morning that had dawned chilly and damp. And there was a strange stillness, a sense of unreality, about an occasion in which Smyth found himself practising 20-yard putts on the putting green while Faldo worked on sandwedge pitches. After the call to action, Faldo proceeded to hit his approach to a birdie position, seven feet below the pin. Soon both players were on the green, but, as Smyth walked towards his ball, he suddenly stepped away. 'I became extremely nervous and had to settle myself,' he said. Finally composed, he stroked the ball down the damp, sloping green to send it within three feet of the target. Faldo, meanwhile, couldn't agree with his caddie, Andy Prodger, about the line to the hole. While the player thought it was right-half, the caddie was convinced it was right lip. The caddie was correct, though Faldo may have pulled it slightly. Either way, the ball missed the hole on the low side and Smyth then stroked his three-footer home for the match. Ireland were through to the final against Australia.

As if destined to be a hero, Smyth was again at the centre of things when the decider drew to a climax. Rafferty always seemed to have the measure of Graham while, by his own admission, Darcy caught Norman on a hot day, with the Shark producing a sparkling 63 to win by eight shots. Two strokes behind Davis with three holes to play, Smyth closed the gap by sinking a 15-foot birdie putt on the sixteenth. He then hit his best drive of the day to leave the ball a yard in from the left-edge of the fairway on the treacherous seventeenth.

Recalling those critical moments, he said, 'Rodger had been hitting low cuts all day and, with the wind left to right at the seventeenth, it was always going to be a tricky drive for him.' In the event, Davis cut his drive disastrously into the hotel grounds – out of bounds. Smyth, meanwhile, played the hole beautifully, sticking to his game plan of hitting a three-iron second shot to the left of the Road Hole Bunker, from where he got down in two putts for an exemplary par. The hapless Davis made seven.

Now, almost miraculously, two strokes clear playing the last hole for the second time that day, Smyth wedged to eight feet and sank the putt for a closing birdie and a round of 71. Though Davis also birdied the hole, it was too late to matter. As in so many Open Championships down the years, the fearsome seventeenth had been decisive. After that, it became a matter of containing a desperate urge to celebrate before Rafferty had delivered the winning point.

'Suddenly I realized it was all down to me, so I took a couple of deep breaths on the seventeenth tee,' said the babe of the trio. As things turned out, he handled one of golf's most fearsome challenges like a veteran, attacking the green from the left as Smyth had done, though his three iron finished short of the menacing bunker. From there, Rafferty pitched strongly to 35 feet and then sank the putt for a par to Graham's bogey. All of which made his play of the eighteenth a glorious victory march.

It had been a wonderful team effort under a captain with a novel approach to leadership. In outlining strategy to his colleagues, Darcy adopted a suitably serious tone before instructing them, 'Now listen to me . . . and go off and do your own thing.'

'Looking back on my career, I consider myself to have been a really good tournament player, but I was never a superstar,' said Smyth with typical modesty. 'So it is really special to be able to reflect on wins over Nick Price, in the final of the 1979 European Matchplay Championship, Ian Woosnam, in the Epson Grand Prix, and Jose-Maria Olazabal and Faldo in the Dunhill Cup.' He went on, 'As the only Irish-based member of the team at that time, however, there was a price to be paid. I was the one who got caught up in all the receptions and functions for almost an entire year after our win. But it was worth it for the wonderful boost it gave Irish golf. Players like Darren Clarke, Padraig Harrington and Paul McGinley were just beginning to make their way in the game at that time and I like to think that what we did in 1988 may have sharpened their appetite for success.'

Despite his protests, Smyth embraced the celebrations with enthusiasm. Still, he got quite a surprise on dropping down to his club, Laytown and Bettystown, for a quiet drink after returning home from Edinburgh within hours of the final. Noeline Quirke, a member of the club's victorious Irish Senior Cup team, was in a position, as an employee of Aer Lingus, to inform her L and B colleagues of his travel plans. Suffice it to say that the anticipated drink proved to be anything but quiet. And this was only the start of what became a decidedly protracted process at a time of deep depression in the Irish psyche, not least because of a desperate economic climate, which led to the Tallaght Strategy in 1987. So, in terms of national morale, the Dunhill Cup success was timed to perfection.

In this context, it was interesting to note the splendid mileage Charlie McCreevy, in his capacity as Minister for Finance, got from his 2002 tax-concession scheme for professional sports-people who remained faithful residents of the auld sod and not a mention of the colleague who first floated the notion a full fourteen years previously.

Back when the sports portfolio merited only a junior ministry, the incumbent, Frank Fahey, latched onto the Dunhill Cup triumph in the best Fianna Fail tradition of shamelessly leaping on bandwagons. Indeed, in the wake of St Andrews, he proposed that Ireland's leading professional golfers should be exempted from tax, as honorary ambassadors for the country. The move created quite a stir, especially since Smyth, as the only Irish-based member of the winning trio, paid considerably more of his $100,000 prize in tax than Darcy and Rafferty, who were both English-based. There was even talk about Smyth and Christy O'Connor Jnr becoming tax exiles.

Enter Minister Fahey. After much initial ballyhoo, however, the proposed scheme died a death, not least because of the country's horrific unemployment figures at that time. Minister

McCreevy was, of course, a much shrewder political animal than Fahey, who lost his seat at the next general election, and thoughts of emigrating were soon discarded by Smyth and O'Connor Jnr.

Conquering Clark

At a time when David Feherty happened to be drawn with both of them in a British tournament, Howard Clark was given to notoriously black moods and Colin Montgomerie was often rather cruelly derided for his matronly manner. Later, on being asked how he had enjoyed the experience, the ever-mischievous Feherty engaged in humorous hyperbole when jokingly replying, 'How would you enjoy spending an afternoon with Charles Manson and Dame Edna Everage?' In fact, Feherty said considerably worse things about Montgomerie, which would have given the Scot added pleasure in a second-round victory over him in the 1991 Dunhill Cup. But there had been no revenge for Clark in a pulsating climax the previous year, when Ireland captured the trophy for a second time.

Unlike the events of 1988, there was no talk of money after this latest Irish success, which was perhaps a measure of the trio's standing in the professional game. Where Darcy, Smyth and Rafferty had gained the most unlikely of victories, Rafferty was the only survivor two years later, when he joined Philip Walton under the captaincy of Feherty. 'I hit that three iron to the extent of my ability,' said Feherty of the shot which effectively sealed victory. 'From my position on the fairway, which was just about perfect, I had no option other than to go for the flag.'

He was talking about a shot of 199 yards into a right-to-left wind on the fateful seventeenth hole of the Old Course. The moment was perfect in every detail. Feherty's shot of a lifetime set up a winning par in a sudden-death play-off with Clark, which had lasted three holes as shadows lengthened across the Home of Golf. Those of us who had the good fortune of being there in 1988 wondered if the magic could be the same the second time around. In the event, a critical difference was that the Irish were highly respected, even feared, as the number three seeds on this occasion, though the quality of Feherty's victory compared with anything which had gone before.

Pressure of rare intensity bore down on the then thirty-two-year-old from Bangor, as he came to the seventeenth in the afternoon phase of the thirty-six-hole final against England. The sides had gone to lunch level at one and a half points each, after Walton had halved with Mark James in the top match, Rafferty had beaten Richard Boxall at number two and Feherty had lost to Clark in the anchor position. Now, with the end in sight, Walton had lost to James in their afternoon match and Rafferty had again beaten Boxall, while Feherty was a stroke ahead of Clark with two holes to play.

Just when he seemed likely to carry that lead down the last, a nasty three-footer from Feherty hit the lip of the seventeenth hole and stayed out. Then Clark suffered the pain of a missed six-footer on the eighteenth, with the result that they both went into sudden death. The decisive strokes for Feherty were that memorable three-iron approach, followed by two putts from 18 feet behind the hole for an exemplary par. And when it was all over, his opponent said with typical Yorkshire bluntness, 'Anyone who enjoys this must be a masochist. I am desperately disappointed, especially after coming from behind.'

There were moments when one wondered which player had won, especially as Feherty remarked with undisguised emotion, 'I never want to do this again. It is the enigma of golf that it's going to hurt if you're to do well.' As time elapsed, however, and the nerve-ends began to return to normality, one suspected that the sense of panic had been replaced by feelings of profound satisfaction. Meanwhile, there was an appealing synergy in the fact that Rafferty (in his 1988 win over Graham), Smyth (in beating Davis in 1988) and Feherty (in his play-off triumph over Clark) all used three irons for their approach shots to the fateful seventeenth. In the 1984 Open on the Old Course, the general view was that Tom Watson destroyed whatever chance he had of outscoring Ballesteros for the title by hitting a two iron through the back of the seventeenth, where he should have used one club less.

It was also ironic that Rafferty should have performed so well, given that on the eve of the tournament he had questioned whether it was right for him to be competing in it at that time. 'I would like to emphasize that I'm not indifferent about playing for my country,' he said. 'Indeed, I can still vividly recall the special feeling I had coming up the eighteenth two years ago when I knew I had played my part in capturing the trophy for Ireland. But I have got to consider my career and that means playing in the events that suit me, and the Dunhill Cup has come at a time when I am attempting to get into the top three in the Order of Merit so as to strengthen my chances of playing in the US Open and the PGA Championship next year. When I suggested I might miss out on the Dunhill, people began to make a big thing of it. But there was no mention of the fact that Spain have a team here without Seve Ballesteros and Jose-Maria Olazabal.' He concluded, 'One thing is certain: I won't allow this situation to happen again.' In the event, Rafferty responded admirably to the call to arms, starting with the offer of playing at number one against Korea in the opening round. Then, with rounds of 70, 71, 68, 71 and 71, he gained the distinction of breaking par in each of his matches, including victories morning and afternoon over Richard Boxall in the final against England.

As for the tournament's swansong: there was an inescapable feeling that after sixteen stagings from its launch in 1985, a hugely popular event had run its course. This was brought home forcibly by the appearance in 2000 of Larry Mize as a team-mate for John Daly and Tom Lehman in the American line-up, reflecting a marked downturn in their interest since the appearance of Tiger Woods only two years previously. For Ireland, it was a bitterly disappointing finale to be no better than runners-up to South Africa in their group, given that they produced the best cumulative scoring of the qualifying stage. From their nine matches, the trio of Smyth, McGinley and Harrington were a total of 30 under par, compared with 26 under from Spain, 22 from South Africa, 17 from Wales and 16 from the fourth semi-finalist, Argentina. Still, a 3–0 win over France in their final match of the group was sufficient only for runner-up position and cheques for £15,000 each, a far cry from the rewards of 1988 and 1990.

Ireland's Dunhill performances year by year were:

1985: Des Smyth, David Feherty and Christy O'Connor Jnr lost 2–1 to England, first round.

1986: Smyth, Ronan Rafferty and Feherty lost 3–0 to Scotland, second round.

1987: Smyth, Rafferty and Eamonn Darcy lost 2–1 to Scotland, second round.

1988: Darcy, Smyth and Rafferty won.

1989: O'Connor Jnr, Rafferty and Philip Walton lost 2–1 to US, semi-finals, and 2–1 to England in third/fourth place play-off.

1990: Feherty, Walton and Rafferty won.

1991: Darcy, Feherty and Rafferty lost 3–0 to Scotland, second round.

1992: O'Connor Jnr, Walton and Rafferty second to US in group.

1993: Feherty, Rafferty and Paul McGinley won group, lost 3–0 to England in semi-finals.

1994: Walton, McGinley and Darren Clarke second to US in group.

1995: Walton, Clarke and Rafferty won group, lost 2–1 to Scotland in semi-finals.

1996: Clarke, McGinley and Padraig Harrington second to South Africa in group.

1997: Clarke, McGinley and Harrington third to South Africa in group.

1998: Clarke, McGinley and Harrington third to Spain in group.

1999: Clarke, McGinley and Harrington second to Spain in group.

2000: Smyth, McGinley and Harrington second to South Africa in group.

Individual records (appearances, matches, won, lost, halved):
R. Rafferty: 9, 30, 15, 14, 1
P. McGinley: 7, 22, 12, 10, 0
D. Clarke: 6, 19, 12, 7, 0
D. Smyth: 5, 12, 8, 3, 1
D. Feherty: 5, 14, 8, 6, 0
P. Walton: 5, 19, 12, 6, 1
P. Harrington: 5, 15, 9, 6, 0
E. Darcy: 3, 8, 5, 3, 0
C. O'Connor Jnr: 3, 8, 5, 3, 0
Highest success rate: Smyth: 71 per cent
Leading stroke average: Smyth: 70.08

Confronted by the Fifth Amendment

In his dealings with the media, Padraig Harrington is renowned as a particularly helpful sportsman, often giving of his time above and beyond the call of duty. By way of explaining this welcome attitude, he has said, 'I want the outcome to be good, like everything else I do.'

By comparison, Ronan Rafferty could be characterized as someone for whom the media seemed generally to be an unwelcome intrusion. And his attitude was shaped in no small measure by events at St Andrews in June 1981, only four months before he turned professional.

Over subsequent years I found myself torn between admiration for the player's marvellous skills and utter exasperation at trying to communicate with him in my capacity as a golf writer. The closest I got to an understanding of his position was, ironically, in the wake of an unscheduled departure from the US Open at Hazeltine in 1991, which generated a torrent of unwanted publicity for the player.

This was the occasion when, in a second successive appearance in the blue riband of American golf, Rafferty carded an opening round of 79 and then departed the scene midway through a second round in which he had Corey Pavin and Craig Parry as playing partners. You can imagine the scene in the media centre when his action came to light and he was nowhere to be found.

The only word we had was from his playing partners, who suggested that he had told them at the turn that he was going to the toilet. As a wag remarked, 'He forgot to explain that the toilet was in a 747 bound for London.' I remember when Pavin was asked what he thought of Rafferty's behaviour, he replied, 'No guys. I'm pleading the Fifth [Amendment] on this one.'

The European Tour were horrified by the withdrawal at a time when they were desperately anxious to get more players into the US Open. In that particular year, for instance, there were only seven European competitors – the regular 'big five' of Nick Faldo, Seve Ballesteros, Sandy Lyle, Bernhard Langer and Ian Woosnam, along with Jose-Maria Olazabal and Rafferty. And the Tour's anger was later expressed in a fine of £5,000.

In the absence of any explanation from Rafferty it remained a very topical issue throughout that summer. Which led *The Irish Times* to send me to the Scandinavian Masters in Stockholm in early August, when an interview was arranged. It turned out to be the most satisfactory interview I had with the player during a working relationship spanning almost twenty years.

Regarding the US Open, he admitted that he had neither expected nor received much sympathy from fellow professionals, who had grown largely to view him as a remote, enigmatic figure. He said, 'It has seemed to be very easy to be critical after the event and to come up with all sorts of ideas as to what I should have done. The thing that people don't seem to understand is that I would not deliberately have done something silly – something that was going to harm my career.'

He went on to claim, 'At the time when I asked the match referee [Ed Gowan of the USGA] what the procedure was, he said [and according to Rafferty this was verified by Tony Gray, the European Tour's Director of External Affairs, who was at Hazeltine], "When you get back, write them [USGA] a letter." And I thought, "great". So, as I understand it, when the tournament was over I could write them a letter and nobody would bother further about the matter. The truth is I was very low at that time. It's not often that I don't want to go out and play, and that was one of the times when I didn't want to play.

'I know now I should never have done it. My respect for golf and for golfing authority is very high. This is borne out by the fact that I have never been in trouble with the European Tour over a period of eleven years. My only justification for my actions was that I understood the referee to have given me a way by which I could leave quietly. At the time I didn't feel I was being discourteous, but I realize now that I was. I don't think it is something I would do again. Since then I've spoken to some members of the European Tour committee about the matter and I've had some of the strangest reactions. One of the guys said to me, "Why didn't you just say you were injured. That's what I always do." '

So, did he consider himself to have been a victim of his own honesty? 'No,' he replied. 'Whatever else, I wasn't going to lie about the matter. My mistake was that I should have said something to the USGA at the time, but for a variety of reasons it never occurred to me. I had a lot of things going on.' His final words on the matter were, 'I fully accept now that, as a professional golfer, there was no justification for my behaviour. I should have known my duty, but it is an unfortunate fact of life that you must make mistakes to fully understand these things.'

It was suggested at the time that had a player with a more popular image, a player such as Lyle, Woosnam or Sam Torrance, experienced similar difficulties, the press and public might have been far more sympathetic. Rafferty, on the other hand, remained highly suspicious of the media and, as a consequence, his public image had suffered.

He admitted to me that this problem had its roots in an incident when he was on Ireland's six-member team competing in the European Amateur Championship at St Andrews ten years previously. That was when Joe Carr, the non-playing captain, found it necessary to discipline him for an alleged breach of curfew, while there was also Rafferty's insistence on playing the big (American) ball in foursomes with Arthur Pierse, at a time when both the big and small balls were optional under R and A rules. More than twenty years later, Carr, who was not known to bear grudges, steadfastly refused to forgive Rafferty whom he accused of ruining the team's winning prospects. Carr was tempted to send him home, but didn't do so because he knew it would destroy the player's prospect of appearing in the Walker Cup.

'When the matter was reported, nobody bothered to get my side of the story,' Rafferty told me in Sweden. 'And that has applied in many other matters since then.' When I pointed out to him that, with an ex-directory telephone number, he was not the most accessible of people, he replied, 'There are always ways of finding out the truth if somebody is prepared to make the effort. I always make myself available during golf tournaments.'

Little more than a year after he had uttered those words, Rafferty finally exhausted my patience. It happened during the World Cup at La Moraleja in Madrid, where he represented Ireland in partnership with Christy O'Connor Jnr. In my report for *The Irish Times* on the Sunday evening, I noted that the pair, tied seventeenth, had recorded Ireland's worst performance in the event since 1971. I then wrote, 'Not that Rafferty had time to ponder such matters insofar as he made one of his now familiar hasty exits from the scene.'

My report went on, 'To my request for a brief interview immediately after he had signed his card for a 73 for a four-over-par total of 292, he replied he could give me only a minute which, in effect, became no more than ten seconds. I cannot remember ever being treated like that by an Irish sportsman in a working situation. When I informed O'Connor that his partner had refused to speak to me, I was told, "I would be angry if he had. Why should he talk to you when he wouldn't talk to me?" Incidentally, Rafferty's comments to me were, "Putted very badly; next tournament in Japan."'

To his credit, it should be noted that Rafferty attempted to repair any existing damage with the USGA by travelling to America earlier in 1992 to qualify for the US Open. Which he did, only to miss the cut at Pebble Beach by two strokes, after a second-round 78.

As for his attitude towards the scribes at St Andrews: it always struck me as odd that I received the same treatment from him as my colleagues, despite the fact that I wasn't even there. I had travelled on that particular week to Troia in Portugal to cover the conflicting European Women's Team Championship, in which Ireland were defending the title.

● ● ● ● ● ● ● ● ●

CHAPTER 6

Golden Girls and Golden Memories

'An experience of ladies' golf running into close on twenty years has convinced me that the ladies are much keener on everything connected with the game than are the men.'

LEADING IRISH GOLF WRITER J. P. ROONEY, 1931

In the wake of a marvellous Irish triumph at Cruden Bay in 1980, Violet Hulton was moved to write to Maureen Madill, a member of the successful team. The letter, from her home near Trowbridge, Wiltshire, on 14 September, indicated a strong and remarkably steady hand for a writer at the advanced age of ninety-seven years. It read: 'Dear Miss Madill. Just a line to say I am delighted at Ireland winning the Home Internationals. I send my congratulations to you and all the team. 72 years ago [sic] since Ireland won. I think it was the last time Mrs Ross captained the team and she and I both played in it. With all the best of luck to future triumphs, Yours sincerely.'

Beneath her signature, the writer had in brackets 'née Hezlet'. And the Mrs Ross to whom she referred was none other than her sister, May, arguably the country's greatest ever woman golfer. Two years after writing that letter, the last of the amazing Hezlet sisters died, at ninety-nine.

On 6 May 1907, the *Belfast Newsletter* carried the headline 'Irish Ladies Secure Triple Crown at Newcastle'. This was the occasion to which Violet Hezlet referred in her letter and it provided a truly memorable finale to a week in which May Hezlet had made the climactic stage of the British Women's Championship a family affair, by beating her other sister, Florence, 2 and 1 in the final at Royal Co Down. The Irish team, whose triple crown achievement was eventually equalled by their male counterparts eighty years later at Lahinch, was: Florence Walker Leigh (Foxrock), May Hezlet (Portrush), J. Magill (Co Down), M. E. Stuart (Portrush), Florence Hezlet (Portrush), Mrs Durlacher (Romford) and Violet Hezlet (Portrush).

The image of May Hezlet as an emancipated woman golfer long before her time is conveyed in her book *Ladies' Golf*, published by Hutchinson in 1904. She wrote, 'Nothing looks more untidy or unsuitable for games than a long skirt – the hem gets drabbled in mud. In wet weather, the long skirt hampers every movement; it gets soaked with the moisture off the grass and in consequence becomes a considerable weight. A short skirt – really short, not simply a couple of inches off the ground – looks infinitely nicer and more workmanlike, and makes an inestimable difference in comfort.' It was a time when weights were sewn into the hem in winter and wire was threaded into it in summer to keep the skirt from being blown about in the wind.

Later, a piece of elastic, known as a 'Miss Higgins', kept around the waist and pulled down around the knees when playing a shot, helped prevent the skirt from being caught up in the swing. Corsets and combinations of leg-of-mutton sleeves and starched stiff collars further impeded the players' freedom to swing. Miss Hezlet's plea for shorter skirts was entirely understandable, given the prevailing fashion of heavy tweed or serge clothing and thick-soled boots with studs or nails, which must have been decidedly uncomfortable and tiring on fine days. In wet, windy weather they would have been sheer torture.

Born in 1882 in Gibraltar, where her father served with the Royal Artillery, 'Miss May', as she was known to her family, was reared near Portrush where she began golf at the tender age of nine. By the time she was eleven, she had won her first com-petition, playing with a cleek, mashie and putter. From then on her progress was dramatic, not least because of her intense love of the game. By her estimation, golf was an antidote to brooding, depression and nervous sensibility – a path to self-reliance and serenity.

In developing splendid skills she was helped greatly by the environment created by three golfing sisters and a golfing mother. Indeed, all five played together in a challenge match in April 1901 against a selected side from the other women members of Portrush, including the illustrious Rhona Adair. This was the lavishly gifted contemporary from Cookstown, Co Tyrone, who learned her golf during family holidays at Portrush, where her father was captain in 1895 and where, aged eleven, she won a bag of clubs in a mixed foursomes tournament. The outcome was a win for the Hezlets by a margin of 4½ to ½, the whitewash being averted by a half from a certain Miss Knox against Mrs Hezlet.

A similar match took place in 1907 when May was at the peak of her powers. On that occasion T. H. Millar, a male vice-president of the LGU, believed the Hezlet sisters had enjoyed so much success that it was 'time to put them in their place'. So, he brought over three other men from Britain to challenge the sisters at Portrush. In what proved to be an ill-conceived venture for the men, May thrashed the said Millar by 10 and 8, and later recalled that he had insisted they should continue playing until he had won at least one hole. Which he failed to do. In fact, he was 16 down after sixteen and, though he succeeded in halving the remaining two holes, we can assume this had more to do with Miss Hezlet's generosity than his own resurgent skills. The other three men were also beaten, albeit by less disastrous, but nonetheless decisive, margins.

After being runner-up in the Irish Ladies' Close Championship at Malone as a fifteen-year-old in 1898, May achieved one of the high points of her career. At sixteen, she beat Miss Adair by 5 and 4 to capture the 1899 Irish title at Newcastle. And the following week, having just celebrated her seventeenth birthday, she captured the British Championship, which meant that both trophies resided at her home club, Portrush. In fact, when May was presented with the winner's medal, her mother, the then Lady

President of Portrush, accepted the trophy on behalf of the club. Shortly afterwards, the men's council at Portrush commissioned the artist Harry Douglas to paint a portrait of the young champion with her trophies, which hangs to this day in the Royal Portrush Ladies Club.

For her part, Miss Adair provoked a decidedly sexist comment from Old Tom Morris at St Andrews later that year. 'I'll no' be licked by a lassie,' vowed the seventy-seven-year-old midway through a thirty-six-hole challenge match against Rhona, whom he led by the narrow margin of one hole. Even back then, male golfers quaked at the possibility of being outscored by a woman and the notion of a 'lassie' actually out-driving them was too grave to even contemplate. Yet we're told that Old Tom had to withstand a spirited rally before winning the match on the final green.

In 1900, the focus of the women's game was Westward Ho! GC in south-west England, where the British Championship had its eighth staging and the precocious May was defending the title. On this occasion, victory went to Miss Adair, who gained revenge for Newcastle. By this stage, the pair had become known as the Golden Girls of Irish golf, for the manner in which they had launched the twentieth century. And as an Irish bonus at Westward Ho!, the defeated finalist was Miss Leigh from Foxrock.

May Hezlet won further Irish Close titles in 1904, 1905, 1906 and 1908, and was British champion in 1899, 1902 and 1907. Meanwhile, Miss Adair won the British title in 1900 and 1903, and captured four successive Irish Close titles from 1900 to 1903. And while the Golden Girls were leaving their mark, Miss Hezlet became noted for her stamina, which she developed through regular twenty-four-mile round trips on a bicycle from her home to her golfing activities at Portrush. Though lacking the prodigious length of Miss Adair, she had a classic swing which delivered splendid accuracy tee to green. In fact, she was widely acknowledged as 'the most finished golfer, man or woman, of her day'. This was quite an accolade at a time when the men's amateur game in these parts was dominated by such luminaries as John Ball and Harold Hilton.

A further distinction came in 1905, when May and Florence

played in a British and Irish side which beat an invited American line-up by 6–1 at Royal Cromer. This is the Norfolk club where Oscar Wilde, who stayed in the area to write *A Woman of No Importance*, played golf with Lord Alfred Douglas in 1892. We're informed that Wilde found Cromer excellent for writing and even better for golf. As it happened, May played Margaret Curtis, whose sister Harriet was also a member of the visiting team. Afterwards, a lengthy discussion between May and Florence Hezlet and the Curtis sisters is said to have prompted the Americans, years later, to donate the Curtis Cup for biennial transatlantic competition. Incidentally, that particular match at Royal Cromer stemmed from a triumphant visit which Miss Adair had made to the US two years previously, when she won no fewer than sixteen trophies.

At the peak of her powers May Hezlet had a domestic handicap of plus seven, and was held in such esteem by the LGU that in 1913 they listed the handicaps of herself and Miss Adair as scratch, for life. All other women players of that time, whatever their achievements, were given scratch handicaps for up to six years at the most. In 1909 she married the Rev A. E. Ross, the Church of Ireland minister at Portrush, and it was as Mrs Ross that she represented Ireland for the last time in the Home Internationals of 1912. Her husband, who was an army chaplain during the First World War, later became Bishop of Tuam, but he died in 1923, leaving May as a forty-one-year-old widow.

She later moved to England where she worked for the Society of the Propagation of the Gospel and, though childless, she also became president of the Mothers' Union. All the while, she kept in touch with happenings at her beloved Portrush. Sadly, all of her trophies and golfing memorabilia were destroyed by a fire in a Belfast warehouse after the Second World War.

Having been captain at Portrush Ladies in 1905, she became its first president in 1922 and held the post until 1951. She was also a life vice-president of the ILGU. For most of her final years May shared Violet's house, before moving to a nursing home in Kent, not far from Deal, the scene of her second British triumph in 1902. Then in her nineties, she told her niece, Rosemary Hoare, how she still remembered a particular putt she holed during that victory.

She died in the winter of 1978, having been the most influential figure in Irish golf through the formative early years of the last century.

A first taste of the Curtis Cup

Mary McKenna had her first experience of the Curtis Cup in June 1968. At nineteen, it seemed the thing to do to travel to the matches which were being staged up the road, as it were, at Royal Co Down. When I interviewed her some years later, she made the remarkably candid admission that she wasn't especially interested in the event, despite the presence in the GB and I team of such great luminaries as Belle Robertson and Vivien Saunders, who was to turn professional the following year. In the event, her visit was limited to the Saturday, probably because she didn't want to take time off work.

She recalled, 'My main reason for being there was to be with my Donabate club-mate, Vivienne Singleton, whom I later beat in the final of the Irish Championship at Lahinch in 1974. She was one of the players picked for flagging and ball-spotting duties, and I remember watching the matches she was "working" on. Though I had been runner-up in the Irish Championship earlier that year, I didn't really know many people in golf at the time. And I certainly knew nothing about the American players. Looking back on it, I suppose it would be nice to say that the sight of those teams, who started the second day on level terms and were battling for one of golf's great trophies, fired my ambition to be part of it all. But it wasn't like that. I was no more than a moderately interested spectator.'

She went on, 'The Curtis Cup didn't even enter my thoughts when I made the Vagliano Trophy team in 1969, after winning the Irish Championship at Ballybunion. I was conscious that there were up to twelve players on the Vagliano team at that stage, whereas only the elite eight from these islands got into the Curtis Cup. But everything was to change in 1970, when I went to Sunningdale's Old Course for the Curtis Cup trials. It was a huge thing for me at that stage of my career. There was a total of fifteen of us there, playing three rounds of three-balls in round robin competition.

'Elaine Bradshaw was also there and I viewed her as the senior Irish challenger for a place in the side, especially since she had beaten me in my first Irish final at Lahinch two years previously and was a member of the 1969 Vagliano team. If only one Irish player was going to be in the team, it had to be Elaine, not me. The selection procedure was that four players qualified automatically from the trials while the other four were picked. If I remember correctly, Ann Irvin missed it through illness and by the Thursday afternoon – in other words with one day to spare – Belle [Robertson] and myself had qualified. She was on 21 points and I was on 19. No matter what combinations won or lost the following day, nobody could catch us.

'All of which came as a total surprise to me. I suppose the fact that I really didn't have any great expectations lessened the pressure. And being my first time on the course meant I had no hang-ups about it. In fact, I had never been to that part of England before: everything was totally new. After being there a little while, however, the significance of it all began to seep in. There was a trip to the States at stake and, as it happened, Dinah Oxley also got one of the automatic places and we went on to form the number one foursomes partnership in the side at Brae Burn, winning on the first day and then being beaten on day two.

'The biggest influence on my golfing career from then on was Belle, right up to the time of our last Curtis Cup appearance in 1986, as members of the team which made history by winning at Prairie Dunes. Because of those trials, going back to Sunningdale always held a great appeal for me. The course seemed to suit my golf and I was fortunate in having further success there in the Sunningdale Foursomes in which I partnered Maureen Madill to three finals, one of which we won in 1984.

'That was a memorable year also for the fact that I went to

Sunningdale after winning the Avia Foursomes, with Belle, the previous week. So, the Avia with Belle and the Sunningdale with Maureen were two special wins with two special people. Meanwhile, on the way to nine successive Curtis Cup appearances, there were times when I had to battle hard to make the side. Which was quite a contrast to the first occasion, when it all seemed to fall into my lap during those trials at Sunningdale. And only a week before my twenty-first birthday.'

Picturing the shot

Several male members of Curragh GC would have empathized with Old Tom Morris and his concern over the possibility of losing to Rhona Adair. It is arguable if this country has produced a player, man or woman, more naturally gifted than Lillian Behan. Among her wealth of talents was an ability to work the ball at will, in either direction. As she explained to me, 'I picture the shot in my head and my hands do the rest.' There was no mechanical adjustment. 'When I discussed this with Christy O'Connor Snr, he told me he did the same thing,' she added with justifiable pride. This was the talent which she brought to Ganton in 1985 when, with Waterford's Evelyn Hearn as her caddie, she shocked the golfing world by capturing the British Women's Matchplay Championship.

By women's standards, Lillian hit the ball prodigious distances, yet we shouldn't have been surprised. The great Glenna Collett Vare recorded a 307-yard drive prior to the 1922 US Women's Amateur. And Babe Zaharias was through the green with a four-iron second shot at a 540-yard hole in the 1947 British Women's at Gullane Number 1.

A very good year

So many wonderful things happened to Claire Dowling (née Hourihane) during the 1986 golfing season that it had to stand apart as her most memorable in the game. Having started with a win in the Hampshire Rose, things seemed to get progressively better for her as the months went by. Twelve years later, she recalled to me, 'I suppose my friends would probably consider the highlight to have been winning the British Strokeplay at Blairgowrie. Certainly it was a significant milestone in my career, but the curious thing is that I don't remember very much about it, other than the fact that the great Jessie Valentine caddied for me.

'Come to think of it, she must have been in her seventies at the time [she was actually seventy-one]. A wonderful woman and such great fun to be with. Maureen Madill introduced me to her in 1982 and, when the British came around four years later, Mary McKenna and I stayed with her. But I couldn't believe it when she offered to pull my bag. And she was so enthusiastic about it that I've no doubt she helped me enormously through the tricky moments that inevitably arise when you're trying to win a championship of that nature. It was really lovely to share the victory with her when I beat Trish Johnson at the first hole of a sudden-death play-off.

'Anyway, strange as it may seem, the winning of a much-coveted British title didn't compare as a golfing thrill with events two months earlier that year, when the British Matchplay was played at West Sussex. It was June and the importance of the championship was heightened by the fact that we were playing for places in the Curtis Cup team to travel to Prairie Dunes, Kansas. And like most of the international players in Britain and Ireland, I very much wanted to be a member of the side, particularly having played in 1984 at Muirfield and in the Vagliano in 1985.

'So I was determined to do well. My prospects of a long run, however, didn't look too bright when I struggled to a first round win at the seventeenth against Claire Duffy. It wasn't a classic; far from it. In fact, I remember she scratched the ball around in the most amazing way, playing out of bushes and bunkers, and pressuring me through sheer grit and determination. But I got through.

'For me, survival gave promise of a second-round match against Marie-Laure de Lorenzi. Not only was she one of the best amateurs around, but I envied nearly everything about her – her golfing talent and her femininity. Though she was invariably courteous, she was also somewhat aloof, typically French. From a golfing standpoint she had a fantastic rhythm and was just so elegant in everything she did. I remember watching her in the British at Woodhall Spa and I knew instinctively we were going to have a good match. And so we did.

'I realized I would have to play well if I was to beat her. In the event it went all the way to the eighteenth and, when it was all over, I remember walking off the green as high as a kite. It was as if I had won the championship, yet I had actually been beaten. With a Curtis Cup place at stake I was knocked out of the championship in the second round. But there were compensations. In fact, we had a fantastic match which produced a better-ball of 13-under-par for the eighteen holes: I was six under and Marie-Laure was seven under. By the very nature of that performance, I had secured my place for Prairie Dunes, even though I was beaten.

'Kansas was a marvellous experience, particularly with Mary McKenna and Lillian Behan also in the side. It's not often you get the chance in golf to be a part of history and we were in the first British and Irish Curtis Cup team to win in the US. Afterwards, we played in the US Amateur, where I lost in the second round. Then it was home and off to Blairgowrie.

'Little did I imagine that the year still had more to offer. It came in the Home Internationals at Whittington Barracks, where the Irish side, captained by Ita Butler, won the title. So, I had come through a year which delivered personal victories in the Hampshire Rose and the British Strokeplay, and team wins in the Curtis Cup and at international level. And I know this must sound daft, but the match against Marie-Laure still stands apart. It proved that losing can also be an enriching experience.'

The only women golfers I know

The success of the 1986 Curtis Cup team had been forged, effectively, during the Vagliano matches in Hamburg the previous year. That was when the nine-member British and Irish line-up combined in a splendid 14–10 victory. The only problem was who to leave out of the eight-member Curtis Cup side. In the way of successful teams, fate took a hand. Maureen Madill, whose distinguished contribution in Hamburg would have made her a front-runner for Prairie Dunes, decided to turn professional in April 1986. So eight players remained and of those the selectors decided to bring the youthful Karen Davies into the side in place of Linda Bayman.

Ireland had three representatives; England had Jill Thornhill and Trish Johnson; Wales had Vicki Thomas and Davies; and Scotland contributed the indefatigable Belle Robertson. The veteran Scot, who shared a room with Davies, later recalled the youngster's selection as something of an inspired decision, especially in view of her success on the US college scene. 'Listening to her talking about the American girls was most reassuring,' said Mrs Robertson. 'On our side of the Atlantic, we had read only of their more spectacular feats, but Karen was able to tell us how so-and-so had an 85 in some college event and played thoroughly badly.'

More than a decade later, when Mrs Dowling was chosen as non-playing captain of the Vagliano Trophy team, she knew that advice from a certain source could be invaluable towards doing the job well. And the person she turned to was a former captain who had been responsible for one of the greatest disappointments of her career. Diane Bailey created a major controversy in 1988 by omitting the then Claire Hourihane from all four series of matches in defence of the Curtis Cup at Royal St George's, Sandwich. To some, the decision was unjustifiably harsh; to others it was simply inexplicable.

But this was the same skipper who achieved the unthinkable at Prairie Dunes. Where all other teams – Walker Cup, Ryder Cup and Curtis Cup – had failed up to then, she had broken new ground by leading the first British and Irish line-up to victory on

American soil. It seemed too much of a coincidence that the Ryder Cup breakthrough should come only a year later at Muirfield Village and that the Walker Cup players would achieve their piece of history at Peachtree, Atlanta, in 1989.

So it was that, in a remarkably pragmatic move, Mrs Dowling put personal feelings aside and focused on the broader picture when the Vagliano matches were played at North Berwick in July 1999. 'I was on five teams with Diane and I knew how difficult some of her decisions must have been,' she recalled. 'I told her I didn't have a problem with what had happened at Sandwich, which she was glad to hear. Apparently she had felt badly about it for more than ten years. Sure, I was terribly disappointed not to have got a match, but from my own experience of captaincy I can now see that you have to weigh things up and do what you believe is best. I know that certain people remain convinced there was some hidden agenda at work during the 1988 matches, but I'm satisfied that was never the case.'

At fifty, Belle Robertson also had good reason to be grateful for Mrs Bailey's leadership qualities at Prairie Dunes, not least for the fact that it became a wonderful swansong in the representative arena, after she had played her way into the side by winning the Scottish Championship at St Andrews. 'During practice out there, Diane discovered that there were four of us who weren't particularly good at the soft flop-shot that would be crucial from rough around the greens,' said Mrs Dowling. 'So she piled the four of us – Lillian, myself and two others – into a large buggy and drove us out to the middle of the course. She then said we would stay there and work on the shot. Lillian seemed a bit miffed at this and demanded that Diane should show us what she meant, and our captain did just that, perfectly. So we stayed there for more than an hour. And we got it right.'

According to Mrs Robertson in her book *The Woman Golfer*, Miss Behan's background was quite similar to her own. The Scot wrote, 'She, too, had country connections, albeit her work was as a stable girl at the Curragh. Lillian has a positively regal gait and the look of a champion.' Of Mrs Dowling, she commented, 'Claire is a wonderfully tidy little golfer who should never be underestimated.' And she wrote of Miss McKenna, 'Mary has been a great friend of mine for many years and I am perhaps too close to her to give a fair appraisal of her career. However, I have always been a great admirer of her talent and, in particular, the length she commands with her long irons.'

As it happened, the visitors achieved a clean sweep of the first day's foursomes and after Miss Johnson, Mrs Thornhill and Miss Behan had gone on to take the first three singles, the score stood at 6–0 before the Americans registered their first point. Indeed, such was the quality of the GB and I performance that they were not flattered by a 6½ to 2½ lead at the end of the first day. And they were assured of a tied match, at least, when Mrs Robertson holed a 12-foot putt on the eighteenth to secure a half in the third foursomes on the following morning.

Having lost by 2 and 1 to Cindy Schreyer on the opening day, Mrs Dowling gained revenge with a 4 and 3 win over the same player in the last match on the course. So the Irish contribution was significant: Miss Behan had three points from two foursomes and a first-day singles; Miss McKenna shared two and a half points from three foursomes with Mrs Robertson; and Mrs Dowling got a point from two singles matches.

Almost incredibly, the winning margin was a whopping 13–5. But to fully grasp the magnitude of the team's achievement, it is necessary to look at the results of previous matches in the US since the current format was adopted at Royal Porthcawl in 1964. In five transatlantic trips from 1966 to 1982 inclusive, British and Irish teams not only lost every time, they never got closer than within five points of their rampant hosts. The nadir was reached in the matches immediately prior to Prairie Dunes, when they were thrashed 14½ to 3½ in Denver in 1982.

So the triumphant British and Irish players flew back to London having written a new chapter in team golf, but there was to be no time to celebrate just yet. From there, they headed to the British Women's Strokeplay Championship at Blairgowrie, where Mrs Dowling would write a stunning postscript to Prairie Dunes. Having flown to Edinburgh, she and Miss McKenna hired a car and drove the 60 miles together to the famous Rosemount stretch.

The Woodbrook player recalled, 'Having driven to Blairgowrie with the Curtis Cup in the car, we had another trophy [British Women's Strokeplay] with us on the return journey. And knowing our baggage would be way overweight when we got back to Edinburgh Airport, we decided to dress up in our Curtis Cup blazers and skirts. Then, as luck would have it, we ran out of petrol, so I volunteered to head off down the road for help. Next thing I was at a roundabout and a police car had stopped to see what the problem was. When I explained our predicament, an officer concluded from my uniform that we were golfers.

' "The only women golfers I know are Belle Robertson and Mary McKenna," he said. Whereupon I declared, "Come with me and I'll introduce you to one of them." So it was that we got our petrol and this Scottish policeman met one of his golfing idols.' With that, the Irish duo headed home to a wonderful reception at Dublin Airport, with further celebrations to follow at their respective clubs. While Woodbrook hailed a team and individual triumph, Donabate toasted yet another McKenna success and the Curragh had follow-up celebrations to the British Championship victory of Miss Behan the previous year.

Aloha, Ms Madill!

Three years after Prairie Dunes, I met Maureen Madill at Aloha on Spain's Costa del Sol, where she was competing in the Benson and Hedges Trophy, a mixed event involving men and women professionals. She was just completing her fourth season as a professional and had reason to be pleased with tournament earnings of £26,923 for fourteenth position in the Order of Merit, an improvement of six places on the previous year.

She talked about the importance of family and how she kept in touch with her sister Patricia Davies, a golf writer with *The Times* and living in Birmingham as the wife of former *Guardian* golf correspondent Dai Davies, who, sadly, died earlier this year. She also talked affectionately of her father, Jim, who was a familiar figure as her caddie when she competed in amateur events throughout Britain and Ireland.

'Though he was always there to encourage me, he was never intrusive,' she said. 'I remember when Patricia and I were teenagers, he promised us each a new set of golf clubs if we succeeded in beating him, which wasn't easy insofar as he was a useful seven-handicapper at the time. But on a certain trip to Rosslare, I think it was 1972, Patricia beat him. And on her arrival home, a new set of clubs were there waiting for her.

'I couldn't wait to get mine. As it turned out, I had to wait only six months. As a fourteen-year-old I beat him in a level match around Portstewart and shortly afterwards duly took possession of a new set of clubs.' Those were embryonic years when golf always seemed to produce a new adventure. Like the time, as a fifteen-year-old, when she was to realize the dream of every youngster by sharing a fairway with Fred Daly, whom she had known about since her earliest days as the Open champion of 1947.

She recalled, 'It was a thirty-six-hole pro-am at Bangor where all the amateur competitors were women and, as the big moment approached, I became really nervous. I remember my anxiety on seeing no sign of him as I headed for the first tee and then fearing that he wasn't going to show up at all. But he finally seemed to appear out of nowhere and was very courteous when introduced to myself and my local female partner.

'She was also quite young, probably no more than twenty, and she had this curtain of hair which covered her entire face when she addressed the ball. As a consequence, she could have seen very little of what she was doing. And to make matters worse, it was windy, which meant her hair was all over the place. Then, as we set off up the first fairway, I suddenly noticed she was in her bare feet. Fred said nothing, but I felt I should make some attempt at conversation so I asked her, "Do you always play in your bare feet?" To which she replied, "Oh yes," putting a swift end to that particular line of conversation.

'Being older than me, she was given the task of marking Fred's scorecard for the professionals' individual competition. He was still a wonderful striker, but a bloody awful putter. In fact, before hitting a putt, he would wave the putter over the ball, back and forth, back and forth. I counted him doing this exactly forty-three times on every putt. Naturally, he wasn't too pleased about his putting and I remember as he walked off the green having taken six at a particular par four, she called after him, "Fred, what did you have there? What did you have . . ."

'He was getting progressively incensed at this and by the eighth hole he informed me he was no longer going to communicate with this girl. So from then on he would say to me, "Tell her I had a five; tell her I had a four." So I would say, "Fred had a five; Fred had a four." And so on. Realizing what was going on, she wanted to know why Fred wasn't talking to her. And there was I caught in the middle, which was horrendous. But on we went for what appeared to be an interminable round. Little did I know there was worse to come.

'Although Fred was playing off the very back tees, his drives were invariably the furthest out on the fairway, while I was usually the middle one and she was last. We finally got to the eighteenth, where she hit her second and I then hit what turned out to be my only decent iron shot of the day. Remember, this was 1973 and Fred was something of a legend at the time, so we had quite a gallery following us and by the last hole it had become a really big crowd. Anyway, to great applause, I hit this eight iron into about eight feet. But when we walked the 30 yards to the next ball, Fred looked down at it and then at me before saying, "You played the wrong ball, sweetie."

'I'll not tell you what sweetie said. Suffice to say that I was mortified. So I had to hit another shot to the green and, when it was all over, I remember turning to my father and, close to tears, telling him, "I can't play with those two again." Of course there was no way my father would hear of such a thing, which meant I was back with them the following day. This time, Fred didn't speak to the other girl at all, but she was prepared for it and every time we finished a hole she would say to me, "Did he have six?" Or whatever.

'Though it wasn't especially pleasant at the time, when I look back now at that tournament in Bangor, I treasure it as a memorable experience, particularly the way Fred could hit brassie shots out of the rough. My only regret is that I was too young to fully appreciate the artistry of a wonderful player.'

When she moved into professional ranks in 1986, her parents became regular observers at Maureen's tournaments and it became a particularly rewarding exercise in 1989 when she won three pro-am events, was sixth over three rounds in the Rome Classic and finished in the top ten on four occasions over seventy-two holes. Her best performance came in the Woolmark Ladies' Matchplay tournament, in which she earned her biggest cheque of the season, £8,000, as runner-up to Denise Hutton. Another sizeable cheque was £2,968 when finishing fifth in the Ladies European Open.

Meanwhile, strong ties with Ireland were strengthened by the arrival as executive director of the women's tour of Joe Flanagan, whom she referred to affectionately as 'Postman Pat', for his care in ensuring that competitors received their mail at the various stops on the circuit. 'Ireland is never far from my thoughts,' she said. 'Indeed, I'm often surprised at the number of Irish people I meet who have followed my career, many of them from Dublin where they knew me as an amateur. Then there are the telephone calls I receive from Mary McKenna, Claire Hourihane and Sheena O'Brien Kenney giving me all the gossip. I sometimes feel there would be a greater interest in the women's professional game if we could get a tournament going in the Republic. Up to now, there have only been three of us – myself, Lillian Behan and Yvonne McQuillan, and Yvonne has since left the tour to return to the US.'

She went on, 'Claire had the game to be a successful professional, but I don't think the travelling appealed to her. Where other Irish players are concerned, however, it must be emphasized that the standard is very high. It is also very demanding. I would reckon that I have played more over the last four seasons as a professional than I did in the previous ten years as an amateur.'

Given that she completed her club-professional exams at Lilleshall in 1988, I wondered if she would consider returning one day to Portstewart GC, as its first woman professional. 'Oh no,' she laughed. 'I don't think I'm quite ready for that just yet.' Interestingly, there was no mention of broadcasting, which she has since turned to with splendid success as an on-course golf commentator, notably with the BBC.

It was as a professional coach, however, that Miss Madill went to Ganton for the Curtis Cup in 2000. Her objective was to help her friend Claire Dowling regain the trophy which compatriot Ita Butler had brought home as skipper at Killarney four years previously. Acknowledging her own appointment as a 'wonderful honour', Claire added the typically candid comment, 'I haven't a clue about the US team, apart from Carol Semple and Robin Weiss. But we'll soon find out, won't we?'

Unfortunately for her, the trophy remained in the US. But it was a memorable occasion for another Irishwoman, Suzie O'Brien. Five years previously, Suzie's brother, Jody Fanagan, played in the Walker Cup at Royal Porthcawl where he and Padraig Harrington had a foursomes win over none other than Tiger Woods and John Harris. So the Fanagans had now joined luminaries Roger and Joyce Wethered, and Michael Bonallack and Sally Barber as brother and sister gaining Walker Cup and Curtis Cup honours.

And it was nice to discover that Lillian Behan was remembered with great affection at the venue where she had stunned the golfing world by capturing the British Women's in 1985. 'We get a Christmas card from her every year, which is really very nice,' said the assistant secretary, Jean Matthewman. 'We think the world of Lillian. Don't forget to give her our best regards.'

Memories of Broadstone

In 2001, Kitty MacCann appeared more than a little bemused by all the attention as she sat in a position of honour. Yet the presence of so many old friends, admirers and former rivals left the organizers in no doubt about the success of the occasion. Tullamore GC had encountered predictable difficulty in persuading their most famous member to agree to a special function to mark the golden jubilee of her triumph in the British Women's at the Broadstone club, Dorset, on 7 June 1951, but the player, famously shy about her golfing achievements, had eventually agreed to the celebration.

So it was that she was reunited with Moira Earner, Irene Holland, Anne Crowley and Roly O'Neill, four colleagues on Tullamore's triumphant Irish Senior Cup team of 1958. Grace O'Brien, the sixth member of the side, sent apologies. Distinguished contemporaries Philomena Garvey and Clarrie Reddan also sent apologies. But Lillian Behan was there, sixteen years to the day since she had become the last Irish winner of the British title at Ganton. Indeed, earlier in 2001, Mrs MacCann had watched Miss Behan lose the final of the Midland Championship on a sixth tie hole at Tullamore.

Kitty's one-time caddie, Dinny White, was also there. So was former Irish international colleague Aileen McCarthy, who had made an unavailing challenge at Broadstone. And Cathy Smith, president of the ILGU, attended, as did Albert Lee, representing the GUI as the then Leinster Branch chairman. All of which reflected the organizational skills of Tullamore's Leonard Dolan. It was a time for fond reminiscences by Mrs Holland who, as Irene Hurst, had been guided by Kitty during her formative golfing years at Tullamore. And Mrs MacCann recalled a 'very happy foursomes partnership' with Mrs Earner at international level.

As a footnote to events at Broadstone, the *Sunday Press* of 10 June 1951 carried this fascinating little tale: 'Proud father of Kitty, Mr G. S. Smye, timed his retirement as manager, Bank of Ireland, for last Wednesday. He chartered a plane for a family party to see Kitty play, but the plane landed at an unauthorized British airport and there was hell to pay.' It concluded: 'After placating angry officials, Mr Smye saw his daughter win with 82 for the first eighteen and two over fours for the last fifteen.'

A remarkable meeting by the Boyne Estuary

When I called on Clarrie Reddan in the summer of 2006, she was sitting just inside the downstairs window of her Baltray home, looking out over the Boyne Estuary at low tide, while eager gulls swooped down to pick juicy morsels off the sun-splashed mud-flats. As she stood up to greet us, it was difficult to imagine her being one month past her ninetieth birthday.

'Vicki and Des live only around the bend down there,' she said, prompting talk of her son-in law, Des Smyth, and his upcoming role as a vice-captain in the Ryder Cup. But her priority seemed to be the Curtis Cup, which she had watched from Bandon Dunes in Oregon the previous weekend. 'It's very hard to judge from television, but I thought the course was disappointingly flat,' she said. 'I didn't see any exciting shots from sand dunes like you'd expect in seaside golf.'

And what of the sweeping 11½ to 6½ win by the US? 'I was disappointed with the way both teams played, but I'm glad the Curtis Cup is to be extended over three days, just like the Ryder Cup,' she replied. 'Mind you, I don't know if it will give our girls a better chance.' She went on, 'I love to watch golf on television, mainly because I'm too old to do anything else. And I can get tired watching, unless I happen to know somebody. I think Tiger Woods is a great boy. Terrific. And himself and the other fellows now have these great big trucks going around with them, giving them massages. It's a different world from the one I knew.'

Though not necessarily disapproving of change, she expressed annoyance at certain aspects of the modern game. 'Now you see this [Michelle] Wie lassie, wanting to play in men's events,' she said, with a distinct edge to her voice. 'I think very badly of her for that. Her parents should take her in hand and stop all this nonsense. She's only encouraging the men to react, like some fellow [Jean Van de Velde] who says he wants to play in ladies' competitions. And I think he's quite right. I don't know what that lassie is thinking about, especially with the big ladies' professional tour in the US and lots of money to play for. Does that not satisfy her?'

Clarrie's ninetieth birthday, on 3 July, was celebrated with dinner at Co Louth GC in the company of her family and friends. As she observed, 'There's a great fellow up there, Michael, the chef. He does a lovely meal.' This was the club to which, seventy years previously, she returned in triumph as Clarrie Tiernan, winner of the Irish Ladies' Close at Ballybunion, in 1936. A year later, she went on holiday to relations in the US and came home with the New Jersey State title.

On that trip, she made her debut in the US Women's Amateur at Memphis CC, where Estelle Lawson Page beat Patty Berg in the final. This was the Estelle Page who won the prestigious North and South title on no fewer than eight occasions, and was to cross paths with Clarrie in another part of the US a year later. 'I loved Tennessee, which was a beautiful place,' she recalled. And how did she get off work for all this travelling, especially at a time when trips to the US were made by boat? 'Oh! I never worked a day in my life – other than in the kitchen, that is,' she replied. 'Anyway, I was there only about three weeks on that occasion, including a trip to Canada, where I saw the Niagara Falls.'

Her New Jersey win was largely responsible for securing a place in the Curtis Cup team at Essex CC, Manchester, Massachusetts, in 1938, when she felt 'very honoured' to be paired in the top foursomes with Helen Holm, the reigning British champion. 'And you know, we beat the crack American pair, Page and Maureen Orcutt, by two holes in a wonderful match,' she recalled. 'Helen was a lovely golfer and you couldn't have played with a nicer person. She encouraged me with "marvellous", "great shot, Clarrie": most supportive. So it was a great disappointment to me that she lost her singles [against Page] the following day.'

In fact, with only nine points at stake at that time, Clarrie gained the distinction of becoming the only visiting player to win both her foursomes and singles matches, beating Orcutt by 2 and 1. This was quite an achievement against a player who, while combining amateur events with golf-writing for the *News York Times*, was reckoned to have won sixty championships throughout the US and Canada.

Due to the Second World War, the Curtis Cup didn't resume until 1948 at Royal Birkdale, where Clarrie was joined in the home team by her great Co Louth rival, Philomena Garvey. I reminded her about the epic 1946 Irish Close final at Lahinch, where Garvey beat her on the thirty-ninth. 'Oh that!' she laughed, as though it were but a minor hiccup. 'I believe they've changed that hole now [the short third, where it ended].' I told her it has gone altogether. 'Well, that's good,' she replied. 'I was laid a stymie on that hole, and the stymie was later removed from the game, which was also a good thing. Phil and I always got on well, though she lived in Dublin most of her life, working in Clerys. Now she lives out here, on her own.'

Clarrie named Babe Zaharias as the greatest woman player she ever encountered, having lost to her en route to the British title at Gullane in 1947. 'Babe was great, a really nice girl, and we were all terribly sad about the way she died [of cancer in 1956],' she said. 'Unlike the rest of us, she was a complete athlete who could have been good at any sport, because of all the exercises she did.'

The mudflats in the estuary were disappearing from sight as I headed off into the gathering dusk and thought of the wonderful contribution Co Louth had made to golf, and how fortunate I was to have spent time with one of its finest champions.

Playing in disguise

On hearing I was from Ireland, she identified herself as Mary Beth Lacy of Adams Golf and insisted she had a fascinating story about playing at Portmarnock. It all started back in 1987 when, as a college graduate from Furman University (the alma mater of Dottie Pepper, Beth Daniels et al), her parents asked what she wanted by way of celebration.

'I told them I would love to make a golfing trip to Ireland,' she recalled when we met at Sawgrass. 'Since I was a fairly useful player at the time, my father thought it was a great idea, provided himself and my mother could tag along. And that's what happened.'

After landing at Shannon, they stayed the night at Dromoland Castle and played Lahinch before travelling on to the popular Kerry courses. Then the trip was to be topped off by a visit to Portmarnock. 'That was when somebody told my father it was an all-male club and girls couldn't play there,' she said.

Armed with this misinformation, they duly arrived at Portmarnock, where Mary Beth's father told the caddie-master that he and his son wished to play a round. 'By that stage, I had tucked my hair under my cap and wore a loose sweater,' she said. 'Nobody passed any notice, though I think the caddie knew, from my hands.'

She went on, 'Anyway, I played off the men's tees and shot 79, which was a real thrill, both for myself and my father.' Having later learned that the disguise was unnecessary, she had vowed to return there one day as a woman. 'But to have any hope of breaking 80 again I'd need to play off the ladies' tees,' she concluded with a smile.

The apparel oft proclaims . . .

During the British Women's Senior Open at the Powfoot club near Dumfries in 1998, the question of proper golfing attire raised a decidedly interesting response. And it was a great pity that club officials from all over this fair land weren't present to hear the exchange. It happened when an elegant Spanish competitor arrived on the first tee dressed in jeans. Yes, those vile garments made from the dreaded serge de Nimes which, however well cut and tailored, are viewed by committees as a threat to the very fabric of their club.

Aware of this ban, Lewine Mair, the golf correspondent of the *Daily Telegraph,* mischievously enquired of the Ladies' Golf Union officials as to what they intended to do about the denim-clad senora. Would she be asked to change? The answer was no; they would do nothing. Indeed, the LGU president, Bridget Jackson, gently suggested, 'Maybe it's up to us to change.'

Apparently there was a growing awareness in women's golf that rather than being encouraged into the game, youngsters are actually frightened off by outdated rules regarding dress. And it's high time that the game's menfolk had a similar, serious look at the so-called dress code in clubs. We are all familiar with those golfers who dress down to play the game. They arrive at the club in perfectly respectable garb, only to reappear from the locker-room in creased, even ragged apparel more associated with gardening. Ah, but it's not demin. So everything's fine.

I know of a young woman who had to leave the mixed lounge of a Dublin club at lunchtime, because the honorary secretary considered her to be improperly dressed – in a designer denim suit. As it happened, she was a university graduate whose reaction was to pity the people who came up with such an anti-social rule. Bridget Jackson is right: it's time for the golfing establishment to change at all levels, but especially with regard to young people, for whom denim is almost like a second skin. Neatness of dress should be the requirement. And if that were the case, some male golfers I know wouldn't get past the front door.

My golfing heroine

If I had a golfing heroine it would, unquestionably, be Anne Tunney. Having previously witnessed her skills as an administrator, especially at championships, I found myself lost in admiration for the manner in which she discharged her duties as president of the Irish Ladies' Golf Union when their centenary celebrations were held in 1993.

At the official dinner to mark the occasion, she delivered arguably the finest speech I have ever heard in such circumstances, irrespective of gender. What made it truly remarkable, however, was that she did it on the day her mother died. As word of her loss filtered through the gathering, people were stunned at how she handled the huge emotional strain. But keenly aware that the occasion was far more important than any personal sorrow, she was simply magnificent.

I had many delightful chats with Anne, but one I especially liked concerned her reflections on the staging of the European Ladies' Team Championship at Hermitage in 1979. This was how she remembered it, twenty years on: 'As the oldest national ladies' union, we in the ILGU were always conscious of our responsibilities at a broader level. So when it was suggested to us that we might stage the European Championship, we took the idea very much to heart. Clearly, it was going to be a huge undertaking from a financial standpoint, but we were greatly encouraged by a formal agreement that was already in place with the Ladies' Golf Union (LGU). They promised us that if the event went ahead, they would split the cost with us fifty–fifty.

'So it was that we agreed to stage the European Ladies' at Hermitage. Initial estimates put the cost at £12,000, but we had promises of courtesy cars from Mazda and help from many other sources. Indeed, we encountered quite incredible generosity. It meant that the figure eventually worked out at £5,400 with the result that ourselves and the LGU paid £2,700 each. Yet it remained a daunting challenge at a time when we had only 21,000 members in 223 clubs.

'The championship was to provide me with wonderful memories that have not only endured, but are certain to be with me for the rest of my life. Even the July weather was unusually kind to us and Hermitage never looked more beautiful, in brilliant sunshine. I was treasurer of the ILGU at the time and a member of the organizing committee. Naturally, we did our best to cover every eventuality, but difficulties arose just the same. Like getting the wrong national flags for the opening ceremony.

'Then there were the problems caused by the large galleries. Twice daily, a huge Guinness tanker could be seen heading through the course towards the clubhouse. But there was none of the black stuff on board. Through the generosity of Guinness it was ferrying water to supplement the existing supply, which was stretched beyond capacity.

'At an individual level, there was the problem of one of the visiting players being whisked off to Holles Street hospital with a miscarriage. And the instruction from her team captain that she was to bring her clubs with her, because she would be needed for play the following afternoon. Which she did. And I remember the wonderful ladies of Hermitage, preparing breakfasts at five-thirty so that the players would be well-fed before setting off the first tee at seven. They did it for the simple reason that the hotels wouldn't.

'I remember the German team being captained by a man. And the fourteen-year-old Austrian player who had an albatross at the long second. And I recall the fact that none of the 126 caddies let us down. But, of course, the crowning glory of the week was that Ireland won. From the fourteen competing nations, we emerged as champions, beating West Germany by the wide margin of 6–1 in the final.

'That was on Sunday, 8 July and our supporters did us proud. Indeed, they turned up in such numbers that I remember struggling to get a glimpse of our champion scrambler, Susan Gorman, getting the decisive point. Appropriately, it came at the nineteenth, but with my lack of inches I could see little more than Susan's curly head. Still, it was enough. The cheers of the crowd gave me all the information I needed. And when the excitement eased, I remember experiencing a curious mixture of joy, satisfaction and relief. We had embarked on a huge undertaking, which became a resounding success.'

She concluded, 'Given the wide, international nature of the event and the consequent language difficulties, it would have been enough for most of us that the event had gone well. But for Ireland to emerge victorious was truly amazing and ensured it would become an historic occasion, packed with precious memories.'

CHAPTER 7

● ● ● ● ● ● ● ● ●

Amateurs Tell Different Tales

'That Irishman is so popular in the United States that he could stand for President. What's more, he'd probably be elected!'

GENE SARAZEN ON JOE CARR

On a comfortably cool night in Florida, far from the wintry winds of his beloved Sutton, Joe Carr became the first Irishman to enter the World Golf Hall of Fame. It was November 2007 and amid all the emotion and fanfare there was an awareness of how fitting it was that this, the ultimate accolade, should have come on American soil, for no nation other than his own took Carr more to its heart.

This was exemplified beautifully by the presence of a true American icon, Jack Nicklaus, giving the introductory address. In typically clear, confident tones, the Bear spoke for seven minutes about a man he described as a great friend and one of the greatest amateur champions the game has seen.

Six new inductees – Carr, Hubert Green, Kel Nagle, Charles Blair Macdonald, Se Ri Pak and Curtis Strange – brought the Hall of Fame's number to 120. And from an Irish perspective, it seemed especially apposite that Carr and Green should have been honoured together, given their close association with Portmarnock GC. In fact I was bold enough to suggest to the new inductee,

'There, isn't it nice to be rewarded for winning the Irish Open back in 1977.' Green, it should be noted, won the US Open that year and later the USPGA Championship in 1985.

Of course that Portmarnock occasion was in August 1977, two months after a rather more significant event for the Alabaman at Southern Hills, where he captured the US Open. Still, Green had the generosity of spirit to chuckle, 'Oh, I loved Portmarnock, a great golf course with the wind, the pop-up shots, the horrible breaks . . . The frustration of it all. That's what golf's about. It takes a real man to overcome that. And I remember a really great short hole, the fifteenth. And, of course, Jimmy Kinsella, who gave it a real run that year.'

The Bear's memories of Carr also had much to do with links terrain. Indeed, they first became acquainted when Nicklaus made his Walker Cup debut for the US against Britain and Ireland at Muirfield in 1959. This is what the great man said on that memorable night in Florida:

'During my career I was lucky enough to play with many of the game's legends. That included our next inductee for lifetime achievement, Joe Carr. Joe was a great champion. As a matter of fact, he was one of the greatest amateur champions the game has ever known. His list of career highlights is long and distinguished: three British Amateurs, six Irish Amateurs, Walker Cup team member a record ten times, the first Irishman to play in the Masters, the captain of the R and A. Those are just a few of Joe's many accomplishments. So it is fitting and appropriate that he is honoured here tonight as part of the class of 2007.

'The first time I met Joe, I was just a nineteen-year-old kid making my first trip to Muirfield, Scotland, for the Walker Cup matches. We didn't get to know each other real well there, but we really got to know each other two years later in Seattle, where we played together during those Walker Cup matches. That same year, we played practice rounds at Pebble Beach before the US Amateur. Joe and I were in different brackets, and we talked all week about meeting in the finals.

'Perhaps he wanted that match a little bit too much, but we both advanced to the semi-finals in different brackets. Unfortunately he lost. I guess it was just not meant to be. However, the great consolation for both of us was that we walked away from Pebble Beach enriched with a friendship that each of us would share for the rest of our lives.

'Each and every tournament after that when Joe and I were in the same field, I made certain to reunite during those practice rounds. Just like in 1962. I made my British Open debut at Troon and found myself teeing off in the opening round at three forty-five with a marker. Not the greatest way to begin a tournament, let alone a major championship. Thankfully, my good friend Joe went to the R and A and told them that it wasn't right to do that to the US Open champion. They moved me into a threesome, and right there in a nutshell is Joe. He always thought about what was best for the game and his fellow competitors before he thought about himself.

'Joe was a great friend. I'm certainly not alone in that assessment. He had a wonderful sense of humour and was a champion on the course. Joe was also a champion needler and full of fun, on and off the course. He was a cheery, fun-loving guy who was always willing to exchange barbs with you. He wore a smile and offered a kind word, but more often than not he offered an opponent more than just the riches of kindness.

'Joe, like many of us, never shied away from a friendly wager and I must have played about, I suppose, fifty practice rounds of golf with him, including for the British Open. It was almost as if Joe knew that at each Open Barbara wanted a new sweater, and he was always very accommodating to fund that purchase. But trust me, Joe still got in my pocket plenty of times.

'In 1967, Joe played in the Masters, becoming the first Irishman to play at Augusta. Well, in 1967 I was defending champion, and he and I found ourselves paired together from the first round. Only one of us saw the weekend that week. And it wasn't me. The next year, Joe got paired with Arnold. You know, the same thing happened to AP [Arnold Palmer]. You [directing his words to Palmer] didn't make the weekend and he did, right?

'Anyway, after that, Cliff Roberts said that they were going to invite Joe back, but they were afraid nobody wanted to play with him. Nothing could be further from the truth, though. Everyone loved to play golf with Joe. But, more importantly, everyone simply loved being around Joe.

'With his induction here tonight into the World Golf Hall of Fame, generations will come to be able to learn more about and share a little bit of the Irishman who gave so much to the game he loved and gave me so many warm and cherished memories. Tonight I'm proud to pay tribute to my friend Joe Carr, recipient of the Lifetime Achievement Category, so fitting, because Joe's truly was a lifetime of achievement.

'On behalf of Joe's family who are here tonight, including his wife Mary, his sons and his daughter, who are all here with us tonight, and Jody back in Ireland, as well as his fellow Irishmen, I'm grateful for the opportunity to speak on their behalf as the Hall inducts its first member from the proud country of Ireland, Joe Carr. Thank you.'

On meeting Nicklaus earlier that day, I wondered how he had come to be giving the Carr address. 'To be honest, I had no idea Joe was being inducted,' he said. 'But the Hall of Fame people knew I'd be here for this and that I was a great friend of Joe's. And I was tickled to death when they asked me to do the address. I told them: "Absolutely."'

Then, reflecting on the Carr era, I wondered how Nicklaus felt about many of today's players, who tend to view their amateur past as some form of disease which they were pleased to rid themselves of by turning professional. The Bear chuckled at the notion. 'It's ridiculous,' he said. 'What they seem to think is that it doesn't count any more. It certainly counted for me. I had a great amateur career. I loved it. Maybe it has to do with such a big focus being put on the professional game nowadays and not much attention being given by the press to the amateurs. But it's still ridiculous.

'When you're growing up, you're playing against the best competition there is available. And for me, that included Joe Carr. Generally speaking, you'll find that the US Amateur, the British Amateur or the NCAA are really difficult tournaments to win. And I can tell you that you don't have to play a whole lot better to win a US Open than to win one of those. If, in fact, you have to play better.' Would Joe have made a success of a professional career had he decided to go that route? 'I often wondered if Joe would have had the temperament,' he replied. 'He was essentially a fun-loving guy with a matchplay temperament. Mind you, he sure as the devil didn't like to lose, which is what made him a great champion.'

Meanwhile, for Joe's widow Mary and the children of his marriage to his first wife, Dor – Roddy, Sibeal, John, Gerry and Marty (Jody had to remain in Dublin for a family function) – it was an unforgettable experience. I noted it was eight o'clock as they went to thank Nicklaus after the ceremony and, as if to order, stars shone brightly in the night sky. 'It was all so emotional, especially seeing so many of Joe's things on display,' said Mary, about what had been both a difficult and enriching two days for her and the Carr family. 'But they did it all beautifully. I was so proud of him.'

On Sunday they attended the Night of Legends Tribute Dinner, held in the upstairs area of the Hall of Fame building, where two glass cabinets contained memorabilia of Joe's career, ranging from his golf clubs and Walker Cup blazer to two remarkable letters. The first was written by the great Bobby Jones on 1 February 1967. It began: 'Dear Joe. To my delight I have just found on my desk your letter to Cliff Roberts saying that you will play in the Masters this year . . .' The other, from John O'Connor, President of the Old Head of Kinsale, was written on 5 June 2004, three days after Joe's death. It began: 'My dear friend Joe. I have just this morning learned of your passing and I feel quite overcome with emotion as I sit here on the terrace of the Old Head. I have written this letter to somewhat comfort myself on receiving the bad news. But also, I want your family, on reading this, to be reminded of one of the two things that they may not know about the great Joe Carr . . .'

During Sunday's meal there were regular visits to the Carr table from friends and admirers anxious to meet Mary and the family. Among them was former USGA president Bill Campbell, whom Joe beat in the quarter-finals of the British Amateur in 1958 and who, remarkably, lost again to Joe's son, Roddy, in the Walker Cup thirteen years later. 'Joe was loved everywhere,' he said. 'There was a quality about him which made him wonderful company.'

Later, in an after-dinner speech, American golf-writer George Peper gave a fascinating perspective to Carr's latest achievement when he said, 'Since that first shepherd struck the first pebble on the links, my guess is that the total number of souls who have attempted this crazy, fascinating, frustrating game is around one billion. One billion golfers . . . and how many of them have made the Hall of Fame? One hundred and twenty.'

From my own perspective, the honour didn't really hit home until the flag-raising ceremony on the Monday morning. That was when the Carrs were joined by GUI president Tommie Basquille, Mairin Byrne, president of Sutton GC, Bill Twamley, captain of Portmarnock GC and Des Fitzgerald, president of Mount Juliet GC. Long-time friends of Joe's from Sutton GC, Brian Wallace and Bill Thompson, were also present. At eleven thirty, all gathered before a silver flagpole which carried the plaque inscribed to Joe Carr, Ireland. Then, in delightful sunshine, Mary, along with Gerry Carr, ceremoniously raised the Tricolour. Ireland, described by Nicklaus as a proud country, now stood among only fifteen of all the world's golfing nations to be so honoured.

So a newly formed semi-circle of flagpoles in front of the Hall of Fame comprises (clockwise, with individual winners) Ireland (Joe Carr), Canada (Marlene Stewart-Streit), Zimbabwe (Nick Price), Germany (Bernhard Langer), Norway (Karsten Solheim), Argentina (Roberto de Vicenzo), United Kingdom, US, South Africa, Spain (Seve Ballesteros), Australia, Japan, Sweden (Annika Sorenstam), Fiji (Vijay Singh) and Korea (Se Ri Pak).

Inside, in the lobby of the Hall of Fame building, the same flags hang from the ceiling. And the fact that the facility had 280,000 visitors in 2006 gives some idea of the significance of Carr's inclusion on golf's ultimate roll of honour. That afternoon, there was the opportunity to meet Nicklaus in the newest exhibit. Titled 'Jack Nicklaus: Golf's Golden Champion', it covers four rooms, marking the great man's life and times. The centrepiece of more than 250 items is a recreation of Nicklaus Drugs, one of the drug-stores his father owned in Columbus, Ohio, evoking Middle America in the 1950s.

Clearly happy to recapture the mood of those far-off days, Nicklaus gave a press conference while sitting on a red-covered stool, his feet on the rung. Behind him was a counter with two juke-box display units and soda dispensers, where the Bear took a metal beaker and pretended to fill a milkshake as he once did as a boy.

When it was all over, an elderly volunteer who drove me in a golf buggy back to the car park, expressed the view: 'I think it's a pity they present these things post-humorously [sic].' He had a point. The fun of meeting all his old friends in such glittering circumstances would have been right up Joe's alley.

A letter from the Hawk

Ben Hogan, one of the most distinguished of Hall of Fame members, died on 25 July 1997 without ever having trod the fairways of this fair land. It was an omission which, fortunately, he shared with only one other player from the game's all-time greats – Bobby Jones. Still, the man from Dublin, Texas, came close to playing in Dublin, Ireland, when the Canada Cup was staged at Portmarnock in 1960. Hogan was originally named to partner Sam Snead as America's representatives, but he stepped down in favour of Arnold Palmer.

When I was in Killarney for the Curtis Cup in 1996, Finbarr Slattery, a local golf enthusiast, showed me copies of two replies he had received to letters written to Hogan. The first was dated 6 June 1989 on the headed notepaper 'Ben Hogan, Chairman of the Board'.

It read: 'Dear Finbarr. Thank you for your very nice letter and for thinking of Valerie [Hogan's wife] and me. We are well and hope that you are too. I received a copy of the *Golf Monthly Supplement* and when I read it, it brought back a lot of pleasant memories for me also. I doubt Valerie and I will ever make a trip to "the old country" as we just don't travel anymore, but thanks again for writing. With all good wishes, I am, Sincerely, [signed] Ben Hogan.'

Tales from the West

When reflecting on the West of Ireland Amateur Championship, it can be difficult to escape the notion that since first moving to its Easter slot in 1931, the weekend was designed as the ultimate test of physical endurance, with long nights of pint-drinking being followed by competitive golf in stinging winds from the wild Atlantic. Kilkenny's J. D. Murphy, father of European Tour player Gary Murphy, famously said of it, 'You go there feeling like Jack Nicklaus and come home like Matt Talbot.'

In this context, it is interesting to note that Joe Carr won ten of his twelve West titles before taking his first alcoholic drink in the summer of 1961. Incidentally, that was the year Carr was joined on his annual pilgrimage to Rosses Point by the distinguished English amateur Gerald Micklem and the finest golf-writer of his generation Pat Ward-Thomas of the then *Manchester Guardian*.

The extent of a player's self-inflicted punishment often became a matter of grave concern for the indefatigable Dominic Rooney, the unofficial bookmaker of the West, which remains the only amateur golf event in Ireland where a full-scale 'book' is still in operation. Not noted as a morning man, Dominic prefers to do business at night. Indeed, there's a story told at Rosses Point about the time when, as club steward, he received a knock on the back door of his living quarters at eight fifteen one morning. Rubbing sleep from heavy eyes, he opened the door to be confronted by a giant of a man. 'Say, guy,' the American visitor boomed, 'I want to pay the green fee.' To which Rooney replied, 'It'll do when you come in.' 'But I am in,' came the retort.

Dominic had been known to urge certain players to leave the bar and head for an early bed, in the hope they might upset the favourite and deliver a profitable book. Though a long-time West devotee, Declan Branigan, insisted, 'He never had to do that to me, because while I was always the first in and last out, I could still play with a hangover. Interestingly, I had probably my worst experience there before I ever took a drink.'

The West of Ireland champion of 1976 and 1981 explained: 'It was my first West and I stayed at Harte's Pub, which is now Nifty's Bunker. I remember on the Good Friday night – there was only one round of qualifying on the Saturday – I went to bed at about midnight. And despite the night that was in it, I could still hear them all down in the pub, singing their heads off. Then the bedroom door opened and there was a bit of shuffling in the room. I wasn't sure what to make of it.

'Next thing the clothes were pulled back and somebody got into the bed beside me. I was afraid of my life to look around to see who it was. Then this man's voice mumbled, "Tell me, who do you think will qualify?" Needless to say, I didn't sleep for the night. But he was out to the world. I later discovered he was a guy from the North.'

Branigan went on: 'I remember 1978, which became known as the Alaskan Open, and I was off at seven thirty in qualifying. As I stood on the first tee, I got a belt of a hailstone which nearly took the eye out of me head. And the starter piped up: "Begob you're getting the best of the day." My first reaction was to hit him, but as things turned out, he was right. After horrific conditions for the first three holes, it cleared into a summer's morning and I shot 75.

'In the afternoon, however, snow came in and it wasn't even hitting the ground, the wind was so bad. Barry [Reddan] was out late so I caddied for him. And I remember saying to him on the ninth tee, "Ten over after eight is very good. You're nearly qualified at this stage." And I'll never forget the look he gave me. But that's how bad the weather was. And Barry went on to win the title that year.'

Weather for the West has always been a major talking point. And while conditions at Rosses Point over Easter could be notoriously unpredictable, I remember them as pretty horrendous for the most part. Which revives a glorious memory of Tom Cryan, known as the Squire during his many years in the Independent Newspaper Group.

During a certain West, the Squire had surfaced from his bed in Hollands at about eight thirty in the morning to dictate an early piece on to a copy-taker in the *Evening Herald*. After a glance out the window, he commenced: 'Rosses Point was bathed in sunshine this morning, as competitors set off in the West of Ireland Championship . . .' About 600 words later, he looked out the window again. 'Holy mother of Divine Jaysus,' he exclaimed. 'It's f***ing snowin'.' Whereupon he re-started the piece: 'Rosses Point was swept by a vicious snowstorm this morning . . .'

In my own experience of recent decades, 1986 stands apart, and not because the title went to a portly Garda named Paul Rayfus from Trim. It had to do with a second-round match on the afternoon of Easter Sunday in which Woodbrook's Liam MacNamara beat the 1983 champion, Colin Glasgow, at the twenty-first. With the flagsticks bent almost to breaking point by the ferocity of the elements, MacNamara eventually sealed victory through a double-bogey seven at the long third, where he required no fewer than five, well-struck woods to cover the 503 yards to the green. When I sat down with him afterwards, he was honest enough to admit that he was actually 23 over par for the twenty-one holes played. That, from an international playing off plus-one at the time!

Local player Francis Howley, who competed six times in the West before turning professional, vividly recalls the day in question. 'I caddied for Eoghan O'Connell that year and he was nine over for the twenty-nine holes he needed in the first two rounds,' said Howley. 'Though the appalling weather obviously made the golf a bit of a lottery, I imagine it must have been a wonderful test of patience. In fact, after experiencing those conditions, you would never again feel intimidated by the elements.'

On reaching a certain age, anniversaries are often viewed with a distinct lack of enthusiasm. Yet Barry Reddan still relished the thought of another visit to Rosses Point in March 2008, thirty years after the 1978 triumph to which Branigan alluded. Indeed, Reddan had made his first appearance in the West ten years previously and now, at sixty-two, he would be the oldest player in the field by some distance. And he wasn't in the least affronted by my suggestion that he might be better employed at home, praying for the grace of a happy death. 'I'm playing off one [0.5 to be exact] and I like to think I can still mix it with the youngsters,' he said.

Whatever about conceding distance, it's not often that a golfer concedes forty-four years on the first tee, but that was Reddan's experience in the West in 2005, when, as a fifty-nine-year-old, he lost by 5 and 4 in the opening round to a fifteen-year-old upstart named Rory McIlroy. The Louthman laughed at the memory. 'I should have beaten him,' he said, before making an immediate retraction. 'Championship golf is a pretty serious business these days, with so many youngsters looking towards a pro career. It was rare to hear an amateur talk of turning pro thirty years ago.'

In field sports, competitors over thirty-five are thought to be past their sell-by date, while the age profile is considerably lower in pursuits such as swimming and tennis. But the less strenuous nature of golf poses something of a problem in defining competitive limits. Which Reddan proved by reaching the semi-finals of the South of Ireland Championship as a fifty-six-year-old in 2002.

Branigan highlighed superb course management as one of the reasons for his friend's golfing longevity, but I feel it may also have something to do with his keen sense of fun. Like in his plan to arrive at Co Sligo GC on the Wednesday, 'so as to have time to acclimatize' before the first strokeplay qualifying round on Good Friday on a course he knew like the back of his hand. 'The first thing Dominic's going to say is that I cost him a fortune when I won in '78,' he went on. 'And when I tell him I want to have a few euro this year on my Baltray club-mate Simon Ward, I'll get the look: "Do you know something that I don't know?" That look has become familiar over the years.'

Then there is the look from Rooney's bookmaking sidekick, Tom Gavin, which Branigan recalled vividly from 2005, when young McIlroy gained the first of two successive triumphs. At an advanced stage of that championship, Gavin enquired off-handedly if any more bets had been laid. 'Yeah,' said Rooney. 'I gave eights on a young fella named McIlroy.' 'Oh, sweet Jesus, we're ruined,' exploded Gavin, with the look of a man who had just caught his foot in a rat-trap.

At this stage of his life, classic West conditions wouldn't have suited Reddan. And so it proved to be, in the 2008 staging. Winds were so severe that the opening round of strokeplay had to be put back to the Saturday. And when thirty-six-hole qualifying was completed on Easter Sunday, winds were still gusting up to gale force and Reddan missed out by a shot, after rounds of 81 and 77.

How long will he continue to make this Easter trek to the West? 'For as long as I can go over there without my golf making a show of me,' he replied. Countless friends around Rosses Point will be hoping that day is still some way off. Meanwhile, is the fun gone out of the event? 'Absolutely,' said Branigan. 'A few years ago, when I went down there with Barry, I qualified despite an eight at the first as a result of being late on the tee. On the Saturday after the qualifying, there was entertainment at the bar. And I was thinking back to when it would have been packed. Now, we were the only two golfers there.'

But huge compensations remain. In a beautiful tribute to the area after that visit with Carr in 1961, Ward-Thomas wrote: 'There is a spell about the land; the welcome and kindness of its people, the eternal entertainment of Irish stories told in voices swift and liquid as a mountain stream, the miracle of bars that fill, although doors remain firmly locked; the growing enthusiasm for golf and, above all, the setting. Mention must be made of an enchanting place that inspired so much of the poetry of Yeats. No wonder Yeats loved this country so . . .'

Emulating Faldo, as a nine-handicapper!

David Feherty once observed that it required a vivid imagination, while for Padraig Harrington it came down essentially to not getting in your own way. The subject? Seriously low scoring in tournament golf. Its fascination lies in the difficulty of pinning it down. Why, for instance, did Darren Clarke, with two 60s on the European Tour, seem to thrive on it, whereas for six-times major winner Nick Faldo it was a rare occurrence?

So what sort of scoring did the double Open and PGA champion admire most. 'Well, if a player shoots 63, 75, it tells me that his 63 wasn't all that great,' Harrington replied. 'I was really impressed with David Duval's 59, because I could imagine him building towards a level of concentration which would allow him to shoot that score. Annika Sorenstam, on the other hand, must really have put herself in a state of mind from the outset, so as to do eight birdies in a row on the way to her 59.'

He paused, before continuing, 'But do you know one of the most impressive scores I've come across in recent years?' In answer to his own question, Harrington recalled the amazing effort of Hermitage seven-handicapper Pat O'Donovan, who carded 18 straight pars in a September Medal at his club.

'I could more easily understand him breaking par, even off seven,' he said. 'Or to have, say, 17 pars and a birdie. But I don't think I've ever managed to shoot 18 pars. I know Nick Faldo did it to win the 1987 Open at Muirfield, but it's a very strange round. Even playing the golf of a lifetime, the pressure on a seven-handicapper would still be unbelievable, especially coming down the eighteenth. Pat would probably have had a better chance of winning the lottery.'

Ah the fateful eighteenth ... It so happens that Pat's an acquaintance of mine who was happy to recount his closing par. 'I pulled my drive into trees on the left,' he said, 'knocked it back out about 20 yards and then hit a seven iron to the back fringe of the green. From there, I bladed a nine-iron chip and the ball banged against the pin before dropping into the hole.' Laughing heartily, he concluded, 'I suppose you could say I was lucky.'

Mulcare in street shoes

At Florida's Bay Hill Club in 1990, a group from Woodbrook GC, including the late Pat Mulcare, watched Jerry Pate hit shots on the practice ground. On spotting Mulcare, who partnered Ian Hutcheon to a foursomes victory over Pate and Dick Siderowf in the 1975 Walker Cup at St Andrews, the American greeted him warmly. Then, having had no success in his attempt at hitting some decent shots with a new driver he had acquired, he asked Mulcare to have a go.

Never one to duck a challenge, the bold Pat was handed three balls. In his street shoes and scorning tees, he threw the balls on the ground, took the troublesome driver and hit three of the sweetest shots imaginable. 'Now you know why he beat me at St Andrews,' Pate told the fascinated onlookers.

Drama on the thirteenth

Those familiar with my 'Golfing Log' in *The Irish Times* will remember that each one ended with a rules teaser. And the most extraordinary rules decision I ever encountered occurred during the Irish Amateur Close Championship at Westport in August 1985. Those familiar with Arthur Pierse's gift for knowing and using the rules to his advantage won't be surprised that he was involved.

It happened on the par-four thirteenth hole in his fourth round match against Pat Lyons of Cork. After they had both driven into the fairway, Lyons hit a three-wood second shot, which he carved into bushes on the right. Pierse then pulled a long iron into a greenside bunker, whereupon Lyons, on the assumption there was little chance of finding the ball, re-loaded. Using the same club, he proceeded to hole out the provisional ball.

'That's my ball in the hole; I'm declaring my first one lost,' said

Lyons, believing he had made four with his second ball. Whereupon Pierse, based on the premise that a player can have only one ball in play at any given time, told him there was no provision in the rules for 'declaring a ball lost'. At this, Lyons said he was not going to search for his first ball, which was his right. But Pierse then set about searching for Lyons's ball, with the help of his fiancée Margaret, her mother and some friends.

As things turned out, they found Lyons's ball in trees, within the stipulated five minutes. Pierse then pitched and putted for a par, which led to a decision being sought. In the absence of an on-course referee, Ivan Dickson, general secretary of the GUI, was called from the clubhouse and, anticipating something fairly straightforward, he arrived at the thirteenth without a *Decisions* book. Recalling the situation, he said, 'It was a very unusual ruling, but I had a feeling it was covered in the *Decisions*. After some thought, I reasoned that had Lyons's ball come up an inch or two short of the hole, he would have been able to bring it into play by tapping it into the hole, albeit playing out of turn. So I felt he shouldn't be penalized for the fact that he happened to hole out his second shot.' On that basis, Dickson ruled that Lyons had made four. But he was wrong, in that Lyons hadn't brought his provisional ball into play. How then could he have done it, since the ball was actually in the hole?

The answer is to be found in Decision 27–2b/2. It poses the problem: At a short hole, A's tee-shot may be out of bounds or lost, so he plays a provisional ball which he holes. A does not wish to look for his original ball. B, A's opponent or a fellow-competitor, goes to look for the original ball. When does the provisional ball become the ball in play?

Answer: In equity (Rule 1–4) the provisional ball becomes the ball in play as soon as A picks it out of the hole, provided his original ball has not already been found in bounds within five minutes of B starting to search for it.

So, in the Westport case, if Lyons wished to bring his provisional ball into play, he would need to have picked it out of the hole before his original ball was found. Which he didn't. So he should have lost the hole. Instead, the half helped him to an eventual 3 and

2 win over Pierse, though the Corkman lost to the eventual run-ner-up, Declan Branigan, in the next round.

'Though my feeling at the time was that if the ball was found, it was in play, Pat and I later had a good laugh about the incident,' recalled Pierse.

CHAPTER 8

● ● ● ● ● ● ● ● ●

The Challenge of Conquering America

'Golf is 20 per cent mechanics and technique. The other 80 per cent is philosophy, humour, tragedy, romance, melodrama, companionship, camaraderie, cussedness and conversation.'

GRANTLAND RICE

Americans were first captivated by the sight and sound of David Feherty when he came into the media centre after a second-round 67 in the 1989 Open Championship at Royal Troon. While he was progressing to an eventual share of sixth place behind Mark Calcavecchia, US scribes were fascinated to learn that he had trained as an opera singer in his youth and had retained a particular affection for Puccini, especially his popular opera *Turandot*. And he talked about his delight in Woody Allen monologues, bowling them over with the line 'I saw hope running towards the horizon with his arse on fire.'

Here was a mischievous, quick-witted Irishman who seemed to have a clever phrase for every situation. And as Oliver Goldsmith wrote of the Village Schoolmaster '. . . and still they gazed and still the wonder grew . . .' Not long afterwards, Americans were to take the Bangor man to their hearts as one of their most popular television golf pundits in his activities with the CBS Network.

Feherty has often maintained that everything he did as a player, including five victories on the European Tour and three others in

South Africa, was by way of leading him to the role he loved most – that on TV. But it wasn't an easy transition, as I discovered on speaking to him early in 1996, when the familiar, razor-sharp responses seemed to lack their normal spontaneity and a strangely subdued Feherty spoke of a painful family upheaval a long way from his Ulster roots.

It was a Sunday morning in Dallas, Texas, a month after the announcement that he was quitting tournament golf. He chose to do so after working with the USA Network commentary team at the Johnnie Walker World Championship in Jamaica. 'I really couldn't see any way I could continue playing, what with a divorce hanging over me and injuries to both my elbows,' he explained. 'I have used so much of myself, physically and emotionally, that I must rest and try and recharge the batteries.'

With that, he put his professional career on hold, pending a resolution of divorce proceedings with his South African wife, Caroline. While he lived in an apartment in Dallas, she was close by in a house they had shared. And he took particular delight in their two sons, Shey (then seven) and Rory (three), staying with him. 'Whatever about the future, America is now my home, for the simple reason that my children are here,' he added. 'I'm tucking my tail in and spending as much time with them as possible. And I'm kind of enjoying being a single parent.'

The four of them, Feherty, his wife and the boys, moved to Dallas as a family in the autumn of 1993, when he secured a player's card on the US Tour. It seemed the only workable solution to chaotic circumstances which saw him commuting between Bangor, mainland Britain and Johannesburg, where Caroline and the children lived. Indeed, I remember him during the Scandinavian Masters in Stockholm, in 1991, talking about phone calls to South Africa which were adding £700 to his hotel bill for the week.

'Then there was the house in Bangor,' he went on. 'It was a charming old mill house which I hoped would be our home. It cost me a fortune. I had workmen in it for more than two years and between the purchase price and the cost of refurbishment, I must have spent close on £700,000. I sold it for £300,000. Meanwhile, my furniture has been earning frequent-floater miles between Ireland, South Africa and the US. That sort of activity can make a bit of a dent in your bank account. And my financial situation is not especially healthy right now.'

He went on to speak of golf, a game he had played sufficiently well to deliver an unforgettable captain's role in Ireland's Dunhill Cup triumph of 1990, before going on to make the 1991 Ryder Cup team at Kiawah Island, where he gained the distinction of a singles win over Payne Stewart, the reigning US Open champion. By 1995, however, his private life was in such turmoil that he found it impossible to concentrate on his game. 'I lost so much weight I was down to 11st 4lbs,' he said. 'But, thankfully, I've since put back about 12lbs and I have to admit that people, including the media, have been very understanding. The truth is that I've had more ink than most players who have accomplished much more in the game.'

In Killarney on 23 June 1991, Feherty's final round in the Irish Open was a record seven-under-par 65 for the Killeen Course. It gave him a share of ninth place behind Nick Faldo for a reward of £7,123 which, as it happened, was sufficient to edge him into the so-called millionaires' club of European players whose career earnings had topped seven figures. Feherty's reaction? 'Where did all the money go?' he wanted to know, with a typically mischievous grin. Had the question been asked in January 1996, there would have been no cause for humour.

From seven European appearances in 1995 he earned only £17,170 and had a best performance of tied thirtieth behind John Daly in the Open Championship at St Andrews. Meanwhile, he picked up a modest US $90,274 from twenty-six events in the US, leaving him down at 166th in the money list for the year. Like Pagliacci, the tragic hero from one of his favourite operas, he attempted to joke his way through what was obviously a very difficult time, but couldn't hide the shocking gauntness associated with extreme weight-loss. The feeling then was that it could only be a matter of time before he quit the US and returned to Europe full-time, so as to be close to established friends, such as Sam Torrance.

'I haven't swung a club since failing at the [US] Tour School,' he continued, 'and with tennis elbow in both arms I need a rest from the game. And the funny thing is that I don't miss it. In fact, I don't even know where my clubs are. They're probably down at the club [his local course in Dallas]. In the circumstances, working with USA Network in Jamaica was a welcome diversion, even if I got athlete's tongue from having my foot in my mouth all the time. I learned a lot and the reaction I've had from people has been tremendous, to the extent that I could be encouraged to consider taking up this line of work some time in the future. I have always thought I would quit tournament golf when I was forty. That gives me three more years, though I hadn't anticipated my present circumstances when I made those plans.'

By that stage, incidentally, he could be said to have adopted a Lone Star state of mind, certainly where local cuisine was concerned. 'Down here in Texas, you see, wine is treated with a salt-like reverence, as it should be,' he remarked. 'So I always say to Rick [the general manager of his favourite eatery], "Bring me a bottle of that red one with the nice label." And he always does.'

Meanwhile, the pull of tournament life persisted. 'I've already had four or five sponsors' invitations into tournaments in the US this season [1996], without even writing to anybody,' he went on. 'Which suggests to me that I could play as many as ten events if I so desired.' People clearly remembered that only eighteen months previously he had been fourth behind Nick Price in the Open Championship at Turnberry – and that he was runner-up to Kenny Perry a week later in the New England Classic in Boston, where prize money of US $108,000 effectively secured his card for the 1995 American season. Indeed, despite playing only a handful of tournaments on this side of the pond in 1994 and 1995, he had amassed £1,585,774 for twenty-fourth place on the European career money list.

Nobody understood the player better, however, than his father, Bill, who had been his greatest fan and who, incidentally, has written a number of charming letters to me over the years. He and his wife, Vi, David's mother, were painfully aware of their son's plight, having visited him and the grandchildren in Dallas a month previously. 'You could say that David is taking a sabbatical from the game,' said Bill, making no attempt to hide his sadness at developments. 'He has suspended his playing career until his marital affairs are sorted out. In his present state of mind, it would be impossible for him to play serious golf.' Meanwhile, the only prediction the player could make with any degree of certainty at that stage was that his golfing future lay in the US.

When I talked with him fourteen months later, the mood had changed dramatically. For a start, the self-loathing had gone. And with the clubs very definitely discarded, he seemed to be happy to demolish imaginary rivals through quickness of thought on television, as a commentator for CBS. I had phoned him to get his views on the Ryder Cup matches at Valderrama later that year, even if he seemed entirely the wrong man to ask about the most pressurized experience in golf. After all, this was the reluctant competitor who railed against everything that tournament golf stood for, after capturing the BMW International in Munich in 1989.

'Anyone who enjoys what I had to go through out there today must be a pervert,' he had claimed. And later, when asked in a television interview if he could describe the pressure he felt while standing over a three-foot putt for victory, he replied, 'Let's put it this way. If you were to place a piece of coal between the cheeks of my arse it would emerge as a diamond in three seconds.' On another occasion he claimed, 'I don't like this game at all. I would rather play tennis or bowls. I enjoy this game only when it's all over, when I can look back.'

That was the key. The blessed relief that only time can bring. So he was bound to have mellowed six years on from Kiawah Island and the infamous 'War on the Shore' in which his level-par figures in beating Stewart gave him the distinction of producing the best golf of the tournament. In truth, the tone hadn't changed much, though the questions were handled more quietly and with a self-assurance gained from his experience in front of the cameras.

'I can only describe the Ryder Cup in the same way that women describe childbirth,' he replied. 'Which is that there's no way of adequately explaining what's involved. It's unique – a lot like what you imagined it to be, yet not like it at all.' He went on: 'At Kiawah, I was fortunate in having had the advice of an old hand in Sam Torrance and, like everything else, there are tricks for survival. For instance, before my singles match, Sam warned me not to walk onto the tee until my opponent was formally announced to the crowd. Otherwise, I would stand petrified, just as the Christians must have felt before being thrown to the lions, while this golfing god, the reigning US Open champion [Stewart], was being introduced like some fabulous prizefighter.

'I was to learn that the Ryder Cup is institutionalized tribalism on a grand scale. It's life and death, delight and devastation, every extreme you care to imagine. And in my experience as a player on both sides of the Atlantic, the Europeans are far better equipped to handle its very special pressures. In Europe, tournament golfers are far closer. There's a greater empathy among players, a sort of male bonding – if that's not illegal!

'In simple terms, European players look out for each other in a way that very rarely happens in the US. During an American tournament, you could see twelve players sitting down to breakfast at twelve different tables. They are insular in the way they think and behave. And, believe me, that's not conducive to good team-spirit. Then there is the American emphasis on winning and losing, with no middle ground, no room for compromise or consideration. The consequence of this sort of thinking was to be seen in the treatment of Curtis Strange and Lanny Wadkins after the 1995 Ryder Cup defeat at Oak Hill. They were vilified; cast into a golfing wilderness. But the European reaction was entirely different when Bernhard Langer had the misfortune to miss that putt at Kiawah. Nobody blamed Langer for failing. Our only reaction was to feel desperately sorry for him.'

But what of the individual pressure? How does it come about? 'Essentially, it is self-induced but in a group situation,' he replied. 'You look around at players you respect and whom you hope respect you. And you sense that they're expecting a certain level of performance from you and that you daren't let them down. And if you don't deliver, you will never be able to face them again. Yet at no stage did I want to get out of the place, to leave all the pressure behind. To walk away would be to deny everything that you are; to deny your reasons for playing the game. Your whole golfing life has been geared towards becoming a member of this exclusive club and now that you're in, there's no turning back.' And when it was all over? 'I experienced a terribly odd sensation, ranging from the extremes of euphoria to utter desolation,' he replied. 'Even now I find it difficult to explain, other than the fact that it happened to be the Ryder Cup.'

While finding time for such wonderfully enlightened reflection, Feherty's television image was being quietly burnished. And those who might have wondered during the winter of 1998 why they were confusing his sparkling delph with Phil Mickelson's, found the explanation in a fairly comprehensive US $20,000 dentistry job, which he had done to his top deck in response to a request from his employers at CBS. 'I'm so pretty, I can hardly keep my hands off myself,' he said with a wicked chuckle.

Indeed, he was pretty much the finished article when I next interviewed him in the week after the US Masters in 2000, when Vijay Singh of the fragile putting stroke became an improbable winner at Augusta National. Most importantly, he seemed to have found love and peace in marriage to his second wife, Anita.

Our meeting place was in an idyllic setting, in a quiet glade down by the sixteenth green on the Harbour Town Links on Hilton Head Island. It was mid-afternoon on a sultry day in South Carolina and there, with his back to the patio glass of a rented house, Feherty sat writing on a foolscap pad. 'This is for the July issue of *Golf* magazine,' he explained, when I disturbed him at his work. He passed me over two photocopied sheets. 'Here, look at this Seamus Heaney poem sent to me from Ireland. It's absolutely brilliant. Wonderful.' After reading Heaney, I wondered if Feherty had listened to the celebrated BBC golf commentator Henry Longhurst, a man of comparable writing skill though more sparing with the spoken word. Could he one day imagine himself being helped up a ladder to the CBS commentary box, full of gin?

'A distinct possibility,' he admitted, 'except that it wouldn't be gin. Vodka, more than likely. Seriously, I don't drink at all [on the job]; I wouldn't even think about it. But to be perfectly fair, it's obviously possible to walk that very fine line and drink to the point where you become a little more creative, as Longhurst did. I think he was probably at his best when he was more than a little on the Anheuser side of Busch, as they say over here. There were people like Pat Summerall, who was frequently plastered up there in the tower. And it worked. If you look at creative people, poets, writers, artists, you know half of them were opium fiends. If it expands your mind to the extent that it might make you more creative, why not? Though I hasten to add I have no great wish to find out, certainly not at this stage of my career.'

The career stage to which he referred was just after he had come through another highly successful US Masters as a member of the CBS team, with responsibility for the pivotal fifteenth hole. In less than two years his impact on the US scene has been nothing short of remarkable. Had he needed help in overcoming his inhibitions? 'Not really,' came the reply. 'But to be perfectly honest, I don't know how I get away with it. I obviously have the ability to say things in a way that doesn't offend people. And, quite frankly, I can't explain what allows me to do that.'

He went on: 'A certain amount of it is due to self-deprecation. If I see faults in a player out there, it's because I recognize them as having been in my own game. I would hate to think that I might ever fall into the trap of criticizing just for the hell of it, without giving the reason why.'

I then mentioned a piece written about him in the *Augusta Chronicle* during Masters week. And how, in describing the size of one of the bunkers on the Blue Monster course at Doral, he had suggested that wars had been started in the Middle East over less sand. He laughed, acknowledging it as one of his better lines. 'Yeah,' he said, with the grin still there. 'That bunker is the size of Kuwait. How the hell do you rake that thing?' It was then that I realized our chat was going to involve quite a few non sequiturs. Keeping Feherty on track was never easy, but it was fun trying.

Was he finally satisfied that in television broadcasting he had found his true métier? 'Yes, I feel that's absolutely right,' he replied. 'I really do. It's almost as if I was supposed to go through twenty years playing the game for a living in order to get here. And the truth is that I couldn't do what I do now unless I had that experience as a player. Especially spending most of my time on the ground [as an on-course commentator], which is where I'm happiest.

'Being down among the caddies and the players is where I always wanted to be from the time I was a caddie myself. First of all I caddied at Bangor, before spreading my wings to go as far afield as Waterville. Any time a European Tour event came to Ireland, I would be off with Jonesey [David Jones] or Peter Tupling or . . . I just loved hanging around professional golfers and I decided that whatever would allow me to continue doing that is what I wanted to do in life. Among other things, it was a wonderful way of avoiding a nine-to-five job. Absolutely. Not only that, I didn't want to be told what to do.'

There was also always a glorious sense of fun. I remember a particular staging of the Benson and Hedges International at St Mellion, where Feherty happened to feel peckish while heading for the sixteenth tee during the final round. So he summoned his caddie, known as Rodders, to head for Yum-Yums, a fast-food facility on the practice ground close by, for the purchase of two hamburgers. In the event, Rodders, who was generous of girth, consumed his own burger on the return journey before handing the other one to his master.

This presented Feherty with a problem in that he would need both hands free when driving off the sixteenth tee. And he left Rodders in no doubt that he didn't trust him to hold the hamburger without sinking his teeth into it. The solution? The bold David put the burger on the ground, stuck a tee in the middle of it, placed his ball on top and then proceeded to whack a perfect drive down the fairway.

Back at Harbour Town, the brow furrowed as he considered his potential as a player. 'I believe I was perfectly capable of winning the Open Championship, or the PGA Championship here [he was seventh behind John Daly at Crooked Stick in 1991], or any tournament if I got my chance,' he said. 'I got close on a couple of occasions but I never felt like I might win. I never reached what you would call the upper echelons of the professional game, probably because I never worked really hard enough. In fact I've never worked very hard at anything. I'm essentially a very lazy person.'

Did he fear he might be found out? 'Oh, I hope not,' he replied. And with a wicked grin he added, 'But I might, if you write it.' With that, he picked up one of the foolscap pages he had been writing when I interrupted him. 'This stuff I write for *Golf* magazine . . . you know, I never learned to type so I end up writing 1,200 to 1,500 words longhand and it takes me . . . well, I'm so lazy I always leave it to the last minute.

'In the process, I probably write about 3,500, there's so much scratching out and notes on the margins and things like that. I enjoy the process, though I find it quite a lot of work, even when I make up a lot of it and pretend it's true. I believe writing is what I am going to end up doing. I know there's a book [smile]. And I'm not talking about an anecdotal toilet book: I've already got about 25,000 words in short articles that could go into that sort of thing.

'No, I'm looking at a novel. Not primarily about golf, though there would be a certain amount of it there. I'm thinking that if Dick Francis can write about racing, I could write about a golfing theme with a central character that could be possibly a private investigator or a . . .' He hesitated. 'Or a broadcaster?' I suggested. 'Yeah, although I don't think a broadcaster would work. The central character is more likely to be a caddie. But then, so much of what I write is more of a side-gag, more of a screen-play than a novel.'

Returning to the written page, he continued: 'I'm writing about spectators here. It's getting harder for me to find topics because you can't be topical in a magazine article that's going to be published in a couple of months' time. Anyway, I start off with European spectators. I've said here: "The Irish are almost the exact opposite to the French in that we dress badly, can't cook, can't stand each other and love everybody else. I hope I'm offending every nation equally here in that I'd hate to have more French than Germans cancel their subscriptions."

'Both of these things actually happened to me at Greensboro,' he went on, with a further excerpt from his article. On being asked by Feherty to be quiet, a fan apparently turned around, 'dropped his drawers and mooned me. He definitely mooned me. Right in the middle of the crowd. So I said, "Fair enough, at least that end of you is quiet." There must be something in the water up there, because later that day I was standing on the fringe of the putting green chipping and answering questions from this old gentleman. He was a very nice old man, and he asked for my autograph. So I turn around and he's wearing this pair of drawstring shorts, but they're around his ankles.

'And he's standing there and he's wearing a pair of Fruit of the Looms that have been rendered antique; holes blown in them and all sorts of baggy. They've been rendered more O than Y-front by the passing of, among other things, time. So that's what I'm reduced to now. I was just so close to the edge, you know. I feel if only I were allowed to use more colourful language, I could write really interesting stuff.'

He went on: 'I have read Peter Dobereiner voraciously. And P. G. Wodehouse. Beautiful language. Thankfully, these days I have the time to read. I work twenty-five weeks each year for CBS and probably another five or six weeks elsewhere. It's wonderful. People are so much more aware of who I am now than when I was playing. So I do a lot of after-dinner speaking for serious money – 20 minutes to an hour. And I talk about home and people seem to love it.

'I miss home. Not a day goes by that I don't think of it. Anita and I had a holiday in Donegal last October and we've talked about it ever since. We can't wait to go back there.' Then there were his family in Bangor, and his friends there and elsewhere around Britain and Ireland. Clearly, he was determined that his heightened celebrity shouldn't cause him to lose touch with reality. 'I never refuse an autograph,' he mused, 'because I remember standing beside players who were better known than I was and people asked for their autograph but not mine.' The shadow of a smile flickered across his tanned face as he concluded, 'That can happen again.'

The Feherty formula remained largely unchanged when, after a lapse of six years, I interviewed him yet again. Mischief without malice but with an unmistakably Irish overlay remained the intoxicating formula while he prepared for his tenth US Masters as a key figure of the CBS commentary team. On this occasion, our meeting place was Isleworth, the exclusive club which Tiger Woods then called his Florida home and which was playing host to the annual Tavistock Cup match against Lake Nona.

He pointed out that the Masters has always had a non-American voice, going back to the halcyon days of the legendary Longhurst. 'Oh, I can still hear that magnificent voice,' Feherty intoned, 'describing Nicklaus holing a putt on the sixteenth with the words "Did you ever see anything like it?" He went on to acknowledge his great good fortune in having embarked on his current career the year Woods burst onto the major scene with his first Masters triumph in 1997. And his impact was such that only a year later the *Augusta Chronicle* thought sufficiently of him to dedicate a full page in the paper's 'Your Life' section on the opening day of the 1998 Masters to the announcer they described as 'the rogue with a brogue'.

As a player, Feherty made his only Masters appearance in 1992, when rounds of 73, 72, 77 and 70 delivered an aggregate of 292 – four over par. 'Like most people, I was shocked when I first saw the course,' he said. 'Television didn't prepare me for those dramatic changes in elevation and the wide-open spaces. I remember walking out there thinking, "This is surreal – like a Dali picture." I expected to see a clock hanging from a pine tree. So perfect.

'A lot of people watch only one golf tournament. In the British Isles it could be the Open, but they definitely watch the Masters. I still love it, though it's a hard week for me because I can't really be myself. Players approach it differently, too. They're a little more serious that week. My fondest memory of 1992 was of the short sixteenth, where I nearly holed my tee-shot. I hit it to the edge of the hole and as I tapped it in a frog jumped out of the hole, almost bringing the ball with it. It had been very wet. It was just the oddest thing. I was left wondering what the ruling would have been had the frog stopped the ball going in.'

He was tied forty-eighth and two strokes ahead of him on that occasion was Lanny Wadkins, who later graduated to the commentary tower with CBS before being replaced by Nick Faldo. And sixth-placed Ian Baker-Finch is another from that year who traded club for microphone, along with Paul Azinger, Curtis Strange and, of course, Faldo. Still, knowledge wasn't enough. As Feherty put it, 'If I can't make people laugh, I want to make them smile.' Meanwhile, the magic of the Masters had remained invitingly fresh. 'Because it's the one major championship which comes to the same venue every year, people become comfortable with that,' he said. 'They understand it.'

But would they understand the changes that had seen Augusta become a potentially brutal battle of 7,445 yards? 'While it has got longer over the years, they don't always play it all the way back,' he responded. 'I understand what they're doing. Whether you agree with stretching out a classic golf course is another matter, but Augusta has always been a work in progress. I doubt if there were two successive years in its history when it remained the same, so there's a strong precedent for change.

'For me, holes like the eleventh, which was already one of the hardest holes in the world, now has a tee in South Carolina. As far as these guys are hitting it, I believe you've got to put it back there to make it relevant. When I played the Masters, the emphasis was on the greens. And it's always going to be that way. The longer and the harder they make it, the more likely it is that one of the top five or six players in the world is going to win. It makes it perfect for Tiger. If you want to make the course Tiger-proof, you make it shorter and easier.

'Clearly, the objective is that competitors will be playing longer clubs into the greens, but however long they make it, the Masters will only play its most difficult when it's hard and fast – and it's been some time since we've seen it that way. In fact, I've seen it only once in my ten years with CBS. When you miss a green and the ball finishes 40 yards away, that's when it becomes a real challenge. So the extra yards won't be a problem. These guys are just enormously long.'

But what other option did the organizers have? Feherty responded with a fascinating solution to a problem which is the source of ongoing torment for golf-course architects. Instead of limiting the initial velocity of the ball, which would almost certainly bring a litigious response from the leading manufacturers, why not make it bigger? 'I think the governing bodies lost the ball-battle a few decades ago, when Nicklaus warned them of what was happening,' he said. 'Apparently he's not an expert. Some dentist or stockbroker, or whatever, decided he knew more than the game's most successful player. So the genie got out of the bottle.

'My belief is that they need to make the ball bigger. We've done it before. I switched from a 1.62 to a 1.68 [inches in diameter] and it's more fun, especially for amateurs and beginners, in that the ball sits up better. And it's harder for pros. I'd increase it to 1.70 or 1.71. It's an odd game, so maybe it needs an odd number. Leave everything else the same. The ball won't go as far, so old hazards become relevant again. And with the ball spinning more, it's more difficult to hit it straight. Then let the manufacturers continue to do their thing commercially. They're talking about velocity restrictions and all the rest, but this one small change would solve most of the current problems at a stroke.'

In his early years as a commentator, Feherty would play the course on the Sunday of Masters week to familiarize himself with the various changes. But no longer. 'I don't play at all now,' he explained, his right hand moving to the small of his back. 'I've got arthritis down here. I could play after a few swings but I wouldn't be able to walk the following day. They've had to make a special [six-inch] waistband for me so I can carry the various equipment for on-course commentary, otherwise the pain would be crippling.'

He continued: 'With knowledge of the course acquired over the years I'll head out on Monday or Tuesday and follow a group. I only have the fourth and fifteenth to worry about. They're my holes, which I putt every morning of the tournament at about nine, before the players. And I'll do sixteen for Verne Lunqvist [his fellow commentator]. The thing about Augusta is that there are no let-ups. There's not a single shot on which you can relax, which explains why it's so exhausting, mentally and physically. You have to be at an absolute peak for four days in a row.

'And of all its demands, the second shot to the third and the third shot to fifteen [as Padraig Harrington discovered in 2007] are probably the most difficult shots in the world. That's why players keep going for the green from the top of the hill at fifteen, even when they can't hit it, because they don't want to face that 75- or 80-yard third shot which is off a downhill lie into that little sliver of a green. It's going in low and if you hit it through the back, which is the tendency, you could chip it into the water. I've seen people make 11 there.

'They're the most interesting shots. People don't often think about the short shots, which have to be struck so precisely from perfect surfaces. If you mistime them by a fraction, you can run up 6 or 7. Faldo had a lovely touch with them. Everything was very soft and predictable. In fact, all of the Europeans, with the possible exception of Woosie and Sandy [Lyle], had wonderful touches around the greens. Players like Langer, Ballesteros, Olazabal, Faldo. Magnificent imagination with chip shots.'

We then talked of Jean Van de Velde and his extraordinary win in Madeira the previous Sunday, despite a double-bogey on the last. Feherty appeared genuinely pleased for him. 'I've always thought he should have come over here and worked in television. They'd love him. I think it's something about the public identifying with failure.'

Curiously, talk of Van de Velde and failure led us to the player who has dominated Feherty's commentating career. 'You know, Tiger frequently makes my job impossible,' he said. 'He's so good that I sometimes can't predict what he might do. People love to see him win but they also love to see him lose, because he's so superhuman most of the time. It makes ordinary people feel closer to him when they realize he can fail.

'I've never seen anything like him. He's a different species. There's never been a person like him in the history of the game. If Tiger Woods plays well, he wins. Period. It doesn't matter how well anybody else plays. And if he plays very well, he wins by 12, as he did in my first Masters with CBS.'

On leaving him, it struck me that I had known this remarkable man since 1980, when I first made his acquaintance at Royal

Dublin, while he was gaining the first of two victories in the Irish Professional Championship. There had been triumph and failure on the golf course and public pain in what should have been his private life. And he had come through it all with amazing equanimity. Which probably explains why meeting him has always been an enriching experience.

Matchplay at its finest

On the presentation podium of the Volvo Masters at Montecastillo in November 1998, third-placed Colin Montgomerie spoke to an interviewer while looking across at the newly crowned champion, Darren Clarke. With his voice barely rising above a whisper, Monty generously acknowledged of his rival, 'He's good. He's very, very good. He has as much talent as anyone in world golf.' Then the Scot, who had retained his position as Europe's dominant player by securing the Order of Merit title yet again, couldn't resist adding, 'But he's got to learn to use it.'

Sixteen months later, in far off San Diego, Clarke's manager, Chubby Chandler, stood before me in the media centre at La Costa and said candidly, 'It is only now that I can look you in the eye and say with absolute honesty that Darren is not an underachiever. There is an inner calm about him that hasn't been there before. It's a wonderful transformation.'

The transformation to which Chandler referred had been wrought through six rounds of matchplay competition at the highest level, culminating in a sensational victory over Tiger Woods in the final of what was then the Andersen Consulting (now Accenture) World Matchplay Championship. And in becoming the first Irish sportsman to win a prize of $1 million, Clarke had given me one of the greatest thrills of my golf-writing career.

Though the camaraderie of colleagues is very much a part of the enjoyment of covering sport, I have to admit that I always took a special pleasure from being on my own. And this was invariably heightened by the prospect of putting one over on journalistic rivals by being the only Irish representative at a significant success. For that reason, my week at La Costa at the end of February 2000 will always be very special.

In a way, it seemed odd for *The Irish Times* to send me on such a trip. Twelve months previously, European invaders at La Costa had experienced arguably their biggest rout since Washington crossed the Delaware, with the last survivor, Jose-Maria Olazabal, losing to America's John Huston at the quarter-final stage. And in the world rankings, Ireland's top challengers, Clarke (nineteenth) and Padraig Harrington (fifty-sixth), were now some way removed from the top ten. Still, as Edward G. Robinson's poker-playing character, Lancey Howard, observed in *The Cincinnati Kid*, rewards can be huge for doing the wrong thing at the right time.

Woods, of course, was number one and the tournament happened to coincide with a report in *Golfweek* magazine touting him as potentially sport's first billionaire. They estimated his worldwide tournament earnings during 1999 at US $15 million, including overseas appearance fees of US $3 million. Significant endorsement income, however, enhanced the figure to what was then a staggering US $50 million. Which meant the twenty-four-year-old's net worth was set at US $150 million, prompting American financial analysts to hail him as a billion-dollar man in the making.

The previous autumn he signed a five-year contract with the Buick arm of General Motors for more than US $30 million. And the magazine further claimed that he was in the process of renegotiating a five-year US $40 million contract with Nike, which was due for renewal in August 2001. So, having earned close to US $90 million over 1998 and 1999, his star remained very much in the ascendant. 'I told Phil Knight [Nike chairman], "That's chump change: you'll make it back in one year," ' the player's father, Earl, was quoted as saying. And Knight was reported to have replied, 'I know, Earl, I know.'

Perhaps the most revealing aspect of the *Golfweek* story, how-ever, was that despite his wealth, Woods was seen to be largely unaffected by money. His attitude at the time was, 'I just feel if you work hard to get something, it's nice to reap the benefits of it.' This was the player who stood between several leading aspirants at La Costa and a coveted title. And his competitive well-being could be gauged from eight victories in his previous eleven tournaments. In fact, 2000 would become the most notable season of his career so far, in that he captured the US Open, Open Championship and PGA Championship in successive months that summer.

As a premier tournament venue, La Costa had staged the Mercedes Championship from 1969 to 1998. The 1997 tournament was especially memorable for a play-off between Woods and Tom Lehman. On the first hole of sudden-death, the short seventh, Lehman hit his tee-shot into water and Woods proceeded to nail his effort to within four inches of the pin. Justin Leonard considered the course to be better suited to matchplay than strokeplay. 'There's a lot of risk-reward and the guy who plays best should win,' he said. Designed by Dick Wilson and Joe Lee in 1964, the tournament course was a composite from the resort's thirty-six holes. It could be described as largely straightforward, though several key holes on the homeward journey had to be treated with caution, especially the narrow, dog-leg fifteenth (378 yards) and the 569-yard par-five seventeenth, where water on the right threatened the second shot all the way to the green.

As for the matchplay format, it was only through attending such a tournament that one could fully appreciate why crowd problems tend to arise at Ryder Cup stagings in the US. It was obvious that the majority of American spectators had only a very sketchy idea of what was actually going on. And their newspapers were not especially helpful. For instance, Thursday's issue of *USA Today* that week informed its readers in a specially prepared panel that Ernie Els beat Bernhard Langer by '2 and 1 (20 holes)' and that Miguel Angel Jimenez beat Brent Geiberger '1 up (19 holes)'.

Sports columnists were even less helpful with their patronizing and somewhat hyperbolic treatment of the subject. For instance, Nick Canepa of the *San Diego Union-Tribune* started by describing matchplay as 'sudden-death golf'. So what happens on the nineteenth? He went on, 'Every day you go out there with clubs, a blindfold and a cigarette. I'm surprised the organizers . . . don't consult with the golfers beforehand and ask them, "What would you like for your last meal?" In some cases, crow is appropriate. Or just plain dust.' As a notable exception, however, Steve Scholfield of the *North County Times* made a timely plea for sanity from the La Costa spectators. 'After the horrible showing by American sports fans during the Ryder Cup [the previous September] . . . it is time for Americans to start showing visitors from the rest of the world we aren't a bunch of animals.'

Then there were the television and radio commentators, among whom Peter Alliss cut through the waffle with some typically pithy comments. 'Matchplay,' he declared, 'is the heart of the game.' He then explained how it had waned in popularity and how professionals could lose the rhythm and feel of the format, just like Woods was experiencing at that moment in a second-round match against Retief Goosen. How did he see this one working out, Alliss was asked by an ABC colleague. 'Oh,' replied the pride of the BBC, 'Woods could shoot 72 and get stuffed.' Which was precisely the sort of matchplay language we Europeans understood.

Except that Woods didn't get stuffed. Not by Michael Campbell, Goosen nor by Shigeki Maruyama. Which meant the favourite was through to a quarter-final meeting with Paul Lawrie in the top half of the draw. 'It's always more difficult to win a matchplay event, because you can go out there and shoot a great round of golf and somebody just outboatraces you,' said the Great One. 'In medal play, the same thing can happen, but you have three other days to make it up. That's the big difference. You always have to be on your game in matchplay. There have been days when I have shot six or seven under par and lost. But there are times when you go out there and you boatrace somebody, and just blow them out of the water and you get done early. Matchplay is always a different type of animal, because you know it's eighteen holes and anything can happen.'

Watching Clarke that week, I thought of his carefree, amateur days, when he had blond highlights in his hair and a sinister-looking, black-clothed caddie by his side. And when inches were mentioned in his company, it generally had to do with a rather generous girth. He was more concerned, however, with becoming a fully paid-up subscriber to the Bobby Jones notion that the most important inches in golf are those between a player's two ears. After infrequent tournament wins, he conceded, 'There's always been one major piece missing and that's been my attitude. It's been the main thing that's been holding me back. But the message is beginning to get through. I'm now more patient than I've been in the past, when I went bull-headed at the game, desperate to try and make things happen.'

Millennium year marked the beginning of what was being vaunted as a golden age for Ireland's international rugby team. Nothing short of world dominance seemed to be acceptable for Brian O'Driscoll et al. Clarke might have been part of that scene had he taken a different route at the Royal School, Dungannon, where his sporting heroes were local rugby internationals Willie Anderson and Jim McCoy. And he was in fairly impressive company on the school's 1st Rugby XV of 1985–86. Colleagues in the pack were two lads who would become English Premiership professionals, winning sixty-seven international caps between them – Paddy Johns and Allen Clarke (no relation).

According to a report in the school magazine from rugby master Keith Patton: 'Understandably, Darren's golfing prowess restricted his rugby season, but, when he played, he left his mark.' Johns had no doubts about Clarke's potential. 'Darren was a very good player and a lot slimmer then than he is now,' he said. 'He could easily have played for Dungannon in the All-Ireland League and probably for Ulster. He was a lively back-row forward, an excellent support player with good hands, good at taking the ball on and breaking the first tackle.'

For his own part, Clarke recalled, 'I played rugby at school all the way through to the Upper Sixth and loved every minute of it. We went on tour and had some great times. Schoolboy stuff, but as they always say in rugby, what happens on tour stays on tour. Then came the time when I had to choose between rugby and golf. We had a very good 1st XV and giving it up was a very, very difficult decision to make, but at that stage I couldn't afford the risk of being injured playing rugby. I couldn't take the chance of breaking a wrist or something and being out of action for four or five months. I could have been captain in that last year, but, in hindsight, I think I made the right decision.'

Though he missed the cut at Riviera CC on the Friday prior to La Costa, Clarke saw this as a bonus rather than a setback. 'Travel is a big thing, especially coming over here to the west coast,' he said. 'The eight-hour time change is one of the reasons I came over early this year. I certainly don't want to be making another early departure. Though I'm still getting rid of some winter cobwebs, my game is in good shape.'

As it happened, Harrington lost in the first round to Jesper Parnevik, but Clarke fared considerably better against Paul Azinger, who was fresh from a victory in the Sony Open in Hawaii the previous month. It was a particularly welcome boost for a player who, by his own admission, had a poor record in matchplay since turning professional. This was all the more surprising given his virtual invincibility on the amateur scene which he departed in August 1990, after beating Harrington in the final of the Irish Close at Baltray.

'It's true, my record is bad,' said the player for whom the only bright spot was a win over Langer in the European section of the Anderson event in 1998. 'It's a mental thing. When I turned pro, I geared all my thinking to medal-play, but given the importance of events like this, I realize I must change.'

In the event, dismal European weather of the wet February variety provided a familiar backdrop to an opening round in which Langer joined Harrington among the casualties. But for Clarke a 2 and 1 victory over major championship-winner Azinger in their first-ever meeting was an important confidence-builder. 'It certainly makes a pleasant change from last year when I was heading home at this stage,' he remarked. Azinger commented, 'I had one of those days when I didn't putt well and didn't hit it very good.'

Then came a crushing 5 and 4 win in the second round over another major winner, Mark O'Meara, in what Clarke described as 'a very professional performance'. He added, 'I got my nose ahead of Mark early on and made no mistakes. That sort of matchplay golf is very hard to beat.' In fact, it was reminiscent of the ruthless nature of his amateur victories. After turning two up, Clarke went on to wrap up the match with a run of four threes – par, eagle, birdie, par – from the short eleventh. The eagle was the product of a 30-foot chip-in after he had powered a three wood of 239 yards, left to right around an obtrusive tree.

By this stage, Clarke's progress was beginning to arouse the interest of the European contingent and there were rumours of a few interesting bets being struck. And while nobody was making any serious predictions, particular significance was attached to Friday's victory over Thomas Bjorn, not least for the manner in which it was secured. A beautifully judged six-iron approach of 169 yards sailed arrow-straight into a gentle cross-wind before finishing 10 feet right of the eighteenth pin. In the event, Clarke didn't need the putt to see off the doughty Dane and he had a rapt audience when remarking afterwards, 'I feel very much at ease with myself and the hope now is that I can keep it going.' A buoyant mood had been set as early as the 526-yard second, where he nailed yet another glorious three wood, this time of 255 yards to within three feet of the pin, which he holed for an eagle.

'My swing felt good in the first round and as the week has gone on my scoring has got better, mainly because I haven't missed many greens,' said Clarke. And if performances on the first three days were admirable, Saturday proved to be a day of extraordinary achievement. That was when he exuded so much composure in a quarter-final win over Hal Sutton, followed by a semi-final dismissal of David Duval, that he could indulge in some self-mocking about failed attempts at trimming down his girth.

'All the hard work I've done in the gym during the winter is standing me in good stead,' he declared with a big grin and heavy irony. In fact, two years previously he had a fully equipped gym specially installed at his new home in Sunningdale, where the equipment had since been gathering dust, except when his neighbour, Paul McGinley, called to use it. If the intention was to lessen the pressure on himself before tilting with Tiger in the thirty-six-hole final, the strategy seemed to be working. And the mood was maintained into the evening through a quiet meal with Chandler and Butch Harmon, the coach he shared with Woods at that time.

In the morning's quarter-finals, Woods beat reigning Open champion Lawrie by 1 up and Clarke recovered impressively from the shock start of 3 down after 4 to beat Sutton, also on the eighteenth. Along the way, the Tyroneman had reason to be especially proud of his play of the long 541-yard twelfth, where he went ahead for the first time by hitting a solid tee-shot down the middle and then, with the driver still in his hand, smashed the ball the remaining 265 yards into the heart of the green for a winning two-putt birdie. In beating Sutton he had avenged a Ryder Cup defeat by the world's eleventh ranked player at Brookline the previous September.

Then, in the afternoon, while Woods crushed Davis Love by 5 and 4, Clarke was only marginally less impressive in a 4 and 2 win over world number two Duval. Birdies on the tenth and twelfth, which he had also managed against Sutton earlier in the day, proved to be decisive blows. So we had the dream final of Clarke against Woods – and I could look to a terrific story for Monday morning, whatever Sunday's outcome.

'Darren is like a big teddy bear,' Harmon remarked on the Saturday night. 'You just want to go up and hug him. He's a great kid with a great personality. He's playing the best I've ever seen him play and if I could get him to lose 20 pounds, he'd be even better. Thirty-six holes is a bit of a test for him, but I see him as the product of his environment. When I saw him at Las Vegas recently, I said, "What have you been doing; hanging out in the pubs, drinking and smoking cigars?" He replied, "Yeah." The Irish are laid-back, good-time people.'

An unshakeable belief in the quality of his own ball-striking left Clarke far from overawed by the clash with Woods. Indeed, reputations always counted for very little with him. His respect for opponents was based essentially on how they hit the golf ball. Either way, he had guaranteed himself an Irish record haul of US $300,000 in prize money by lunchtime on Saturday and at the end of the day the figure had gone up to US $500,000 – a record by any player in an official European Tour event. In his own words, it had been achieved by 'hitting greens and knocking in a few putts'.

Determined to maintain the magic, he went to the practice ground on Saturday evening only to learn that Woods had arrived there some time earlier to hit shots under Harmon's guidance. It provided an opportunity for Chandler, a former European Tour campaigner, to boast, 'I now hold the distinction of being the last player to beat Darren.' This happened the previous weekend on the other course at La Costa where, receiving four strokes on each nine, Chandler covered sixteen holes in 2-under-par gross to win $165 from his charge. If it had contributed even in a small way to knocking Clarke's game into competitive shape, it was arguably the player's best investment since turning professional.

On Sunday morning, Harmon devoted most of his time on the practice ground to Woods, prompting Clarke to tease with a wave and a grin, 'I'm fine, Butch. I don't need anything.' Before the players headed for the first tee, however, Harmon went to his other client and talked to him about confidence. 'That's generally all he talks about,' Clarke later explained. By way of response, the underdog then proceeded to deliver a performance of astonishing control and quality in a 4 and 3 victory over Woods. In the process, he nudged the game's elite in Ireland, Britain and the world to make way for a new arrival. After being hit with 12 birdies in the thirty-three holes played, the world number one graciously conceded, 'To be honest, Darren just flat outplayed me. I think he missed only one fairway, while I just couldn't quite hit the shots the way I wanted to. I just wasn't able to put pressure on him.'

Victory placed Clarke firmly alongside two legendary Irish figures of the game in fellow Ulsterman Fred Daly, the Open champion of 1947, and Christy O'Connor Snr, whose twenty-four European Tour wins included a world record £25,000 cheque for the John Player Classic in 1970. And though it has since become commonplace, the US $1 million prize really captured the imagination in 2000. Though it may have been no more than a standard appearance fee for Woods in a tournament outside his native shores, it set Clarke apart, not only in the history of Irish sport, but as the most lucrative winner on the European Tour at that time.

What would he do with this bonanza, given that he already had two Ferraris and two BMWs? 'Spend it,' came the predictable reply. 'It won't be lying around for long.' Meanwhile, as coach to both players, Harmon found it impossible to maintain a detached view of events. 'It was very much a mixed day for me in that I felt so happy for Darren, but really sad for Tiger,' he said.

From my own perspective, my dominant memory is of Clarke being remarkably composed about his achievement. 'Tiger was always going to be a tough opponent and it's a fantastic feeling to have played so well against him,' he said. 'I now feel comfortable with matchplay once more, after some indifferent results as a professional.'

I walked the full eighteen in the morning and the key from Clarke's standpoint was some stunning putting on the front nine, where he needed the blade only ten times. But the match remained extremely tight and from the time Woods squared with a birdie at the short seventh, they stayed level for the rest of the round. All the while there was an obvious warmth between them, even though Woods claimed afterwards that they never talked. For instance, when Woods declined to concede an 18-inch putt for a half on the short fourteenth, Clarke enquired with a smile, 'Are we playing medal?' Indeed, the Great One's intensity was further emphasized by an innocent young voice in the gallery remarking, 'Gee, Mommy, Tiger uses words just like Daddy does when he's golfing.'

Yet there was the sense of a battle moving up a gear when they went to the first tee the second time around. And we wondered whether, at 18st 7lbs, Clarke might find fitness to be a problem. As an American spectator remarked, 'I didn't know a fat man could walk so far.' Chandler put the weight issue into perspective afterwards, however, when he said, 'Darren is clearly not fit, but he's very strong.'

In the event, the world number one made his intentions abundantly clear by powering a huge drive down the nineteenth, fully 50 yards beyond his rival. It meant Woods was hitting only a soft wedge to the green compared to a full eight iron from Clarke. Yet its potential impact was scuppered when Clarke proceeded to hole a 15-foot putt for a winning birdie to claim the honour for the first time since the seventh tee in the morning. The fact that Woods happened to draw level with a birdie at the long twentieth proved to be only a temporary setback. From there on, Clarke took almost complete control. While driving the ball impeccably, it didn't bother him to be conceding yardage to Woods, in the knowledge that he could maintain the pressure through quality approach play.

So it proved at the twenty-second, where a seven iron was followed by a winning eight-foot putt. Even more impressive was a majestic four-iron approach at the 446-yard twenty-third, where he holed from a foot for another win. Then a 12-footer found the target to extend his lead to three up at the short twenty-fifth. And when Clarke sank a 10-footer to go four up at the next, it meant that from the last seven holes of his semi-final victory over Duval to that point he had shot fifteen birdies in thirty-three holes against the two best players in the world. Needing only thirteen putts for an outward journey covered in thirty-one strokes, Clarke resisted the temptation to look to the finishing line.

Woods, meanwhile, prowled menacingly around the greens, like a grandmaster coming to grips with a chess conundrum. And keenly aware that he was running out of holes, his torment with the blade reminded me of Nick Faldo's remark when an emerging Woods was being hailed as unbeatable. 'Let's see what happens when he starts missing a few putts,' said the Englishman. Ironically, the ultimate killer blows were two attempts at a bunker recovery on the long thirtieth, which he lost to a par. Two holes later, it was all over.

On the following morning, the *San Diego Tribune* carried the headline, 'Tiger meets his match,' with the sub-heading 'Unintimidated Clarke beats Woods handily.' Harmon painted a more graphic picture with the words, 'Darren did to Tiger Woods what Tiger's been doing to other people.' Meanwhile, the more corpulent US scribes delighted in the self-deprecating attitude of the Tyroneman to his generous frame. But after supplying them with more than enough one-liners for some tasty morning pieces, Clarke showed himself to be as aware as anybody of the need to change.

Even Woods, clearly in friendship, felt moved to remark, 'Darren obviously has the ability to play great golf. It's just dependent on how dedicated he is to his work ethic. Butch has been trying to get him to work a little bit harder and when he does it shows in his play.' And Harmon warned: 'Unless he changes, he's not going to achieve the longevity his talent deserves and that would be a great pity, because I've now seen a Darren I hadn't seen before.' All of which prompted Clarke to acknowledge, 'While I was actually surprised at how strong I felt during the second eighteen against Tiger, I think I have to get in better shape. I've been lax over the winter and I'm going to get myself onto a programme and do the work.' Those close to Clarke felt his first move should be to seek a more demanding dietitian than a man with the sobriquet of 'Chubby'. Yet from a business standpoint, there was no denying the enormous investment in time and emotional support which Chandler has made in Clarke's career.

Woods, meanwhile, said of his own game in the final, 'I got stuck out there and I was trying to figure out what it was. I wanted to hit the right golf shot and put pressure on my opponent.' Which got me thinking that the Great One was blinding himself to an inescapable fundamental of matchplay golf. Joe Carr, the great Irish amateur, claimed that in most matchplay situations your opponent will play as well as you let him. The truth about the final was that Clarke, through superb iron play and an irresistible putting touch, pressurized Woods on almost every hole, causing the American to question his own ability to stem the tide. And when no cracks appeared in Clarke's armoury as they entered the final nine holes, we saw Woods make the ruinous mistake of trying to force the issue, culminating in his two shots from a greenside bunker at the long twelfth.

He admitted, 'I was trying to put a soft little bunker shot in there and I didn't accelerate the blade properly. I didn't release it the way I should have and came up short.' He could also have said that he didn't play the shot he wanted to, because the pressure of the situation led to uncertainty. The fact that he had by then established himself as probably the best ball-striker since Ben Hogan didn't guarantee him sound thinking under pressure. As

Clarke suggested, 'Tiger's length worked to my benefit by giving me an opportunity of hitting into the par fours first. When I got it in there close, the pressure went on Tiger.'

Given the nature of the prize fund, there was a lot of talk about money at La Costa that week. And among all the would-be experts, Louis Martin stood apart. While the rest of us looked from match to match more in hope than expectation, the then chief executive of the South African Tour had the courage to back Clarke at 66/1 for the title. The extent of his wager was not disclosed. Nor, for that matter, was the amount Chandler bet on his charge winning the second-round match against O'Meara, which he considered to be the greatest certainty of the championship.

Meanwhile, it was hardly surprising to find Las Vegas resident Harmon relieving certain London bookmakers of a reported US $10,000 in various bets by the Saturday. It was also a very reward-ing exercise for Clarke's caddie Billy Foster, then a remarkably boyish-looking thirty-four-year-old. When caddying for Seve Ballesteros, Foster was famously described by Mac O'Grady as one of the great pacifists of our time. 'Billy deserved the Nobel Peace Prize for what he put up with,' said the American, who claimed an unparalleled knowledge of all matters golfing.

Against this background, the oftimes volatile Clarke had to be something of a soft touch. 'They have totally different tempera-ments and it was a much greater strain working for Seve,' said Foster. Interestingly, he reluctantly parted company with the illus-trious Spaniard after the 1995 US Masters, because of the player's notoriously demanding attitude towards caddies in general. And the contrast with Clarke was never more marked than in the wake of the La Costa triumph, which guaranteed Foster the standard, 10 per cent pay-off of US $100,000. But did he actually receive more than that? 'That's really confidential,' replied the native of Bingley, who added, 'It doesn't get any better than beating Tiger with the whole world watching. It's a dream come true.'

Since Clarke didn't have a club contract at the time, it was intriguing to note the variety of implements which Foster carried to victory. There were MacGregor VIP Tour irons, a Titleist 975D driver with a 9.5-degree loft, Callaway number three and number five woods, and a Scotty Cameron Putter which, incidentally, he picked up at the local factory in Carlsbad only on the Monday before the event.

Back in Dublin, as a former captain of the Royal and Ancient, Joe Carr was understandably reluctant to downgrade Fred Daly's achievement as the only Irish winner of the Open Championship. But after some thought, he concluded, 'Our sporting achievements never fail to amaze me and what Darren Clarke did last weekend has to be the greatest ever performance by an Irish golfer. Consider the facts: he beat six Ryder Cup players in a row, including the number one and number two in the world. Nobody has done that. And while I accept that it's very difficult to compare one generation with another, golfers nowadays are unquestionably better, technically, than in my day. There's no doubt in my book: Darren stands alone.'

And into the category of words a scribe would gladly have retracted went a report in the *Los Angeles Times* on the Sunday of the final which started thus: 'Now that he can almost smell the ink on the $1 million winner's cheque, it's time to ask this question: is there anyone in the world better at matchplay than Tiger Woods? If there is, he wasn't there Saturday at La Costa.' Still, Woods had the last word. On the Sunday evening, after all the interviews had been completed, Clarke went to the locker room. There on the door of his locker was a pinned note. It read: 'Congrats Big D. Well done. Be proud. Best wishes, T. PS You're still a fat f***k.'

This is a round-by-round analysis of Clarke's route to victory, by leading American statistician Sal Johnson, who is now to be found on GolfObserver.com.

Match	Holes	Won	Lost	Birdies	Eagles	Bogeys	To par
v P. Azinger	17	5	3	2	0	4	+2
v M. O'Meara	14	5	0	4	0	0	-4
v T. Bjorn	18	6	5	4	1	3	-3
v H. Sutton	18	4	3	4	0	2	-2
v D. Duval	16	6	2	6	0	1	-5
v T. Woods	33	9	5	12	0	1	-11
Totals	**116**	**35**	**18**	**32**	**1**	**11**	**-23**

Final: hole-by-hole

First 18
Front nine

Par	4	5	3	4	4	4	3	4	5	36
Clarke	4	4	3	3	5	3	3	3	4	32
Woods	4	4	2	4	5	5	2	3	4	33
Match		1dn	a/s			1up	a/s			a/s

Back nine

Par	4	3	5	4	3	4	4	5	4	36	72
Clarke	4	3	4	4	3	4	4	5	4	35	67
Woods	4	3	4	4	3	4	4	5	4	35	68
Match											a/s

Second 18
Third nine

Par	4	5	3	4	4	4	3	4	5	36
Clarke	3	5	3	3	3	4	2	3	5	31
Woods	4	4	3	5	4	4	3	4	4	35
Match	1up	a/s		1up	2up		3up	4up	3up	3up

Fourth nine

Par	4	3	5	4	3	4
Clarke	4	3	5	3	3	4
Woods	5	2	6	3	3	4
Match	4up	3up	4up	Clarke wins 4 and 3

Card of the course

Hole	Yds	Par		Hole	Yds	Par
1	412	4		10	450	4
2	526	5		11	180	3
3	187	3		12	541	5
4	386	4		13	410	4

5	446	4	14	204	3
6	365	4	15	378	4
7	188	3	16	423	4
8	398	4	17	569	5
9	538	5	18	421	4

Out: 3,446 Par 36   In: 3,576 Par 36

Overall: 7,022 Par 72

As a postscript, probably the most gratifying letter ever written about my work appeared in *The Irish Times* the following Saturday, 4 March. Sent to the editor by Terry Purcell of Oak Court Grove, Dublin 20, it read:

Sir, I have been a little short of amazed at Dermot Gilleece's coverage of the golf over the past few days.

From the end of last Saturday's play he wrote a piece on the semi-final, then presumably on Saturday or early Sunday morning wrote the bones of Monday's front page article, leaving space for quotes etc., and another piece in case Clarke was beaten.

A report on the actual game must have been written as play was progressing and another one on the top Irish money-winners written somewhere in between. Add in quotes to be collected after the game, presentation and sending it off, all of which must have been against a deadline which could not have been more than an hour or two after the last putt dropped, presumably working a lap-top modem mobile phone and any other technology required. Collecting enough material for Tuesday's paper before everyone left was another small detail. Getting the facts right is taken for granted. He must also have slept, eaten and travelled to and from his hotel and kept track of the check-in time for his own flight.

Perhaps next year you might ask him to take photographs as well. For God's sake, give him a week or two off and don't dare to question his expenses . . .

Yours, etc. . . .

The generous face of golf

A few years ago, a British colleague of mine who happened to be quite friendly with Greg Norman became redundant from his position as golf correspondent with a national newspaper. When the Shark generously wondered if there was anything he could do to help, the scribe replied, 'Yes. Give me your services for just one day and I'd be set up for life.'

Neither party was too sure whether the suggestion was a serious one. Either way, it came to nothing. But I was reminded of it at Portmarnock Links on Monday, 14 September 1998, when the extraordinarily generous face of golf never looked more appealing.

Initially, Darren Clarke set out to raise about £30,000 to £40,000 for the Omagh Memorial Fund. With some cash still to be counted, the total stood at £342,000. And none of the professionals got as much as a penny for his services or expenses. In fact, it cost Colin Montgomerie about £5,000 to come in his own plane, while Ian Woosnam was about £2,000 out of pocket.

'It was a wonderful example of everybody pulling together in a common cause,' said Andrew 'Chubby' Chandler of International Sports Management, who organized the players. 'For instance, Aer Lingus didn't want it mentioned that they were giving the visiting professionals free flights, but we let it slip. And the hotel arranged everything without a hitch.'

He went on, 'Had we taken more time about it, we might have had fifty-four pros with a concurrent pro-am next door at Portmarnock GC, possibly with people like Ernie Els and Nick Price playing. We might have raised £1 million. But in my view, it was perfect. It was one of the most heartwarming and dignified occasions I have ever experienced.'

Chandler concluded, 'The only people not surprised by it at all were the golfers. Despite the bad press we get from time to time, we know we're part of a very generous and caring sport. We proved that when the right cause is given the right focus – which Darren did – there is no limit to what can be achieved.' Just so.

Sickening halt to a great adventure

On the tarmac at General Mitchell Airport, Milwaukee, the familiar whine of jet engines rose in pitch as the flight for Reno prepared for take-off. Among the passengers, John Morgan teased the caddie in the seat in front of him, while contemplating another instalment in a thrilling adventure. Next thing he knew he was in a hospital bed, mystified by the pain shooting through his upper body.

No, the plane didn't crash, but Morgan's golfing world was about to disintegrate after the sudden return of a cruel illness he believed was consigned to the past. He was only twenty-six.

A month earlier, in July 2004, he had the world at his feet. From a position of five strokes off the lead with only nine holes to play, he had reeled off birdies in a blistering 65 to earn a play-off for the John Deere Classic. And though beaten by Australian Mark Hensby on the second hole of sudden death, a runner-up cheque for US $410,400 was very handsome compensation. Then came US $56,250 for a share of thirteenth place behind Jonathan Bird in the BC Open. And while more recent performances had lacked that sparkle, there was the excitement of a planned Reno reunion with his parents, whom he hadn't seen in six months.

The memory of those events brought a catch to his voice and mist to his eyes. We were talking in October 2006 in Estrela da Luz, Oceanico's luxury apartment complex near Lagos in southwest Portugal where, earlier in the day, Morgan had played as a guest in the John Aldridge Golf Classic. This was social golf, a far cry from the fiercely competitive tempo of the US Tour, but well-honed skills were still very much in evidence in a remarkably comfortable 67. Like the breathtaking shoulder speed which dispatched the ball formidable distances and the efficiency with which he wielded the belly putter, recommended to him by Vijay Singh in New Orleans in 2004.

Milwaukee. 'I can remember being strapped into my seat and the plane leaving the gate,' he recalled. 'Then blank, until I woke up in hospital with tubes hanging out of me. I discovered later that the caddie in front of me thought I was hitting him. And he said,

"C'mon; that's enough," not knowing I was having a seizure. Then somebody told the pilot and the plane turned back to the gate.' He went on, 'The safety belt was keeping me rigid while my body wanted to move. Then, apparently, I broke the strap and finished up in the splits position on the floor between the rows of seats. Hitting myself backwards and forwards and injuring my ribs, sternum and back. After staying overnight in hospital I flew to Reno the following day and met my mum and dad. I was an emotional wreck. They tried to be very strong for me, but my mum broke down.'

Morgan's a big man – 6ft 2ins and 14st 7lbs. I thought of the commotion he would have caused. Such disturbing images were gladly replaced, however, by the recent memory of splendid athleticism I had witnessed at Morgado golf course, where he hit 320-yard drives with consummate ease. Surely he had to win his battle to get back into the big time. Born in Bristol, the son of a docker, on 19 December 1977, he had a promising amateur career in which wild behaviour often deprived him of representative honours. Indeed, it was the disappointment of yet another rejection by selectors which prompted him to turn professional, in April 2002.

After only two months in paid ranks, he finished second to Alex Cejka in a European Challenge Tour event in Germany. A month later, he had his first win, which came in the Challenge Tour Championship at the Bowood GC, close to his west of England home, where he beat the German-based Englishman David Geall on the first hole of a sudden-death play-off. 'When I got the last invitation spot on the Wednesday, I jumped up and down for joy,' he said. 'And when I holed a 40-footer on the last to get into a play-off in front of my home crowd, I jumped even higher. They took a picture of me and I couldn't believe how far I was off the ground. The winning cheque was Stg£26,804 – and that was another story.'

He explained, 'A couple of weeks pass and though the Tour keep insisting they sent out the cheque, I hadn't received it. Then I get this phone call and the voice says, "This is John Morgan." And I say, "But this is John Morgan." And we laugh. Turns out it's the

John Morgan who played on the Seniors Tour and who, sadly, went from us last June [2006, when he died of a brain tumour]. He says, "I seem to be about £26,000 better off." And I say, "I seem to be missing £26,000". And he tells me he'll send it on, which he does. My middle name is Edward and from that point onwards I've called myself John E. Morgan to avoid another mix-up.'

So, a great adventure had begun. By finishing eighth (Peter Lawrie was fourth) in the Challenge Tour Order of Merit in 2002, he earned a European Tour card for 2003. But he also survived all three stages of the US Qualifying School to become only the second player to earn cards on both sides of the Atlantic in the same year, emulating the achievement of Ireland's Richie Coughlan in 1998. 'Next thing I know, Nike come along with a deal and I'm thinking, "Wow! Hello, Tiger,"' he said. 'Which reminds me, I've got one of Tiger's drivers, though I can't hit it.'

In a soft west of England burr, he eases into another story. 'I was drawn with Davis Love and Zach Johnson in the Deutsche Bank Tournament in Boston, and I needed a driver,' he said. 'It was a windy day and the one I was using was hitting the ball straight up in the air. When I went to the Nike caravan, they said that the only one they had was Tiger's back-up. Naturally I was intrigued to hit it. It was seven degrees and the shaft was like an iron rod and just as heavy. Crikey. I nearly broke my back trying to hit it and the ball just went along the ground. With great effort, I could get it airborne, but nothing like the way Tiger could.' He paused and smiled. 'I still have it. I had to nick it. When Nike asked me what I thought of it, I said it was a great driver. Suited me perfectly. I've just bought a nice little house in a fishing village called Portishead on the outskirts of Bristol, looking out over the channel towards Wales. And it's there. A proud possession.'

Morgan wasn't long on tour when he gained the reputation of being a bit of a character. For instance, he dyed his hair blue after losing a bet to the founder of MTV in Miami. Even Woods was intrigued. Which would explain his reaction when seeing Morgan alongside him at traffic-lights on the way to the 2003 Buick Classic. 'We're both in courtesy cars, but I reckon Tiger's is hotter than mine,' he said. 'My mum and dad have come to see me and they're in the car. We're at the lights on a sort of dual-carriageway set-up. With Steve Williams beside him, Tiger looks at me with Schumacher eyes, like, "I'm having you." And I'm thinking, "OK let's go for it." And when the lights go green, the two of us take off. And my mum and dad are having heart-attacks. So I hit the brakes and let him win.

'When we pull into the car park at the course, Tiger is laughing and saying, "I'm one up. I'm one up." And I'm wondering how I can get back at him. Later on, I got a putting lesson off him on the putting green. That was good, very good. On the same day, bad weather kicked in and Jim Furyk, who had just won the US Open at Olympia Fields, was lined up by the television people to fill in time. Ben Curtis was there, too, as the British Open champion.

'Next thing I know, Tiger comes up behind me with a bunch of grapes. "Start peeling," he says. And he tells Scott Verplank the same thing. Then, as the interview is happening, we start chucking these soggy grapes at Furyk and he's covered with them. They're all over the set. And we're having a right laugh. When it's the turn of Curtis to be interviewed fifteen minutes later, he knows what to expect. And he puts up an umbrella so we couldn't get at him.' Fond memories.

By the end of 2004, Morgan has earned US $909,949 on the US Tour, but his career is in ruins. 'After Mikwaukee, I did the stupidest thing imaginable,' he said. 'My play had been fantastic up to that point and I was getting stronger and stronger mentally. Confidence was so high. But from being able to do anything with a golf ball, it now seemed I would be able to do nothing with a golf ball. It was very hard to take.

'It was the first seizure I'd had since I was twenty. Like me, I suppose my parents believed it would never recur. But it was back with a vengeance. And I prevailed upon the physios at the golf course to give me the strongest painkillers they had. And I played. How stupid can you get? Shoot 76 and withdraw. Next week I play only a few holes and withdraw. A week later I shoot 77 and withdraw. I could only half swing, but I kept playing because I felt

I needed another US $20,000 to keep my card. Whereas I could have taken the rest of the year off and got a medical exemption from the tour.

'So stupid! It baffles me still. The biggest rookie mistake I could have made. I was so determined to do well that wild horses wouldn't have held me back, even if I had the right guidance, which I hadn't. I became a total wreck. Eventually I broke down and came home to my parents.' The struggle continued through 2005 until, eventually, it all came apart at the second stage of the Qualifying School in Tampa. 'I turned my hotel bedroom upside down in a physical rage,' he admitted. 'Fortunately, my coach, George Ryall, was there and he told me, "John I have to take you home. You can't take any more." Since then, my only trip back was to this year's John Deere, where I missed the cut by a shot.'

Three small epileptic seizures earlier in 2006 caused him to lose his driving licence. 'I became frightened of being outdoors for fear of another attack and I've been given drugs which don't seem to be working very well, so I'm going to see a specialist when I get home,' he said.

John E. Morgan considered the future. 'I believe I was born to be a professional golfer,' he said. 'Without a doubt. But I've got to learn not to become too intense. I've got to learn to enjoy it. All I need now is an opportunity to prove myself, because I know that the next time I go on tour I'll be ready.' As he walked away, one felt that the nightmare of Milwaukee had been accepted as a lesson well learned; a stepping stone to brighter things.

Footnote: In his first official European tournament of 2008, Morgan earned €3,525 on 4 May for a share of eighth place behind Michael Hoey in the Moroccan Classic on the Challenge Tour.

Broken dreams

In 1998, on the occasion of the sixtieth anniversary dinner of the Association of Golf Writers at Wentworth, I was entertained by some marvellous stories from veteran British colleagues. For instance, John Ingham, the one-time correspondent of the *London Evening Standard*, talked of Bernard Darwin not being overly impressed with the outcome of events at Royal Portrush in 1951. 'Faulkner,' barked the celebrated golf correspondent of *The Times*, 'I understand you've won the Open. Sit there and I'll write about you.'

Ingham recounted that little vignette by way of admonishing us, his successors, for deferring too readily to the current crop of professionals. Naturally, there were also stories about Leonard Crawley, who regularly took Henry Longhurst to task about his manners. It seems that Crawley was especially affronted by his colleague picking up lamb chops with his fingers when dining. Anyway, it resulted in a one-way stream of letters, all of which commenced with the words, 'My dear Henry, It ill becomes you . . .'

Crawley, a Walker Cup representative and long-time golf correspondent of the *Daily Telegraph*, was a wonderful character whom I recall first meeting at the Jeyes Tournament at Royal Dublin in my dim and distant youth. As for dealing with professionals: he always took the view that they should come to him in the clubhouse. He made it a policy never to go in search of them for information.

But there was one very notable exception, which was recalled by Mark Wilson, who wrote on golf for the *London Evening Standard* and the *Daily Express*. It happened during the PGA Close Championship won by Brian Huggett at Thorndon Park in 1967, when the organizers were so strapped for cash that they had to have a whip-round among their vice-presidents to come up with the prize money.

Anyway, with dusk closing in rapidly, only four golf writers remained in the clubhouse. One of them was Crawley who, on looking out of the window, noticed a lone figure on the practice ground in the distance. 'See that young man, all on his own,' he said. 'When practice grounds are full of young men as dedicated as him, Europe will be able to compete with the world.'

Suddenly enthused by his own words, Crawley left his colleagues, got into his distinctive, black Mercedes and drove out over the course to where the young man was hitting shots. There, he lowered the window of his car and said, 'I am Leonard Crawley and I want you to know your efforts have been noted. I can assure you that your dedication will be rewarded.' With that, he wound up the window and drove away.

About ten minutes later, the young man arrived in the club-house, with his bag of clubs cradled in his arms and tears streaming down his face. He wanted to know where the man in the black Mercedes had gone . . . and why he had seen fit to drive over his clubs, smashing every one of them.

Epilogue

During a practice day at Shinnecock Hills for the 2004 US Open, I met with Nick Price on the putting green. I was drawn to him, not so much by his innate courtesy as a leading player but because he had travelled a road during the 1980s very similar to the one Padraig Harrington was now negotiating two decades later. Especially interesting was that the Zimbabwean had endured the crushing disappointment of squandering a winning position in the 1982 Open Championship at Troon and was outgunned by a resurgent Seve Ballesteros at Royal Lytham six years later, before his major breakthrough came in the PGA Championship of 1992.

'Padraig is certainly a potential major winner,' said Price. 'He's very smart and has all the game for it, without a doubt. But sometimes he's a little over-analytical. He tries to play the game too precisely, instead of letting it flow. The more times he gets into winning situations, however, the more comfortable he's going to be and the better decisions he's going to make. One of these days everything is going to fall into place for him, and when he finds that recipe it will be so obvious that he'll slap himself in the face and wonder how he didn't see it before.

'There's no great mystery about it. It's not about trying to win; it's about not making mistakes coming down the stretch. It's a confidence thing. You don't beat yourself. We work on the practice ground to eliminate physical mistakes, but mental mistakes are more elusive.' Price concluded: 'I feel sure he'll make it.'

EPILOGUE

On 10 August 2008, at Oakland Hills, Harrington completed the rare double of Open Championship and PGA Championship in the same year, just as Price had done in 1994. In fact, he even outstripped the Zimbabwean by equalling the hitherto unique distinction of Tiger Woods and added the PGA to his successive Open Championship triumphs. With victories in three out of six successive majors, the stepping stone that had been Carnoustie in 2007 had become a giant leap, setting him among the game's all-time elite.

For Price, the mental process reached a significant milestone in the Lytham defeat by Ballesteros. That was when he realized he had the talent to be a major champion. And it was also while grappling with the pain of defeat that Harrington found his moment of clarity. 'When I walked off the seventy-second green of the 2006 US Open at Winged Foot, Bob Rotella [his mental coach] was there,' Harrington recalled at Oakland Hills. 'And I remember saying to him, "Now I know I'll win a major." Winged Foot was pivotal, even though I had finished with three bogeys.'

This conviction was based on brilliant play from tee to green over the first fifteen holes of that final round. 'If I putted then as I did today, my score would have been so much better,' he mused. 'Up to then, I had wondered if I could play the required level of golf in those situations, whether I had the necessary consistency. Ironically, as one of the losers at Winged Foot, I knew I could. I knew I could play that golf again and again and again.'

The victory scene around the seventy-second green at Oakland Hills lacked the family emotion of Carnoustie and Birkdale, simply because the championship hadn't officially ended when Harrington sank what we all knew was a decisive fifteen-foot putt on the last. He had been with Sergio Garcia and Charlie Wi in the penultimate three-ball, but Ben Curtis, a group behind, could still tie if he holed his second shot on the last. So there was no excited patter of tiny feet by five-year-old Paddy out to the waiting arms of his dad. This would take place out of the public's view.

When the soon-to-be-crowned champion went up the walkway behind the green towards the Recorder's Cabin, he stopped for a few moments en route. First he kissed his wife, Caroline, then the

Wanamaker Trophy which happened to be on a table to her left. He then kissed baby Ciaran before embracing his mother, Breda, who stood there silently, almost bemused at what this great son of hers had just achieved. Then, after signing for a second successive 66, he turned to find little Paddy racing towards him with one of those special, clinging hugs that only children can give; a beautiful manifestation of total, unconditional love.

Moments later, Adrian Mitchell, Harrington's Yorkshire-born manager, was at his side. 'It's hard to believe,' were the only words a normally loquacious player could find. 'It's hard to believe, Mitch.'

In the way of such important sporting events, there were certain official formalities to be gone through – the sort of situations in which the notion of being an ambassador for one's country takes on a profoundly serious dimension. I often wonder if politicians and other public speakers, who use the phrase so freely, ever think about the full impact of such an ambassadorial role. Those of us familiar with Harrington, however, would never consider the possibility of embarrassment or unease arising in these situations.

I will leave an assessment of his post-championship behaviour at Oakland Hills to an Englishman, David Wright, the Director of Regions and Heritage for the PGA of Great Britain and Ireland, of which Harrington is a member as a Ryder Cup player. He told me: 'On the occasion of his Open wins at Carnoustie and Royal Birkdale, Padraig was required to make a formal speech at the presentation ceremony and he obviously assumed the same would apply this time as well, because I could see him stuffing some hastily prepared notes into a trouser pocket as he headed back to the eighteenth. But the PGA of America doesn't give the winner that opportunity.

'A few minutes later, he and his family went back into the clubhouse for the Champions' Reception in the main banqueting area, where Brian Whitcomb, president of the PGA of America, introduced the main guests and their champion. It was a gathering of about two hundred, including representatives of the PGAs of Australia, South Africa, Canada and the European Tour, along with referees from all over the world, including Japan. At the outset, the champion's wife, Caroline, was presented with a beautiful silver pendant carrying the PGA crest as a memento of the week. Then Padraig received a gold money clip.

'At that point, Brian handed the microphone over to Padraig who, totally off the cuff, proceeded to thank the PGA of America, Oakland Hills Golf Club and the PGA of Michigan, who had been involved in the setting up of the golf course. Though lasting no more than about two minutes, it was what I can only describe as a very special speech in which nobody was overlooked, from the staff of the golf club down to the various volunteers who had contributed to the success of the championship.

'To do that unscripted was hugely impressive. Other speeches I have heard were positively mundane by comparison. In its special way, it confirmed the general impression of Padraig as a class act. As I see it, he could be described as a thinking man's golfer, who clearly applies a great deal of discipline to playing the game, while conducting his life in an exemplary fashion – the whole family aspect of it. In my view, these are qualities you can only respect hugely.

'Thinking of what has happened here today, there is one memory that will remain with me. In 2000, I went to Pebble Beach for the US Open. Woods and Els were playing in the final group and the second-to-last twosome of the day was Miguel Angel Jimenez and Padraig. I saw that as a very significant milestone – to be in such a prominent position on the final day of a major championship in the United States. In my view, his career blossomed from that moment.'

The man from The Belfry went on: 'It is gratifying to think that our championship in Ireland at The European Club is acknowledged as having provided crucial preparation for Padraig's Open victories. And Carnoustie was obviously very important for Irish golf when you think that previously Fred Daly was the only major winner the island had given to the game. The immense contribution that players like Christy O'Connor Senior and Junior and Harry Bradshaw have made to the Ryder Cup must also be acknowledged. But suddenly, over a relatively short time, Harrington was quietly stepping up to the plate to the point where he has now emerged as a dominant figure in the most extraordinary way.'

While absorbing scenes of high emotion beneath overcast Michigan skies on that Sunday evening, I, too, thought of all the Irish players who had gone before; of those mentioned by David and others for whom a victory of this magnitude was also an unreachable goal. As David Feherty was honest enough to admit, 'I was one of those players who didn't want to win the British Open. I had my chances at Troon [1989] and Turnberry [1994], but there was one pivotal moment when I always messed up. I just didn't have the mental capacity to go all the way.' Against that background, Feherty's admiration for Harrington's achievement had to be viewed in a special light. 'Padraig is a quality person, very smart and with a tremendous heart,' said the former tournament professional turned CBS television commentator. 'I admire him greatly.'

Watching Harrington through the practice stage at Oakland Hills, there was the feeling that his demeanour was somehow different from what it had been on his previous American visit for the US Open two months earlier. He seemed to have acquired a certain aura that comes only through great achievement. There was no hint of arrogance, which is entirely alien to his nature, but he seemed different nonetheless. Maybe it had to do with the way the locals deferred to him as the man who had recently retained the Open crown in such impressive fashion. Even those of us present at the championship were made to feel honoured by association.

By Friday evening, however, Harrington's image had changed dramatically to one of almost boyish vulnerability. 'It was a struggle for me,' he said with typical candour, after carding a 74 on a day when Justin Rose, for instance, had swept to an impressive 67. 'I did my best to be ready for the week, but clearly I'm not. What can I say? The harder I tried, the worse it got. Obviously I'm still just having a hangover after winning the Open.'

That was it. Since the introduction of the FedEx Cup in the US in 2007, the gap between the Open and the PGA had been reduced from three to two weeks. He needed more time. 'You know, when you're just not mentally strong it's hard to stop your mind from wandering away,' he went on. 'There was no calmness there at all. I couldn't get off the course quick enough. I'm clearly not ready, but if this is a consequence of winning the Open, so be it. I'll give it another go next year.'

Then, almost as an afterthought, he added: 'But there's plenty of golf left to turn it around. Maybe after a night's sleep I'll be better tomorrow. I just need to be patient.' In his way of using the media as a sounding board for his innermost feelings – a sort of exercise in group therapy – that exchange by the clubhouse seemed to lift his spirits, even if desperate, negative thoughts were not banished entirely. As it happened, the problem was later attributed to dehydration in the suffocating heat.

Thunder, lightning and torrential rain wreaked havoc on Saturday's schedule. Harrington was able to finish only the outward journey of his second round, though there was at least the lift of a birdie at the forbidding short ninth to leave him five over par for the championship and apparently battling for no better than a top-ten finish. In a rearranged schedule, the third round was completed early on Sunday morning and, with two-tee starts and players setting off in three-balls, it became possible to complete the championship almost on time.

After rising at 4.30 on Sunday morning, Harrington prepared for battle. Gone was Friday's self-doubt, to be replaced by the fierce determination of only three weeks previously at Birkdale. Four successive birdies from the thirteenth to the sixteenth brought him home in thirty-two strokes for a stunning 66. Now, at one over for the championship, he was back in the hunt.

As the second-last three-ball set off, we wondered how this renewed rivalry with an old foe would pan out. Would Garcia grab this chance of revenge for the sickening setback of Carnoustie, or would we see Harrington emphasize his superiority over the mercurial Spaniard? As a battle of rare intensity progressed towards its climax, Harrington got the breakthrough he had patiently waited for. It came at the treacherous sixteenth, where Garcia dumped an ill-judged second shot into the lake.

Now they were level going to the seventeenth, whose length had been reduced, sensibly, from 238 yards to 216. With the pin back, right, Harrington hit a glorious five iron to ten feet, only for Garcia to respond with an even better one to within four feet of the target. This would decide the destiny of the ninetieth PGA Championship. Over years of matchplay golf on the great courses of his native country, Harrington had become familiar with the old adage: Whoever's first in, wins the hole. That was his thinking as the ten-footer held its line beautifully to find the bottom of the cup. Now, Garcia had to sink his four-footer or face the prospect of going up the last a stroke behind. One could imagine the gasps from millions of armchair viewers as the Spaniard's effort was pulled ruinously onto the left lip.

Both players made mistakes down the toughest finishing hole in American golf; Garcia was in the cavernous front bunker in two, while Harrington also took three to reach the putting surface after visits to sand and heavy rough. Finally, it came down to a fifteen-foot putt with a double-break which meant aiming a few inches outside the right lip. Harrington saw the line instantly. From my position off the back of the green, I remembered a similar situation at Mount Juliet in 1993 when Nick Faldo had a twelve-footer to capture the Irish Open in a play-off with Jose-Maria Olazabal. 'This fellow holes these, you know,' whispered Joe Carr, who was crouched beside me, knowing that great players can make things happen when the need arises.

Now, Harrington confirmed his elevation to greatness by willing that putt into the bottom of the eighteenth cup, just as he had done for birdie at the seventeenth and for a priceless par at the sixteenth. It was all over. With a twelve-footer which had now become inconsequential, Garcia missed and Harrington became the winner by two strokes. The Spaniard would share second place with Curtis, the 2003 Open champion.

In the company of a small group of Irish colleagues on the Monday morning, I visited the sort of luxurious dwelling you would expect to find in one of the ten richest counties in the US. It was where Team Harrington were based for the week, only a five-minute drive from Oakland Hills. Attired in a tee-shirt and shorts, our host served us with drinks from the fridge and then invited us to join him out back, by the swimming pool.

EPILOGUE

There, Ireland's greatest international sportsperson held the Claret Jug and the Wanamaker Trophy in either arm as we gathered around him for a commemorative photograph. 'Here, help me with this,' he said of the weighty Wanamaker. And it was impossible not to smile at the simplicity of it all. And of the glorious golfing summer this remarkable man had given us.

Picture acknowledgements

Frontispiece: cartoon of the author with Douglas, his caddie, at Augusta National, April 1994: by kind permission of Martyn Turner.

Picture section: DG as radio ham: Frank Fennell; DG with Greg Norman: Matthew Harris/www.golfpicturelibrary.com; DG with Nick Faldo: Andy Reddington; DG with Arnold Palmer: Mark Doyle.

Index

INDEX

INDEX

INDEX

INDEX

INDEX

INDEX